Scarvia B. Anderson

Samuel Ball

The Profession
and Practice
of Program Evaluation

Theodore Lownik Library
Illinois Benedictine College
Lisle, Illinois 60532
WITHDRAWN

Jossey-Bass Publishers
San Francisco • Washington • London • 1978

300.72
A549p

THE PROFESSION AND PRACTICE OF PROGRAM EVALUATION
by Scarvia B. Anderson and Samuel Ball

Copyright © 1978 by: Jossey-Bass, Inc., Publishers
433 California Street
San Francisco, California 94104

&

Jossey-Bass Limited
28 Banner Street
London EC1Y 8QE

Copyright under International, Pan American, and
Universal Copyright Conventions. All rights
reserved. No part of this book may be reproduced
in any form—except for brief quotation (not to
exceed 1,000 words) in a review or professional
work—without permission in writing from the publishers.

Library of Congress Catalogue Card Number LC 78-1154

International Standard Book Number ISBN 0-87589-375-9

Manufactured in the United States of America

JACKET DESIGN BY WILLI BAUM

FIRST EDITION

Code 7815

A joint publication in
The Jossey-Bass Series
in Social and Behavioral Science
& in Higher Education

Preface

The Profession and Practice of Program Evaluation is a workbook in at least two senses: It is about the work of evaluation, and it provides some workbook-like materials to help guide the planning and conduct of evaluations and to help deal with professional issues. Beginning with an overview of the field, the book then treats the following topics: the major purposes of evaluating educational and social programs; general methods of evaluation best suited for each purpose; types and sources of evidence frequently associated with the general methods of investigation; targeted dissemination of evaluation infor-

Preface

mation and results; the professional predispositions and preferences of evaluators that may influence what they look at and how they look at it; the complex fiscal and administrative relationships among funding agencies, program directors, and evaluators; ethical responsibilities bound up in program evaluation; defining, instilling, and assessing the competencies of evaluators; and the status and prospects for evaluation as a "profession."

We hope that the codification of evaluation principles and the framework for appropriate practices presented here will lead both experienced and neophyte evaluators to a more systematic approach to their profession and help directors of educational and social programs to a critical appreciation of what evaluation is all about. Such systemization and understanding may also help to combat some prejudices against program evaluation that have been held in both research and decision-making circles.

This book was stimulated by a conference on professional issues in the evaluation of education and training programs held at Educational Testing Service (ETS), Princeton, New Jersey, in late 1974. Participants included Lee J. Cronbach, Stanford University; Joel Davitz, Teachers College, Columbia University; Henry S. Dyer; Henry M. Levin, Stanford University; Robert Perloff, University of Pittsburgh; Seymour Sarason, Yale University; Michael Scriven, University of California, Berkeley; Robert E. Stake, University of Illinois; Judah Schwartz, Massachusetts Institute of Technology; Julian C. Stanley, Johns Hopkins University; Ernest J. Anastasio, Albert E. Beaton, Paul B. Campbell, Garlie Forehand, Norman Frederiksen, J. Richard Harsh, Dean Jamison, Frederic M. Lord, Albert P. Maslow, Samuel J. Messick, Richard T. Murphy, Charles E. Scholl, and William W. Turnbull of ETS; B. J. Farr, Austin Kibler, James Lester, and Harold F. O'Neil, representatives of the Office of Naval Research (ONR); and Donald Miller, the Ford Foundation. A number of the participants also reviewed a preliminary report of the conference.

The conference was sponsored by the Personnel and Training Research Program, Office of Naval Research (Contract No. N 0014-72-C-0433, NR 154-359). We are grateful to ONR for its support and

Preface

to Marshall J. Farr and Joseph L. Young for their encouragement and active participation.

We would also like to thank the ETS staff members who visited the adult training installations and whose cogent observations about evaluation in the real world are reported in Chapter Ten: Clyde Aveilhe, assistant director, Washington, D.C., Office; J. Robert Cleary, associate director, Northeastern Regional Offices; Roy Hardy, assistant director, Southern Regional Office; J. Richard Harsh, director, Los Angeles Office; Richard T. Murphy, research psychologist, Educational Studies Division; David M. Nolan, director, Washington, D.C., Office; Donald E. Powers, research psychologist, Educational Studies Division; Donald Raske, program director, Elementary and Secondary School Programs; and Theresa Strand, professional associate, Midwestern Regional Office.

Finally, we wish to express our greatest thanks to Frances M. Dendy, JoAnne Luger, William I. Sauser, Jr., and other members of the staff of the ETS Southern Regional Office and to Adele Lechowicz, Princeton Office, for research, editorial, and secretarial services that were invaluable for turning some ideas into a book.

Despite all this great and good help, the opinions expressed in this book are ours alone and do not necessarily reflect the views of our advisers or of the Office of Naval Research.

February 1978
SCARVIA B. ANDERSON
Atlanta, Georgia

SAMUEL BALL
Princeton, New Jersey

Contents

Contents

Tables and Figures

Tables

Tables and Figures

Figures

The Authors

SCARVIA B. ANDERSON is a senior vice-president of the Educational Testing Service (ETS), with responsibilities for regional offices, advisory and instructional programs, and international activities. She is also director of ETS's Southern Regional Office in Atlanta.

Scarvia Anderson received her B.S. degree in English and mathematics from Mississippi State University, her M.A. degree in psychology from George Peabody College for Teachers, and her Ph.D. degree in psychology from the University of Maryland (1955). She was also a Fulbright scholar at the Institute for Experimental Psychology, University of Oxford. She began her career in education as a teacher in Nashville, Tennessee, and her career as a psychologist at the Naval Research Laboratory, Washington, D.C. She has been able to combine her interests in both professions at ETS.

Anderson has published numerous articles, technical reports, and manuals, as well as chapters in various edited collections. She has also coauthored two books, *Meeting the Test* (with M. Katz and B. Shimberg, 1965) and *Encyclopedia of Educational Evaluation* (with S. Ball, R. T. Murphy, and Associates, 1974), and edited *Sex Differences and Discrimination in Education* (1972). She is editor-in-chief of a new quarterly sourcebook, *New Directions for Program Evaluation,* launched by Jossey-Bass in 1978.

Scarvia Anderson's work has encompassed such diverse topics as early education, continuing education, the disadvantaged, innovative measurement procedures, and problem-solving processes in children and adults. She has built on her own developments in the assessment of preprimary English-speaking children to initiate measurement devices for Spanish-speaking children, in order to enable valid and useful appraisals of their abilities and educational needs. She is also a recognized authority and consultant in the area of program evaluation.

She is active in the American Educational Research Association, a fellow of the American Psychological Association, a member of the Board of Directors of the National Council on Measurement in Education, and chairperson of the standards committee for the Evaluation Research Society.

SAMUEL BALL is senior research psychologist at the Educational Testing Service, Princeton, New Jersey. He also holds a chair in education at the University of Sydney in Australia—where he was born and educated.

Ball received his B.A. and M.Ed. degrees from the University of Sydney and his Ph.D. degree from the University of Iowa (1964). All three degrees are in educational psychology. He is editor of the *Journal of Educational Psychology* and has authored or edited a number of books, including *Motivation in Education* (1977), *Encyclopedia of Educational Evaluation* (with S. B. Anderson, R. T. Murphy, and

Associates, 1974), and *The Psychology of the Educational Process* (with J. Davitz, 1970). He conducted the national evaluations of "Sesame Street" and "The Electric Company."

He has been involved in many evaluation workshops and conferences internationally, such as in Malaysia for the Van Leer Association, in Indonesia for the U.S. AID program, in Liberia for the Ford Foundation, and in Sweden for the International Evaluation Association.

Ball is a member of a number of professional associations, including the American Psychological Association, of which he is a fellow and a member of the executive committee for Division 15, and the Evaluation Research Society, where he serves on the board of advisors.

The Profession
and Practice
of Program Evaluation

One

Issues in an
Emerging Profession

Once upon a time—not very many decades ago—families and individuals with serious social and economic problems were left to the
uncertain ministrations of private charity. They turned to relatives,
churches, civic clubs, the lady in the big house on the hill, or—in the
case of major disasters—the Red Cross. In contrast, education was considered a public responsibility from the earliest days of the colonies.
However, the disparities and limitations in educational opportunities and services available to our young people were well known even
before the Supreme Court declared separate but equal facilities
unconstitutional and before published accounts of disproportionate
educational spending across school districts appeared regularly.

As our society has become more complex and at the same time

more fractionated, more urban and densely populated, and more vocal and demanding, local or private means of coping with educational and social problems have been recognized as meager at best. In economists' terms, the rationale for undertaking some projects in the public sector is that, under certain conditions, the market system fails to provide the proper level of some goods and services—specifically "merit goods," such as education and health care, "deserved" by all members of society according to the value judgment of that society (Sassone and Schaffer, 1977). Coordinated programmatic attacks on educational and social problems, launched at federal or state levels, are increasingly accepted—indeed *expected*—by the public. No longer is the handicapped child seen as a problem only to his own family or health care considered the province of the rich or economic development construed as a wait for the right company to come along. As public programs have become increasingly massive and expensive, it is not surprising that taxpayers and some of those who authorize expenditures of public money have begun to ask questions about how well that money is being invested and spent and about how much it buys. So, a new enterprise called program evaluation has come on the scene. Even though its record of results is still modest, program evaluation offers enough promise that it is being mandated and incorporated in the planning for both large and small human-service interventions.

The definition of a *program* used throughout this book is paraphrased from Perloff and others (1976, p. 570): that is, a sponsored activity, more often than not from public funds, aimed at mitigating a social or economic problem or improving social and economic welfare. Nunnally (1975) adds that a common characteristic of all such programs is that they are concerned ultimately with *change*.

This definition qualifies a great variety of activities as targets for evaluation—for example, education, job training, community health and mental health, residential treatment, group and individual therapy, certification and licensing designed to protect the public from malpractice, economic assistance, law enforcement, systematic rehabilitation of alcoholics and drug abusers and other violators of societal mores or legal codes, public safety, organized political

2

action, urban planning, and environmental protection. The definition includes programs delivered to groups and to individuals by instructors and other practitioners and through television, books, museum exhibits, and other media. The definition does not restrict the size or scope of the program to which evaluators direct their attention, so long as that size or scope can be delineated. Thus, a program can be defined narrowly (for example, an algebra class, a parent-child center in a particular location) or broadly (say, the national Head Start program, a state immunization program), depending on the information wanted.

Evaluation Purposes and Methods

Most people outside the field of program evaluation, including those responsible for many of the educational and social programs that are evaluated, assume that evaluation has but one purpose: to determine whether a program is any good. Most practicing evaluators, however, subscribe to the formative-summative distinction made by Scriven (1967). The purpose of summative evaluation is to assess the overall effectiveness of an operating program, while the purpose of formative evaluation generally is to help develop a new program. Some evaluators even "specialize" in helping improve programs rather than appraising their impact for policy decisions. We think it is useful to describe the capabilities of program evaluation in terms of *six* major purposes, which are not necessarily mutually exclusive.

I. To Contribute to Decisions About Program Installation

Harless (1973) calls activities oriented toward this purpose "front-end analysis." These activities include ascertaining the need and demand for a program, testing its conception and technical accuracy, and appraising the adequacy of resources for carrying it out.

II. To Contribute to Decisions About Program Continuation, Expansion, or "Certification"

Purpose II corresponds to most definitions of summative

3

evaluation, but it goes further than mere assessment of the overall effectiveness of a program in meeting its objectives. For example, evaluation activities might include determining whether the program is still needed and investigating possible unintended effects.

III. To Contribute to Decisions About Program Modification

We include here such activities as appraisal of the competencies of the program staff and other aspects of the delivery system, as well as examination of program content.

IV. To Obtain Evidence to Rally Support for a Program

V. To Obtain Evidence to Rally Opposition to a Program

Purposes IV and V are stated in appreciation of the real world of program evaluation. Many investigators eschew evaluations designed to serve these purposes—that is, when they *know* what the purposes are. Many people who commission evaluations are unwilling to admit to their real motives. We would not necessarily advise evaluators to avoid all such situations, for there may be times when they can play a legitimate and useful role. However, a number of cautions and qualifications need to be considered, and we will do so later in this book.

VI. To Contribute to the Understanding of Basic Psychological, Social, and Other Processes

Evaluation studies can sometimes be designed to yield contributions to basic knowledge as well as information for program decisions. However, investigators who have agreed to perform evaluation services for a program must make those services the central focus of their efforts. Theses or pet research projects should not be bootlegged on someone else's hard-gained evaluation funds to the detriment of the evaluation.

We realize that there are dozens of so-called models of program evaluation about, with varying numbers of followers. Baker (1976) has suggested that the strength of the following is directly related to the personal magnetism of the model-maker—the "Charisma Coefficient." We tend to reject most of the uses of the word *model* in these applications as pretentious, and we certainly do not claim "model" status for our six program-evaluation purposes. We simply wish to emphasize that evaluators can address many kinds of questions and perform a wide variety of useful services. Evaluators are not limited to trying to provide information to help improve an already-developed program or to appraise the effectiveness of an operating one.

Of course, different kinds of evaluations require different kinds of strategies. For example, evaluation directed toward determining program impact requires experimental designs that allow such inferences, while estimations of program acceptability may be derived from simple survey techniques. Furthermore, the evaluator has to consider the constraints inherent in the situation even before deciding what questions can reasonably be addressed. Constraints may be practical, financial, or political. For example, it may not be practical to assign subjects randomly to experimental and control groups and construct a true experiment. Computer technology in a clinic may not be advanced enough to handle even an analysis of covariance. The staff available may not be capable of conducting in-depth interviews. The cost of obtaining objective observational data may be too great for the evaluation budget. Or certain kinds of data may be too "sensitive" to seek. It is not necessarily better to have tried and failed than never to have tried at all, if "trying" produces data that invite ambiguous or erroneous interpretations or the effort creates serious political or personal problems.

It is also important to recognize that the evaluation strategies and personnel useful in monitoring a continuing program may be quite different from those employed in seeking information about a new program.[1] We tend to equate program evaluation with innovation. Indeed, in many fields relatively little attention has been given to continuous or periodic monitoring of programs that have been around any length of time (see, for example, Messick, 1972, on educational programs). Yet it is frequently important to find out not only whether a once-effective program continues to work but also whether the delivery system keeps on "delivering"—and even whether the needs the program was designed to serve still exist. The keeper-of-the-

5

badger problem is not limited to fiction (Dennis, 1955). We can learn a lesson here from Department of Defense training efforts that maintain monitoring units schooled in systems approaches (see Chapter Ten). They keep more or less constant track of program content and delivery, trainee progress, and the success of graduates, and they provide regular feedback of information to training directors and instructors to enable them to make appropriate program adjustments. Such systems represent a form of quality control for programs that may be significant in size (some deal with a thousand or more trainees a year) or important for national security. The approaches can also be made successfully routine, so that people without advanced degrees in mathematics or social science can handle them.

The intersection of evaluation purposes and methodologies and the quality and usefulness of the evidence collected are the subjects of Chapters Three and Four.

The Roles and Values of Evaluators

There is general, though not universal, agreement that program evaluation involves providing services to decision makers. Whether evaluators can provide such services effectively is not entirely under their control, of course. Sometimes decision makers simply use program evaluators for their own ends, which have nothing to do with making decisions informed by data. But there are areas in which evaluators can perform in such a way as to maximize potential influence, beginning with the initial structuring of their roles in relation to the other parties in the evaluation process. These parties include the agency or individual who commissions the evaluation (who may be the director of the program or an outside monitoring agent), the program staff and participants, and influential people outside the program or evaluation (for example, community members). The evaluator is usually described as "independent" if he or she* does not work directly for the people intimately connected with

*Since there is no common and acceptable term to indicate both the feminine and masculine in the English language, the authors have tried to avoid the stereotypical pronouns *he* and *his* without substituting awkward

the program under scrutiny, and independence in fact as well as on paper is an important posture to maintain whenever the credibility of a program is at stake. However, some efforts to gain information about programs, especially information intended for use in decisions about program installation or improvement, may be enhanced by close or dependent relationships. Whichever is the case, the evaluator is well advised at the outset of the effort to analyze all of the interrelationships that may be important, to try to get clear agreement on lines of responsibility, and to build appropriate communication channels. Such steps form a necessary basis for carrying out the evaluation efforts in an ethical way. We want to stress the ethical responsibilities not only of the evaluator, but also of the other parties, including their obligations to the evaluator as well as to each other once the decision has been made to submit the program to examination. Establishing interrelationships and communications early is also important for dissemination of evaluation results. It helps the evaluator target those results appropriately with respect to timing, mode of presentation, and the degree to which the evaluator's own judgments about alternatives should be included, all of which help determine whether the evaluation results will be used in decisions about the program.

Issues related to internal and external relationships in evaluation are discussed in detail in Chapter Seven; ethical problems and suggested solutions for dealing with some of them are the subject of Chapter Eight; and techniques and strategies for handling communication and dissemination to ensure greater utilization are treated in Chapter Five.

Relationships and the handling of ethics and communications are all influenced by the values the evaluator brings to the situation. The evaluation processes and products may also be subject to the same influence. The social sciences borrowed from the physical sciences the myth that science is value-free. As we know, science is not as value-free as it claims. And program evaluation takes place in about

---

and graceless constructions. Where the word *he* or *she* is used, the reader should interpret it to mean both *he* and *she*.

as value-full a context as can be found. There are the values that *surround* evaluators, and there are the values that evaluators themselves are burdened with. With respect to the latter, at least three kinds of values may influence what evaluators look at, how they look at it, and what they see. All evaluators carry around a set of deep-seated values that on a conscious plane might be called ideologies. Many evaluators, however, are not actively aware of these values because they share them so widely with their associates. For instance, most of us do not stop to question the "rightness" of prenatal care, equal employment opportunity, or the principle that more knowledge is good. Nor do we ponder the "wrongness" of routine corporal punishment in the classroom, limiting museum access to the privileged, or disclosing private information about clients. Thus, most evaluators would be similarly disposed toward evaluation issues that invoke such values. However, there are exceptions and extremes. For example, House (1976) argues that evaluation is a social mechanism for the distribution of resources and, therefore, the evaluator should ensure that the results of the evaluation are not only "true" but also "just." A viewpoint like House's can be expected to lead to an evaluation different from one conducted by an evaluator oriented toward "truth" alone.

At another level, evaluators may have personal preferences related to the content or conduct of particular programs that may threaten their objectivity or their acceptability to program sponsors. Consider an evaluator who is personally against using school programs as an employment resource or mechanism when the programs do not discernibly affect students. If this evaluator is faced with an educational program where the only real purpose, he suspects, is to provide jobs for teachers who would otherwise be unemployed, he may evaluate the program differently from an evaluator who feels that the employment goal is worthy in its own right. Or consider an evaluator who is asked to document the unique contributions of private schooling and who thinks that private schools have little unique to offer. He feels that any superiority shown by private schools can be attributed to the fact that they enroll above-average students and are able to afford smaller classes. It is interesting to speculate how his study would compare to one by an evaluator with a more favorable

8

attitude toward private schools. In general, evaluators need to try to identify any personal values that might affect their activities in a particular program, examine these values, and, in some cases, disqualify themselves.

The social ideologies and personal preferences of evaluators probably exert a less direct influence over their activities than do their professional values. Such values, based in large part on their professional training and favored evaluation "models," are clearly reflected in evaluators' choices of evaluation approaches, methods of investigation, analytic techniques, and the ways in which information is interpreted. In Chapter Six, we propose that a fairly good prediction of evaluation behavior might even be obtained from responses to a self-report measure requiring the evaluator to check his position on scales anchored from phenomenological to behavioristic, absolutist to comparative, independent to dependent, broad scope to narrow scope, and so on.

Research and Program Evaluation

As the reader will have gathered by now, we take a very pragmatic approach to program evaluation. Evaluators do what they have to do to answer the questions posed about a program, within technical and ethical boundaries. Therefore, we are somewhat impatient with the continuing argument over whether evaluation is or is not research. However, the argument does exist, and we would like to acknowledge it, comment on it, and leave it behind in this first chapter.

The stereotypes are as follows: Research is knowledge-oriented; evaluation is decision-oriented. Research derives from theories and principles; evaluation is atheoretical or, at best, diffuse and eclectic in its sources of inspiration and hypotheses. Research provides generalizable knowledge in the form of new theories and principles without necessarily offering immediate practical payoff; evaluation provides immediate practical payoff without necessarily providing generalizable knowledge. Research holds promise for future program development by providing basic information on which to

9

build; evaluation assumes current or past program development. Researchers invent treatments; evaluators do not.

Gephart and Potter (1976) have declared that the debate between "proponents of the research process" and "dissidents who asserted that evaluation was a different process" is settled. "More and more empirical methodologists have recognized that research and evaluation are variants of the scientific method which serve different purposes; are appropriate resolution strategies for different classes of problems; involve different sets of procedures; produce different kinds of results; and, when qualitatively assessed, require the use of different criteria" (p. 5; see also Gephart, Ingle, and Saretsky, 1972). Sommer would agree. His 1977 article in the *APA Monitor* is entitled "No, Not Research. I Said Evaluation!" Millman (1975, p. 2) states that research and evaluation "can be clearly differentiated at a conceptual level" although "there are more similarities than differences" in the skills and competencies that researchers and evaluators need. We think that, in general, the differences between research and evaluation are more often differences of purpose and style than of great substance. And, in particular, some evaluation efforts readily qualify as empirical research and others do not.

Going back into history, we are not sure that Kurt Lewin's (1958) classic studies of nutrition and behavior change in Iowa in the 1940s would not fit the definition of summative program evaluation. Ball's (1957) doctoral thesis was called educational research when it was conducted twenty years ago, but today we would clearly label it program evaluation. The producers of "Sesame Street" asked the formative evaluators this question: How often and at what intervals during an hour show should a letter or number be presented to the young audience? The research literature revealed precious little about the population of interest and nothing related directly to TV viewing. So the evaluators had to undertake studies to find the answers (Gibbon, Palmer, and Fowles, 1976). Did they suddenly lose their status as evaluators by embarking on such relatively basic research? G. Stanley Hall's work (Boring, 1957, p. 568) in the Boston schools in the late nineteenth century was a primitive kind of formative evaluation or needs assessment, but his name is famous in the annals of psycholog-

10

ical research. E. L. Thorndike's work (1924), which exploded the notion that training in the so-called "difficult" subjects developed generalized intellectual power, was a major contribution to learning theory, but the study design was much the same as might be used by program evaluators today and the conclusions apparently affected the school curriculum. J. M. Rice's studies in the 1890s provide another example of evaluation posing as research before people knew that there was supposed to be a distinction (Cremin, 1961; Cronbach and Suppes, 1962). Was the Eight-Year Study of Progressive Education (Smith and Tyler, 1942) research or evaluation?

If we consider the kind of evaluation sometimes called "front-end analysis," where the evaluator's task is to provide information for decisions about program installation, we can readily see that the evaluator might need to take into account the current knowledge base, theoretical expectations, sampling effects, and other factors familiar to researchers embarking on empirical investigations. Finally, while we allow that in many cases researchers invent treatments and evaluators accept treatments developed by others, *sometimes* researchers must use treatments developed by others or else replication, that highly valued scientific endeavor, could not take place, and *sometimes* "front-end" and formative evaluators play a significant role in shaping treatments (programs). As we suggested at the outset of this section, worrying about whether evaluation is or is not research seems to be a particularly unproductive way for evaluators to spend their time.

To Evaluate or Not to Evaluate

The focus of the chapters that follow will be on issues associated with evaluation purposes, methods, and evidence (Chapters Two to Four); dissemination, communication, and utilization (Chapter Five); values, relationships, and ethics (Chapters Six to Eight); and the training of evaluators (Chapter Nine). The two final chapters will focus on the evaluation of adult technical training programs and trends in program evaluation. Before we turn to those detailed discussions, however, one more topic needs to be addressed now.

The Profession and Practice of Program Evaluation

Evaluators tend to assume that all new human-service programs ought to be evaluated. And funding agents, sometimes out of ignorance about what evaluation and evaluators can do, frequently take the same point of view. Of course, it would be foolish to deny that such programs *will* be evaluated, one way or another. We evaluate our physicians' services and disregard their instructions—or change physicians—if we find them wanting. We make judgments daily about the adequacy of garbage collection, police protection, and termite inspection, not to mention the competencies of our children's teachers, the ethics of abortion clinics, and the'cost-effectiveness of psychotherapy, welfare programs, and public service messages on TV. The same can be said for those involved in delivering such services: the sanitation workers, police officers, teachers and principals, or TV producers. They are variously critical or congratulatory of their own efforts and those of their associates. Such informal evaluations are as inevitable as they are fallible. However, they do not correspond to the meaning of "evaluation" advanced in this book—that is, evaluation as a planned, systematic process, frequently with specially earmarked funds and with implementation procedures, roles, and standards for the quality of the evidence presented. Unless program directors and sponsors are willing to leave program evaluation to the vagaries of the informal processes, with the attendant risks of biased and ill-informed judgments, they are generally well advised to encourage systematic inquiries into the validity of program needs and to seek specific evidence of the effectiveness of their efforts.

At the same time, we should recognize that for particular programs there may be reasons why a decision *not* to evaluate in any formal sense might be made: if the program is provided at low cost to very few people; if the program is a one-time effort; if as a result of the "treatment" the clients will not be placed in a position to adversely influence the health, safety, or well-being of others; if the constraints in the situation prevent a professionally responsible evaluation; if there is no possibility that the results will be acted upon in decisions about program installation, continuation, or improvement; or if there is no one interested or informed enough to carry out the evaluation effort required. These reasons for not evaluating (in our sense of

12

the term) are paraphrased from those suggested by Grant and Anderson (1977) to steer administrators of adult training programs away from irrelevant or cost-ineffective evaluation efforts. The authors express the hope that "the last two reasons for not evaluating ... programs will dissipate with time and the persuasive performance of those who conduct evaluations and train evaluators" (pp. 3–4). However, the other reasons are valid. The point to be emphasized here is that decisions *not* to evaluate—to assemble orderly evidence about program needs, processes, or results—should be made as early and deliberately as the decision to evaluate.

Two

Evaluation Purposes

Chapter One listed six major purposes of evaluation. These purposes are stated in terms of a common element that runs through the writings of those identified with the field: namely, that evaluation bears, or should bear, some relationship to decision making. These purposes constitute our definition of *program evaluation*. At the same time, we indicated that there are many other definitions and "models" around, although we specifically disclaim any model status for our simple representation of the various purposes of program evaluation and of the kinds of situations that give rise to them. We recognize further that although these purposes can be separately described, they are not mutually exclusive, and we hope that they do not generate the kinds of confusion about their intent that Baker (1976, p. 2) calls attention to in other schemes. Specifically (and to paraphrase her statement), the six purposes are presented to help us organize the way we think about evaluation, not to control our actions or guide the specific ways in which evaluation is conducted.

Evaluation Purposes

Before we review each of these purposes in detail, it may be well to remind ourselves of some of the things that evaluation is *not*. It is not simply measurement and data collection, although measurement and data collection are usually important precursors to the process. It is also not decision making, although it must be useful for decision making to survive. It does not always qualify as research, although for some questions the closer the evaluation process comes to research the more valid and reliable it will be. It is not necessarily limited to determining how well programs achieve their objectives; it may begin before a program or policy is implemented, or it may touch on issues that were not envisioned at the time the goals or objectives of the program were formulated. It is not the exclusive province of social scientists, although psychologists, sociologists, economists, and others of similar bent have tended more than physical scientists or those in the arts and humanities to gravitate to the field.

The six major purposes of evaluation—or areas of involvement of evaluators—can each be broken down into a number of components. The major purposes and their components are listed down the left-hand side of Table 1. Table 1 also matches evaluation purposes and components to likely general methods of investigation, a match which is the subject of Chapter Three.

The content of this list of evaluation purposes benefited from Scriven's (1974) "Product Checklist." Scriven's list, however, is designed primarily for appraising completed educational products or evaluation proposals, while Table 1 is intended as an aid to overall evaluation planning. Now let us examine each of the six purpose categories in turn.

I. To Contribute to Decisions About Program Installation

Usually, the evaluation process has been thought to begin *after* the decision to implement an education, training, or social-action program. However, a number of the skills and techniques usually associated with existing or planned programs apply to what Harless (1973) calls "front-end analysis." Assessment of the needs for a program, evaluation of the adequacy of the conception, estimates of cost and of operational feasibility, and projections of demand and support

15

are all important precursors to decisions about whether to implement a program and about the size and scope of the installation. Untold waste, wheel spinning, and harm can be prevented by sufficient advance attention to such factors.

Some of our colleagues in engineering have not been caught as often as we have with inadequate investigations into feasibility. They frequently start out by designing software instead of hardware, making plans instead of equipment, using simulations in place of the real thing. Many received their inspiration from advance systems analyses in World War II, which doubled the chances of fighter planes intercepting Nazi bombers and increased the number of U-boats sunk by more than 50 percent (Pfeiffer, 1968). Our colleagues in publishing and manufacturing know what happens when their market research is inadequate. If nobody buys their products or books, they incur enormous losses as well as the wrath of stockholders and overstocked retailers. Experienced cooks try exotic new recipes on the family before they serve them to guests at a special dinner party.

But health officials attempt to distribute family-planning information to populations where the number of children in a family is an entrenched status symbol. A $45 million educational satellite is launched with no programs to be transmitted from it. Developers in countries where few people have cars build schools in locations far from public transportation lines. Legislation requires bilingual education in areas where the "native" language has never been written down. Elaborate experimental programs are launched in schools where, once the initial grant is spent, maintaining the program would take half of the school's total budget. Supplementary funds are allocated to school districts on the basis of the number of children diagnosed as "retarded"; is it any wonder that one county reported brain damage in 20 percent of its elementary school population? Reports indicate that the new closed-circuit TV training programs do not appear to be very effective; no one noted that the television sets were not delivered to some of the groups until the series had been underway for several months. (Guttentag and Struening, 1975, p. 4, have commented trenchantly that "evaluations continue without either raising or answering the primary question: 'Does the program

16

exist?' ") Employee-training programs are installed without determining whether organizational barriers will make it impossible for trainees to apply their newly acquired skills or whether supervisors' attitudes toward a program are so negative that it is likely to be scuttled or ignored. Elaborate licensing programs are pushed through as a means of eliminating competition in the occupation instead of protecting the public. Lengthy written procedures on how to qualify for special community health or economic assistance programs are distributed to a population verging on illiteracy. Horror stories? Yes. But each is an example of what can happen when programs are launched without appropriate concern for the context of the innovation.

It seems obvious to determine if there is a need for a program before one seriously considers installing it. There are at least two aspects to need: frequency and intensity (see IA, Table 1). In general, the more people who are presumed to have a need, the more likely it is that public support can be obtained for a program to fill it (for example, programs to reduce widespread illiteracy in developing countries). However, action may also be taken if the need, although not widespread, is seen as intense or grave. Recent extraordinary concern with mental retardation is a case in point (Anderson, 1973, p. 197).

Evaluators should be able to perform an especially important service in the area of needs assessment, because in the past relatively few program planners have approached degree of need directly, objectively, or even explicitly. If they have been explicit, they have tended to use their own and their colleagues' intuitions, second-hand reports ("Our social workers say that . . . "), general population indices that may not be applicable to the locale of interest, or "carrier" variables (for example, family income rather than actual appraisals of the needs of individuals in the income category). They have also tended to confuse possible solutions with problems; for example, in education, evaluators have defined needs in such terms as "individualization of instruction," "open classrooms," "differentiated staffing" (Blabolil, 1976). Scriven (1974, p. 27) presses for explicit distinction between needs described in performance-deficit terms (which we are stressing) and needs described in treatment-deficit terms. He suggests that

17

the two kinds of needs have quite different implications for evaluation.

Needs may be defined at the level of individuals (the potential clients for an educational, economic, or social-action program) or at a higher level of governmental or organizational requirement. As an example at the governmental level, consider what happened following Sputnik, when we were afraid that we were not going to produce enough scientists, mathematicians, and engineers to meet the technological and defense demands the nation faced. Extraordinary educational and professional interventions, many well funded by the financial standards of the day, were launched. The results were so "successful" that we feared an oversupply of engineers in the decade that followed, but many individuals benefited from the opportunities provided. An organizational need is illustrated by an industry unable to establish plants in a certain area or keep existing installations open without undertaking massive training efforts to ensure an adequate supply of trained workers. In many such instances, partnerships with —and even sponsorship by—state development offices have made such efforts possible. The addition or maintenance of several hundred jobs contributed sufficiently to the economic welfare of the area to encourage such cooperation. And individuals profited from the chance to upgrade their earning ability.

Problems arise if the needs projected from above conflict with the needs of the individuals whom the program must ultimately reach. From time to time there have been proposals to redistribute the population of the United States to relieve congestion in the cities. Such plans have not materialized, not only because of the tremendous logistics and costs involved, but also because of a basic unwillingness of people in a democracy to be moved on any basis other than their own volition. Young and Willmott (1957) describe the unhappiness of families in East London who were moved from their familiar neighborhoods to better housing in a strange district. Commenting on a similar kind of local redistribution effort, the Model Cities projects, Rothenberg (1975) suggests that "complicated social impacts of project activities on motivations, productive capacity, and decision-making processes may well have to be estimated, as well as more conventional notions of living standards, in order to predict continuing-future consequences of . . . projects" (p. 87). But, in the past, program developers have seldom bothered to document their rights to inflict programs on others—or to justify the particular techniques they have chosen. In fact, Chazan (1968) and others point out that such value decisions are outside the scope of evaluative research. However, we suggest that assistance in clarifying the range of alternatives that underlie major value decisions related to possible program installation is an important function for the evaluator at the stage of front-end analysis and properly belongs under evaluation of program conception (item IB, Table 1).

But let us return for a moment to needs assessment "models" (as they are called), whether they are applied to individuals, groups, or institutions. The most usual definition of *need* is "a condition in which there is a discrepancy between an *acceptable* state of affairs and an *observed* state of affairs" (Anderson and others, 1975, p. 254). Scriven (1974) rejects the definition of a need as a discrepancy between the actual and the ideal (although he admits it is a formula he used to like), "because we often need to improve and know how to, without knowing what the ideal would be like" (p. 25). Needs assessments may vary in their degree of objectivity, but they should at least qualify as systematic if they are to be discussed in the literature of program evaluation. Witkin (1976) provides a comprehensive review of approaches to needs assessment in the area of educational planning and evaluation. "Most writers agree," she says, "that a complete model should include at least these components: (1) consideration of goals; (2) procedures for determining the present status of those goals; (3) methods for identifying, describing, and analyzing discrepancies between goals and present status; and (4) methods for assigning priorities to those discrepancies. In practice, one or more of the components are often omitted, and the order of components 1 and 2 may be reversed" (p. 4). She also points to the dilemma that the broader the statement of the goal, the easier it will be to obtain agreement about its importance but the harder it will be ever to find out whether the goal is met.

Some of the key questions to ask in assessment of needs are:

19

What made us think in the first place that there were any needs "out there" requiring mitigation? Whose needs are we talking about? How can we find out whether the needs are frequent or intense enough to justify intervention? How much frequency or intensity is sufficient— that is, how much discrepancy between acceptable state and observed state is intolerable, or at least undesirable? According to whose standards or what criteria?

The problem of standards is a particularly difficult one to deal with in needs assessment as it is in many other aspects of evaluation. We are all aware that standards change with circumstances, expectations, and who is setting them. They also vary with the perceived ability of a society or institution to influence the phenomenon to which they pertain. What is considered a minimum standard of living in this country has risen dramatically in the last generation and is much higher than that considered tolerable in less developed nations. Standards for employability go up during times of widespread unemployment; standards for nutrition go down during times of crop failure.

The field of literacy offers a fairly straightforward illustration of both changing standards and multiple definitions of them (see Corder, 1971). The U.S. Census Bureau definition of "literacy" is "ability to read and write a simple message in any language." For their purposes, individuals with more than five years of schooling are *assumed* to be literate; if people do not have five years of schooling, self-reports of ability to read and write are accepted (a person who claims to be able to read but not write is classified illiterate). In World War I, the U.S. Army adopted "the equivalent of a fourth-grade education" as its definition of functional literacy. Currently, the Army gives literacy training to those who score below fifth-grade level on a norms-referenced test (and "graduates" those who subsequently achieve at that level). Increasingly, objective measures of reading and writing are replacing years of schooling or self-reports, because performance associated with those criteria has been found wanting.

Thomas G. Sticht, of the National Institute of Education's Basic Skills Group, has plotted the relationship between criteria of literacy and the proportion of the population judged illiterate, where the criteria are defined as follows (after Resnick and Resnick, 1977):

20

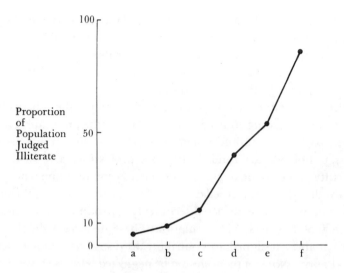

Figure 1. Diagram of the Relationship Between Criterion of Illiteracy and Proportion of Illiterates

(a) writing one's name; (b) reading familiar text aloud; (c) reading familiar text aloud and indicating recognition of content; (d) reading unfamiliar text to gain new information; (e) inferential reading of new text; and (f) interpretive and relational reading of texts. The curve, shown in Figure 1, corresponds closely to one that can be derived from National Assessment data (1972), which includes items corresponding approximately to criteria b-f. One can readily see here how differences in standards can affect the size of a population judged deserving of "treatment."

Even after the case has been made that a particular kind of program is needed, we must be prepared to consider the priority for this particular program in the face of competing needs and limited resources. As a very simple example, should a school system assign its special remedial-reading teachers to the large number of eighth graders reading at fifth-grade level or to the handful of fifth graders reading at second-grade level? Such decisions about priorities probably should go hand in hand with evaluation of the conception of the program—its quality and appropriateness (see item IB, Table 1).

In the same vein, do we have the capabilities—financial, personnel, material, and operational—to deliver the goods? If not, can we obtain them by the scheduled starting date and maintain them for the life of the effort? Whose support besides that of the "clients" and "staff" are we going to need to make a go of the program? The list might be long: community members, parents, educational associations, public officials, funding agencies, professionals. (Consider the difficulty of setting up a nationwide inoculation program when physicians disagree about its efficacy, or of installing a new mathematics curriculum that is considered technically unsound by the National Council of Teachers of Mathematics.) These are some of the elements of evaluation designed to contribute to decisions about program installation. None of them should be neglected. However, we should stress that evaluators tuned more to empirical investigation than to judgmental processes will be even more frustrated in front-end analysis than in pursuing the other five evaluation purposes outlined in Table 1, for Purpose I requires a full measure of wisdom, opinion, speculation, estimation, discretion, and political acumen. Economists talk about the "art" of cost projections at this stage (perhaps through simulation) as contrasted with the "science" they can employ after a project has already been installed. It is obviously easier to evaluate an existing program than one still on the drawing board (Sassone and Schaffer, 1977). However, front-end analysis is worthwhile if only a few potential clients, would-be program directors, and hard-pressed funding agencies are spared a dismal experience—or, conversely, promised a more rewarding experience than a poorly thought-out effort might have provided.

II. To Contribute to Decisions About Program Continuation, Expansion (or Contraction), or "Certification" (Licensing, Accreditation, and so forth)

This purpose is the one usually served by what is commonly called "summative" or "impact" evaluation, which many people, especially those outside the profession, see as the essence of evaluation. For example, Briggs (1976) has said of educational evaluation, "When an administrator, school board member, teacher or parent says, 'X will be evaluated,' he or she usually means that at some future point the question, 'Was X worthwhile?', will be answered." Weiss (1975) allows that "many public officials in the congress and the executive branch sincerely believe that policy choices should consistently be based on what works and what does not" (p. 18). Deming (1975) recognizes the widely shared view "that evaluation is a pronouncement concerning the effectiveness of some treatment or plan that has been tried or put into effect" (p. 53). That many people directly involved in evaluation take a broader view of evaluation processes—and the range of decisions they can contribute to—than do the decision makers they are trying to serve is one cause for tensions in the system. Even though we recognize that problem, our definition of evaluation even within the Purpose II category is somewhat more comprehensive than the general "summative" one (assessment of the overall effectiveness of a program in meeting its objectives).

Investigations under Purpose II may well include some of the same components as investigations under Purpose I. After a program is in operation, it is frequently important to monitor the continuing needs for the program. Some of them may change or even go away. In fact, the major criterion of success for some programs may be a drastic reduction in need for the services. Some health care delivery efforts whose goal is to minimize the need for treatment of disease through positive programs of health maintenance might fall into this category. Unfortunately, it is the nature of bureaucratic structures, which frequently house the kinds of educational and social-action programs we are interested in here, not to discontinue programs under any circumstances. And it is not easy for any structure to dismantle a program that has been shown to be successful. Yet in many cases, evaluation evidence of success, rather than of failure, should contribute to decisions about discontinuing a program.

Two other familiar items from Purpose I appear again under Purpose II: cost (E) and demand and support (F). Both need to be assessed against the estimations and projections made in the planning phase of the program, which may have been too optimistic or too pessimistic. Assessment of popular, professional, and other support for the operating program may help explain some of the impact or lack of impact the program had on its "targets."

Assessment of actual costs can now be related to the effects or benefits the program appeared to achieve: Have we spent $1 on a 10¢ problem? Or have we spent an average of $1000 a child to raise reading levels only one month? Of course, we may be pleasantly surprised to find that we have spent comparatively little and managed to effect important and substantial improvements. Much of the recent discussion of "accountability" in education and other fields assumes as an underlying premise that improved information and delivery structures can contribute to the productivity (and efficiency) of resource use. The economic principle of return on investment applies: Can the same benefits/effects be obtained at less cost? Can greater benefits/effects be obtained at the same cost? Such cost analyses have not figured prominently in many evaluations of education and social-action programs, partly because the evaluators were not sophisticated in the ways of economic analysis, partly because economists have been slow to communicate their techniques to evaluators in these fields and to help in applying them, partly because assigning values—monetary and otherwise—to the outputs of social and educational programs is very difficult. However, the situation seems to be changing. We are promised something beyond the fairly simple economic functions and relationships evaluators have tried to use in the past.

Jamison (1972), Rothenberg (1975), and Levin (1975) are among those who speak directly and understandably to the problems of economic analysis in education and social-action programs. Rothenberg, for example, immediately dispels the myth that cost-benefit analysis is "unitary or definitive," but he maintains that there is still a central focus that must be kept in mind. That focus is "the means-end relationship. . . . Its centrality stems from the existence of scarcity. . . . Under scarcity the productive resources—human and nonhuman—available to the society do not suffice to enable everyone's total wants (needs) to be satisfied. Every possible configuration of use of these resources makes possible a configuration of partial fulfillments. The target of the . . . system is to bring about the best configuration of fulfillments, or at least a configuration not inferior to any other" (pp. 58–59). Levin distinguishes among cost-benefit, cost-effectiveness, and cost-utility analysis. The first, requiring as it does the assignment of monetary values to both benefits and costs, is frequently difficult to apply in such areas as general education. However, it is the "father" of cost-effectiveness analysis, which allows the effectiveness of a strategy to be expressed in terms of "its actual physical or psychological outcome rather than its monetary value" (p. 92). Cost-utility analysis "incorporates the decision maker's subjective views in valuing the outcomes of alternative strategies" (p. 94).

In general, economists recognize the differential applicability of their constructs and analytic strategies to evaluating economic impacts (effects on national economic developments), environmental impacts (changes in physical and biological surroundings), and social impacts (effects on distribution of income and on the psychological, social, and physical well-being of people). It may be useful to sketch out in detail Sassone and Schaffer's (1977) formulation of cost-benefit analysis (CBA) and its relationship to cost-effectiveness and social-impact analyses. They trace CBA all the way back to an 1844 publication on "Measurement of the Utility of Public Works" by Jules Depuit, an engineer, and define CBA as an estimation of net benefits associated with alternatives for achieving public goals. They recommend six steps for a cost-benefit analysis: problem specification, identification of all costs and benefits, research design including development of assessment procedures, calculation of all elements in detail, data collection, and analysis-conclusions-presentation. At the problem-specification stage, the analyst chooses between assuming that the project takes place and estimating the consequences or assuming that the project is not undertaken and estimating the consequences. Although at first glance the second assumption would seem relevant only before a project is installed, analyses proceeding from it are also applied to projects already in operation. Cost-benefit problems are conceptualized in terms of the nature of the decision: accept or reject the project—accept if the "net present value" (NPV) is greater than zero; accept one of several alternatives—where the choice would be of the alternative with maximum NPV; or accept a few alternatives out of many—where capital constraints and dependencies among alternatives would have to be taken into account along with NPV. Other considerations figuring in the type of CBA approach advocated by Sassone and Schaffer include:

- Internal versus external effects, where the former accrue directly to the project; for example, elimination of mosquitoes as an internal effect of a mosquito-control project, with opening an area for recreation as an external effect.
- Measurables versus intangibles. So-called "incommensurables" would have to be made explicit to be included in the CBA, but there is a trade-off between quantification and credibility; some hard-to-quantify variables may be hypothesized to contribute so little that it is not worth dealing with them from the economist's point of view. However, consultations and comments from interested parties are included in typical economic reports of environmental impact studies (see Levin's description of cost-utility analysis above).
- Direct versus indirect effects. Examples of indirect effects might include the cost of unemployed resources (negative) or the opportunities offered by freeing resources for use elsewhere (positive). The analyst might not choose to address certain secondary effects (for example, the effects of a metropolitan transit system on surrounding counties) if such effects would be unlikely to influence project decisions. However, such eliminations must be justified explicitly.
- "Double counting." A pitfall to be avoided is including essentially the same costs or benefits in the analysis under different names.

Cost-effectiveness analysis, according to Sassone and Schaffer, addresses these decisions: determining the least-cost means of achieving a specified level of performance of a given system, or determining the greatest level of performance that can be obtained for a specified cost. Social-impact analysis, on the other hand, deals with and stresses noneconomic effects that might be relegated to the "incommensurables" category in CBA.

Evaluation Purposes

As can be seen, cost-effectiveness relationships are a little easier to conceptualize in Purpose II evaluations when the design pits one approach to mitigating a social or economic problem against another, than they are in the situation where "absolute" appraisals of value received for money spent must be made. When we say, for example, that trainees in program A performed significantly better on criterion tests than trainees in program B and the costs of the two programs are about the same, the decision to continue A and terminate B is fairly straightforward. (We say "fairly straightforward" because nothing is really straightforward in the evaluation business. If influential political forces have some reason for pushing program B, then . . . . But that situation is covered in Chapter Seven.) However, if the cost of A is twice the cost of B, the evaluator and program director must ask: Is the difference in effectiveness worth the extra money? Here economic analysis, using the concepts of productivity and efficiency, may offer some help.

Along this line, Glass (1976) concludes that evaluation in the areas of law enforcement and criminal rehabilitation, with a fairly consistent record of "no difference" findings, has paid off better than evaluation in other areas. He notes: "One feature after another has been altered experimentally, and crime and recidivism rates have remained unchanged. . . . If cutting reformatory sentences in half does not produce increased recidivism, then shorter sentences are 100 percent more cost-effective, *ceteris paribus.* Doing as well as in the past but doing it more cheaply is a gain in value as surely as is doing better at a greater cost" (p. 11).

The more "usual" component of Purpose II evaluation is embodied in item IIB, Table 1: global effectiveness of the program in meeting need. This phrase is generally interpreted to mean effectiveness of the program in meeting the goals or objectives espoused for it, where the goals or objectives are themselves based on the perceived or documented need the program was designed to address. As suggested in the cost-effectiveness example above, evaluation efforts oriented toward component IIB may be conducted in either a comparative or absolutist framework. In a comparative framework, results will be judged in comparison with the performance of another group (perhaps exposed to an alternative program) or with earlier performance by the same group. In an absolutist framework, results will be judged according to some performance standard related to program objectives. Cronbach (1963), early on, discouraged curriculum evaluators from relying on a "horse-race" approach, which at that time generally involved comparing performance of one group exposed to the new curriculum in math, physics, or some other subject with another group offered traditional school courses in the subject. These curricula frequently were intended to accomplish different goals, and the problem of ensuring both comparable and valid measurement for two groups in such a situation—which is something like pitting a Clydesdale against a quarter horse—continues to loom large. However, Scriven (1967) consistently maintains that comparison is an important part of all evaluation and that even if the two curricula are designed for different purposes, the evaluator must attend to relative outcomes across many dimensions. Certainly there are cases when the most meaningful question to be addressed in evaluation is whether one treatment or delivery system accomplishes a certain effect better than an alternative system—especially if the systems differ profoundly in cost or in such factors as ease of execution, popularity, or potential for negative side effects.

The two subcategories under "Global effectiveness in meeting need" in Table 1 are "Short-term" and "Long-term." Ideally the decision whether to look for long-term or short-term effects should depend on the nature of the program and the needs it serves. The effects of a first-term algebra course might best be evaluated immediately at the end of that course, as students prepare to enter second-term algebra. However, the effects of a high-school training program on "parenting" can be determined only after the students have become parents. Short-term effects may be all that we are concerned about in evaluating certain television shows, audio-visual materials, billboard campaigns, and job-training programs. But it is hard to imagine many instances where long-term effects are not the object of community health, certification and licensing, rehabilitation, urban planning, or environmental protection programs. Bronfenbrenner (1975) noted, for example, that "two years was regarded as a minimum for gauging long-range aftereffects" of early childhood interventions such as Head Start (p. 520).

But four problems plague us. First, it is sometimes not feasible to measure the ultimate criterion of program effectiveness. For example, the ultimate criterion of a training course for firefighters is effectiveness in combating fire, but we hate to think of having to wait around for a three-alarmer to test the trainees' prowess (and it would be next to impossible to obtain valid and reliable assessment under those conditions anyway). Furthermore, it would be difficult and certainly destructive to try to simulate such conditions in the training center. Second, it is an awesome task to follow up for any considerable length of time adults who are free to move about the country. For that matter, longitudinal work with school children is not much easier, because moving parents tend to take their children with them. Weinstein (1975) points to some of the complexities involved in maintaining multiyear medical records and in locating medical patients who do not return for treatment. "Lifers" in prison, military personnel with long enlistments, institutionalized "incurables" offer better opportunities for long-term studies, but even there pardons, discharges, and miracles may alter the population. Besides, we spend comparatively little time inventing programs to improve the social and economic welfares of such populations. Third, extraordinary problems of privacy and confidentiality attend many attempts to keep longitudinal records. Fourth, outsiders (government agencies, school boards, and elected officials, to name a few) want—and sometimes demand—evaluation results before the program has had a fair chance to take effect or before apparent effects can be interpreted. This problem alone has probably sent more evaluators screaming from the field than any other.

Evaluators seem more attentive to possible program side effects (items IIC and D, Table 1) than they were a few years ago, partly because of the emphasis placed on side effects by such authors as Messick (1970), Scriven (1967), and Suchman (1967). This concern with side effects is more novel among those working in the educational and social-action fields than those in medical fields, where researchers have long attended to the issue even when distributors and practitioners appeared to ignore their warnings. Of course, not all side effects are negative. When early Head Start advocates could find little comfort in the size of IQ increments among their charges (an inappropriate major criterion of effectiveness of that program in any case, but one used simply because "the tests were there"), they could point with some pride to the involvement of enormous numbers of parents and to the diagnosis and treatment of medical defects for many, many children (Temp and Anderson, 1966; Grotberg, 1969).

Side effects are included on the Table 1 checklist to remind evaluators once again that limiting themselves to estimating how effectively a program meets its intended outcomes may distort or impoverish the picture of the program's impact. Of course, it is not possible for evaluators to list—or measure—all potential side effects of a program. However, once evaluators are familiar with the program, they should be able to make some fairly good guesses about variables that, though not specified in the program objectives, deserve examination. For example, these classes of variables frequently figure in the search for side effects: drop-out (client drop-out, program-personnel turnover), attitudes (of those who receive the program, those who deliver it, and those who are excluded from it for one reason or another), transfer effects (to other content areas or areas of activity). (See Anderson and others, 1975, pp. 364–367.)

Results of investigations of continuing needs, costs, and demand and support should all be considered along with results of impact studies (focusing on both intended and unintended outcomes) in making decisions whether to continue a program, expand it or cut it back, or stamp it "approved" or "disapproved" when certification, licensing, or accreditation is at issue.

III. To Contribute to Decisions About Program Modification

Purpose III corresponds to the one usually ascribed to formative evaluation, although information about program components can also be obtained in the context of a global appraisal of effectiveness after a program is in full operation. Of course, if a program is cast in an unchangeable mold, the evaluator is wasting his time seeking information to help make it better. Fortunately, this is seldom the case. But the role of evaluation in program improvement has been less well sold than its role in overall appraisal of effectiveness, and sometimes the problem is simply to show program directors how useful feedback can be to them. One hypothesis advanced to account for the poor quality of evaluations under Title I of the Elementary and Secondary Education Act, in addition to the lack of technical sophistication in some of those thrown suddenly into evaluator roles, is that local education agencies have not seen any program-improvement benefits accruing to them from the effort. Thus they have done as little as possible to get by and "satisfy the Feds."

A major distinction between evaluation efforts devoted to Purpose III and those devoted exclusively to Purpose II is the emphasis on describing program processes in contrast to program products. As Table 1 indicates, the evaluator may seek information to guide program improvement in a broad range of areas, including:

A. Program objectives. Are the objectives valid and useful for attacking the needs the program is designed to serve? Do they meet with general acceptance from those who can be expected to influence, or be influenced by, the program? "Acceptance" criteria have acquired a bad name in some evaluation circles, because the "smiles test" has sometimes been the only form of evaluation. However, as the listing in Table 1 suggests, information about the acceptability of the program and its components to the parties involved is important for decisions pertaining to program installation, continuation, modification, defense, or defamation (see items IE, IIF, IIIA, IIIB, IIIC, IV, and V).

B. Program content. Is the content relevant to the program objectives and does it cover those objectives adequately? Is it technically accurate and professionally acceptable (that word again!)? Is it overly structured or not structured enough for the sophistication and "styles" of those who must deliver the services and of those for whom the services are intended? Does the program fit the backgrounds of the clients? Are we asking clients to make assumptions or handle materials that are beyond their experience or over their heads? Or are we talking down to them? What about the effectiveness of each of the components and the order in which they are presented, prescribed, or delivered? It would usually cost more than it is worth to evaluate the effectiveness of each tiny program module separately. However, some components that program directors are least sure of probably deserve specific attention; for example, how long the four-year-old audience for "Sesame Street" could attend to TV presentations of letters and numbers (Palmer, 1976, p. 138). Sequence can also be important; for example, offering experience B before experience A could make all the difference in whether clients return for a second visit to a mental health clinic.

C. Program methodology. Here we are concerned not with the "what" but with the "how" of program presentation. How much control do clients have? How much does the staff have? How is the program delivered? Are there better methods than group discussion for dealing with the families of the mentally ill? What about the pacing and length of the program? Would weekly sessions over six months be more effective than an intensive one-week "immersion course"? How are clients reinforced for participating in the program? Are the reinforcements adequate to sustain interest?

D. Program context. Weiss (1975), Tumin (1970), and Campbell (1972) all stress the significance of the political context in which educational and social-action programs are evaluated. Weiss summarizes: "Political considerations intrude in three major ways, and the evaluator who fails to recognize their presence is in for a series of shocks and frustrations. First, the policies and programs with which evaluation deals are the creatures of political decision.... Second, because evaluation is undertaken *in order to* feed into decision-making, its reports enter the political arena.... Third, ... evaluation itself has a political stance.... It makes implicit political statements about such issues as the problematic nature of some programs and the unassailableness of others, the legitimacy of program goals, the legitimacy of program strategies, the utility of strategies of incremental reform" (pp. 13-14). We shall return to this theme often in this book and especially in Chapter Seven. However, under Purpose III, we are concerned primarily with the political and administrative stance and workings of the program itself. A program may be technically sound, but if it is administered badly, if staff working relationships are ill-defined or antagonistic, if facilities and resources are inadequate, if fiscal policies are unsound and support shaky, or if the program's own public relations efforts are insensitive, the program may be doomed. Ah, you say, but most of those things should have been worked out at the planning phase; what happened to evaluation under Purpose I? Of course they should have, we reply, but this is the real world. There may not have been any evaluator when the program was conceived; planning may have been haphazard; or conditions may have changed—the "cup and lip phenomenon" (Weiss, 1973). The evaluator, playing the role of an objective near-outsider, may be in a position to spot problems that program managers in their day-to-day involvement and proximity cannot see. Many management consultants continue to earn their keep because they can get from staff information that has escaped supervisors or can detect poor accounting practices that have slipped into the system. The evaluator may also be able to apply some empirical methods as well as subjective judgment in this general area. We should note that the opposite of the good-program–bad-context combination can exist. We know of instances where a program has received far better press than its merits warrant, because of the charisma of its director, because of enthusiastic if unenlightened support from the community, or because of Hawthorne effects.

E. Personnel policies and practices. Investigations and descriptions in this area go hand in hand with inquiries into program context. With respect to clients: Who is the program reaching? How is it reaching them? Do the clients represent the "needy" population the program was designed to serve? Or are they ever likely to be able to contribute to the societal or organizational needs that the program was designed to serve? With respect to staff: Who are they? How were they selected? Are they qualified to deliver the program initially? If not, is in-service training adequate to qualify them? With respect to both clients and staff: Who stays in the program? Who leaves? What efforts are made to retain "worthy" clients and staff? Are there any attempts to weed out clients who are not profiting from the program or staff who are incompetent? What effects do such personnel policies seem to have on the operation and effectiveness of the program?

IV. and V. To Obtain Evidence Favoring a Program to Rally Support, or to Obtain Evidence Against a Program to Rally Opposition

These two purposes recognize the realities of program evaluation. Many evaluators shun evaluations with these purposes; many people who commission evaluations are unwilling to admit to their real motives. But occasions do arise when decision makers must rally support for a program in order to sustain it or drum up opposition in order to "kill" it and divert funds to other things. We must at least entertain the possibility that the public interest will be served on some occasions by declared efforts to seek support or opposition. We must also consider the possibility that the evaluator might perform a legitimate function on these occasions; that is, if the requirement is not sweeping contrary evidence under the rug, but simply collecting evidence (where none has been collected before) or disseminating existing evidence convincingly. With respect to disseminating evidence, some evaluator may have been at fault in the first place if reports were written in such a way that, even though they contained data favorable to the program director's position, the director could not interpret or use them. A chapter on dissemination follows (Chapter Five), but it should be noted here that the items listed under Purposes IV and V in Table 1 are all oriented toward the groups that the program director is trying to influence. And it is certainly true that the same evidence may be accepted or rejected, depending not only upon the initial inclination of the recipient but also on the way that evidence is presented.

In any case, it is better in the long run if the agency authorizing the evaluation faces up to its real motives and does not hide them from the evaluator. The evaluator's responsibilities, in turn, include defining clearly the nature of the evidence being presented, indicating any lack of representativeness, and ensuring the validity of the evidence even if it is only a partial picture of the total state of affairs.

The situation for the evaluator is happier when decision makers are willing to consider both negative and positive evidence about the effectiveness and operation of a program. The so-called adversary model of evaluation applies directly to this situation (Churchman, 1961; Stake and Gjerde, 1971). Usually, evaluators with roots in the social sciences operate on the assumption that they should gather the best and most relevant data they can, interpret it according to accepted criteria, and then present the results as fairly and openly as possible, no matter what the implications for the program. Thus, the evaluator is charged with both finding and presenting evidence. The adversary model of evaluation has its beginnings in the legal profession, which offers its own approach to reaching "truth." Specifically, the proponents of the adversary model (Kourilsky, 1973; Levine, 1973) suggest including in the evaluation process an adversary who will "cross-examine" all the evidence as it comes in or at least providing for later presentation of evidence on both sides of all important issues. We have tended in the past to reject the adversary model on the grounds that good debating techniques may prevail over good evidence (Anderson and others, 1975, pp. 21–22), but we have come around to the point of view that at times, especially when the results are truly equivocal and much is at stake, this approach may be best. (Another application of the adversary model is discussed in Chapter Six.)

VI. To Contribute to the Understanding of Basic Processes

Pursuing decision-oriented evaluation does not preclude investigating, within the context of the same study, basic processes in at least one of the disciplines listed under Purpose VI in Table 1. In the last chapter, we considered some of the overlaps between research and program evaluation. Nonetheless, evaluators cannot afford to lose sight of two key issues. First, if they have agreed to perform evaluation services for a program, those services must be the central focus of their efforts. It is unfortunate that a few social scientists have given program evaluation a bad name by trying to bootleg their theses, pet research projects, or tests of new methodologies on someone else's hard-gained evaluation funds. Second, in spite of any zeal they may have to contribute to the basic disciplines, evaluators must recognize any limitations inherent in specific evaluations that undercut their ability to test hypotheses or make generalizations, processes important to fundamental contributions to knowledge. Many evaluation scenes present such limitations.

The Profession and Practice of Program Evaluation

Table 1 details the purposes that program evaluation can serve and the variety of variables that are proper targets of scrutiny in evaluation enterprises. The table has forced us to delineate our inclusions and exclusions and has provided a framework for the review of the evaluation-related issues that form the bulk of this chapter. We hope the table will serve another purpose for program planners and evaluators: acting as a systematic reminder of the variety of purposes program evaluation might serve and the variables on which it might focus. No, Eva Baker, we are not suggesting that any evaluator anywhere anytime would attend to all of the components there. Baker (1976) has very reasonably made an impassioned plea for economy and parsimony in evaluation efforts, not to mention conscious control of our impulses to ask questions when the answers cannot possibly be the basis for action. However, we feel that there are many sins of omission as well as commission in program planning and evaluation, and failure to attend to some important issues sometimes results from a lack of reminders that the issues exist. Table 1 can serve as such a reminder.

Table 1. Purposes and General Methods of Program Evaluation

Legend:
— Likely investigation method
▓ (shaded block)

Purpose	Experimental Study	Quasi-Experimental Study	Correlational Status Study	Survey	Personnel or Client Assessment	Systematic "Expert" Judgments	Clinical or Case Study	Informal Observation or Testimony
I. To contribute to decisions about program installation								
A. Need								
1. Frequency								
a. Individual				▓		▓		▓
b. Society				▓		▓		▓
c. Other (that is, industrial, professional, governmental)				▓	▓	▓		▓
2. Intensity								
a. Individual				▓	▓	▓	▓	▓
b. Society				▓	▓	▓		▓
c. Other				▓	▓	▓	▓	▓
B. Program conception								
1. Appropriateness						▓		
2. Quality						▓		
3. Priority in the face of competing needs						▓		
C. Estimated cost								
1. Absolute cost				▓		▓		
2. Cost in relation to alternative strategies oriented toward same need								

Table 1 (continued)

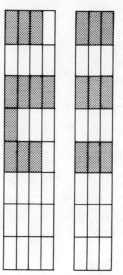
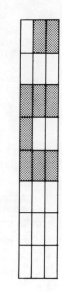

Experimental Study	Quasi-Experimental Study	Correlational Status Study	Survey	Personnel or Client Assessment	Systematic "Expert" Judgments	Clinical or Case Study	Informal Observation or Testimony

D. Operational feasibility
   1. Staff
   2. Materials
   3. Facilities
   4. Schedule

E. Projection of demand and support
   1. Popular
   2. Political and financial
   3. Professional

II. To contribute to decisions about program continuation, expansion, or "certification" (licensing, accreditation, and so on)

   A. Continuing need
      1. Frequency
         a. Individual
         b. Society
         c. Other

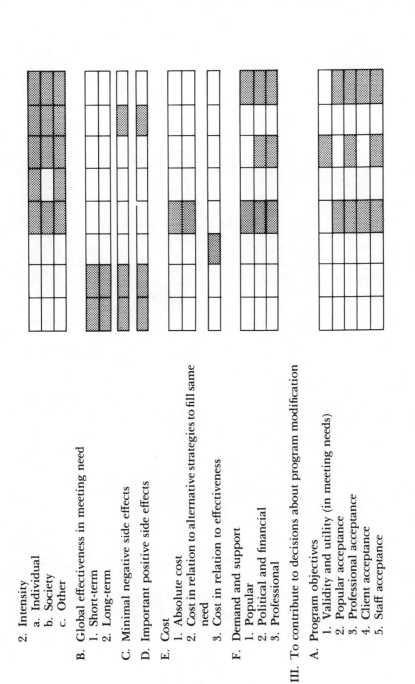

2. Intensity
   a. Individual
   b. Society
   c. Other

B. Global effectiveness in meeting need
  1. Short-term
  2. Long-term

C. Minimal negative side effects

D. Important positive side effects

E. Cost
  1. Absolute cost
  2. Cost in relation to alternative strategies to fill same need
  3. Cost in relation to effectiveness

F. Demand and support
  1. Popular
  2. Political and financial
  3. Professional

III. To contribute to decisions about program modification

A. Program objectives
  1. Validity and utility (in meeting needs)
  2. Popular acceptance
  3. Professional acceptance
  4. Client acceptance
  5. Staff acceptance

Table 1 (continued)

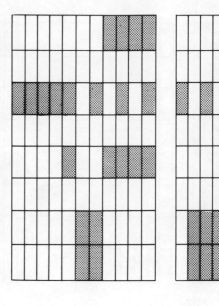

	Experimental Study	Quasi-Experimental Study	Correlational Status Study	Survey	Personnel or Client Assessment	Systematic "Expert" Judgments	Clinical or Case Study	Informal Observation or Testimony

B. Program content
 1. Relevance to program objectives
 2. Coverage of objectives
 3. Technical accuracy
 4. Degree of structure
 5. Relevance to backgrounds of clients
 6. Effectiveness of components
 7. Sequence of components
 8. Popular acceptance
 9. Professional acceptance
 10. Client acceptance
 11. Staff acceptance

C. Program methodology
 1. Degree of client autonomy
 2. Effectiveness of delivery methods
 3. Pacing and length
 4. Reinforcement system, if any
 5. Client acceptance
 6. Staff acceptance

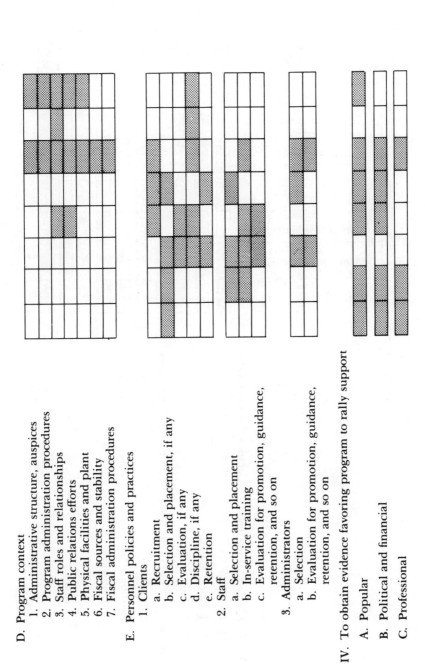

D. Program context
  1. Administrative structure, auspices
  2. Program administration procedures
  3. Staff roles and relationships
  4. Public relations efforts
  5. Physical facilities and plant
  6. Fiscal sources and stability
  7. Fiscal administration procedures

E. Personnel policies and practices
  1. Clients
    a. Recruitment
    b. Selection and placement, if any
    c. Evaluation, if any
    d. Discipline, if any
    e. Retention
  2. Staff
    a. Selection and placement
    b. In-service training
    c. Evaluation for promotion, guidance,
       retention, and so on
  3. Administrators
    a. Selection
    b. Evaluation for promotion, guidance,
       retention, and so on

IV. To obtain evidence favoring program to rally support

  A. Popular

  B. Political and financial

  C. Professional

Table 1 (continued)

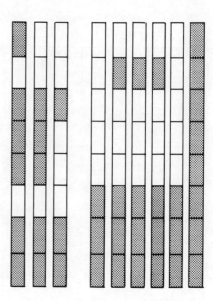

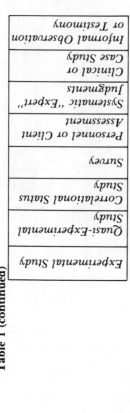

	Experimental Study	Quasi-Experimental Study	Correlational Status Study	Survey	Personnel or Client Assessment	Systematic "Expert" Judgments	Clinical or Case Study	Informal Observation or Testimony
V. To obtain evidence against program to rally opposition								
A. Popular								
B. Political and financial								
C. Professional								
VI. To contribute to the understanding of basic processes								
A. Educational								
B. Psychological								
C. Physiological								
D. Social								
E. Economic								
F. Evaluation (methodology)								

Three

Evaluation Methods

It has been said that researchers fall into two categories: the method-bound and the problem-oriented. The method-bound have a favorite method, analytic technique, or instrument and spend their time looking for a problem to apply it to; if their search fails, they may apply the method anyway—either inappropriately or gratuitously. The problem-oriented may never have any particular technique or scale named after them—and may also occasionally apply methodologies inappropriately—but at least they start with the premise that the choice of methodology should follow from, not precede, the delineation of the purpose of the investigation. Whether or not one recognizes program evaluators as researchers, experience with program evaluators suggests that a similar dichotomy may exist in their ranks: The closer evaluators' names, or those of their mentors, are linked to particular evaluation schemes, the more likely they are to apply those schemes and accompanying methodologies, regardless of the subject of inquiry.

The Profession and Practice of Program Evaluation

Table 1 joins evaluation purposes to general methods of investigation and thus derives from the second school of thought: The choice of investigatory method (and eventually of specific measurement and analysis techniques) must depend on the evaluation's purpose. This statement implies, of course, that the purpose has been well defined. In Szaniawski's (1975) words, "The only criterion of evaluation for a method is its efficiency with respect to a given objective, but as long as the latter remains hazy, the rationality of the procedure must remain in doubt" (p. 446). There are other considerations as well (for example, the nature and context of the program being evaluated), and we shall touch on some of them later in this chapter. But first let us review the eight general methods listed across the top of Table 1. (In making up their own "personal tables," evaluators should leave space to add additional methods, for it is not likely that we have included all possible general approaches.)

Experimental and Quasi-Experimental Studies

First, there are experimental and quasi-experimental methods. If our broad listing of possible evaluation purposes is accepted, then many evaluation questions cannot be answered well by any kind of experimental study. However, experimental studies are almost essential if evaluators are seeking relatively unequivocal answers to certain questions about program or component effectiveness or if they hope that some of their evaluation findings will make fundamental contributions to knowledge of basic processes.

True experimental designs depend in their most precise form on random assignment of the units of concern to experimental and control groups. Where such designs are possible, they will generally be preferred to quasi-experimental designs (and certainly to correlational-status studies), because the results are more directly interpretable and generalizable. As an example, let us use the one provided by Nunnally (1975) about the evaluation of the effect of a drug on the moods of hospitalized and depressed patients: "All of the depressed patients in a hospital are randomly divided into two groups, with equal numbers of subjects in each group. The patients

44

in the [control] group are given a sugar pill which closely resembles in appearance the actual drug. The patients do not know which pill they are receiving, and the persons administering the pill do not know which pill they are administering. Dependent measures concern psychophysiological processes, self-ratings of moods, and ratings by attendants concerning adjustment status of patients. One can see in this simple example [that] all of the major, possible confounding variables are controlled" (pp. 116-117). In other words, we can be fairly sure that whatever results we get can be attributed to the drug and not to extraneous variables such as national events, maturation, selection factors, motivation, or variations in data collection procedures (Campbell and Stanley, 1966, pp. 5-6). Further, we will have defined the type of group to which the results might be generalizable, although since this experiment is limited to a single hospital, generalizations to other settings present some problem.

We have argued elsewhere (Anderson and others, 1975) that failure to employ randomization is sometimes as much a matter of poor thinking or timing as it is of practical pressures. However, there are practical pressures that preclude randomization, even when a true experimental design would probably provide the best answers to the evaluation question. (As one of our professors used to say, all behavioral scientists are not fortunate enough to have identical twins so that they can baptize one and keep the other for a control.) The politics of providing a socially desirable program to one group of people while withholding it from another equally deserving group are formidable. John Tukey (in informal discussion) has suggested that assigning clients at random to "equally elegant *appearing* treatments" may be one way to cope with this problem and still maintain an evaluation design capable of yielding relatively unequivocal causal inferences. For example, an educational evaluator might give a reading program to one randomly constituted group of pupils and extra art supplies to the other. But, apparently, few evaluators have been influenced by Tukey's suggestion (however, see Ball, 1976). Another and more widely adopted approach is to divide the group of "deserving" into random subgroups and offer the desirable program to the subgroups sequentially; that is, hold subgroup B as a control group while subgroup A receives the program, and then offer the program to subgroup B later. Differences in context over time and the possibility of "contamination" from the first group to the second sometimes present sticky problems in this design. (Of course, the problem of contamination is not limited to sequential designs. Gray and Klaus (1970) refer to "horizontal" diffusion, which can occur when simultaneous experimental and control groups in a social intervention simply live in the same neighborhood.)

There may be occasions, of course, when a program is thought to be so valuable that it would be inhumane to deny it to anyone it might help. In such cases, we wonder whether the program needs any general evaluation, for its worth has already been judged. However, evaluators could investigate possible side effects or variations that might improve program delivery. (See the discussion of ethical problems of withholding treatment in Chapter Eight.)

Before we get carried away with attempts to develop true experiments, we should note that in some instances, quasi-experiments may be preferred on other than opportunistic grounds. According to Ross and Cronbach (1976), "The main argument *for* nonrandom comparison, besides that of practicality, is that of representativeness. If one wishes to generalize over diverse communities, only one or two of which consent to a random manipulation, the random experiment may give no better answer to the original question than would comparing nonequivalent groups" (p. 96). There are other instances where assigning eligible clients at random to experimental and control groups, as "eligibility" is usually defined in social and educational interventions, may not allow appropriate generalizations; for example, when eligibility alone does not determine who enters the program. Head Start is a good example. We know that even when families are in the same general economic category, those who send their children to Head Start are different from those who do not. If we want to predict the effectiveness of such a program, the evaluation study should focus on a sample similar to the group that will actually elect the program; that is, the sample should be chosen from those who are eligible *and* likely to elect the program. Ross and Cronbach have noted that Rubin's 1964 article "provides the best general discussion" they have seen "on the trade-offs between random and nonrandom experiments" (p. 96). The Rubin article also discusses matching as an alternative to randomization, one of the most controversial topics in the literature. (See also Campbell and Stanley, 1966, pp. 70–77; Campbell and Erlebacher, 1970, pp. 597–615; and Sherwood, Morris, and Sherwood, 1975, pp. 183–223.) While matching is a controversial means of selecting comparable experimental and control groups, there is general agreement that once one discovers that the experimental and control groups differed significantly to start with, certain covariance adjustments become "quite misleading and even absurd" (Anderson and others, 1975, p. 233; see also Roberts, 1976). If the experimental and control groups are random samples from the same population, it might make sense to ask what the results would have been if the two groups were identical to start with (the covariance technique). But if some self-selection has occurred, and if the two groups are not randomly drawn from the same population, it does not make sense to ask such a question. Could the ants beat the elephants if they were the same size?

Two other areas of general concern deserve mention. First, there are instances when the desired comparison group may not be a random subset from the same population as the experimental group; that is, the comparison group is deliberately selected to represent a "normal" or desirable level of functioning. For example, middle-class children may be used as the control against which to evaluate the effectiveness of compensatory education programs for poor children, or successful managers may be the comparison group in evaluating training programs for those being considered for entrance to the management ranks. In such cases, however, attempts are generally made to "equate" the experimental and comparison groups on as many other relevant background variables as possible; for example, age, sex, geographical location, marital status, ethnic background, and physical or psychological condition (Anderson and others, 1975, p. 86; Anderson, 1973, p. 201).

The second issue pertains to the units assigned to experimental and control groups or, in the case of some quasi-experimental designs, the units that make up the groups to be compared. If the program is designed for individuals, then individuals are the proper units of assignment and comparison. However, if the program is designed for intact groups such as families or classrooms, then those groups must be the units of concern. Again, it is a question of generalization: Do we wish to generalize to individuals or to groups? "A design must reflect the ultimate, substantive question addressed by the evaluator" (Ross and Cronbach, 1976, p. 97). There are some related practical and analytical considerations. Evaluators working in schools, for example, frequently find it impossible to work with less than intact classes because of schedules and management arrangements. More important, the "lawnmower effect" has to be dealt with. All the students in the same class are subject to some common influences that are probably not characteristic of any other class. The teacher is the most important of these, but we might also consider as an example the noise of the lawnmower outside the classroom, which makes important instructions inaudible to all the students. Need we remind the reader that the units of assignment and comparison in the study should also be the units of analysis?

A number of intriguing quasi-experimental designs have been presented in the literature; for example, time-series designs, pretest-posttest nonequivalent-group designs, and the regression-discontinuity model (see Campbell and Stanley, 1966; Cook and Campbell, 1975; Anderson and others, 1975, pp. 301–310). All of these designs have comparison groups of sorts—sometimes the target group at earlier times (time-series designs), sometimes specific groups judged to be roughly comparable to the treatment group (nonequivalent-group designs), sometimes groups that differ from the treatment group in one significant and continuous dimension such as family income (regression-discontinuity model), sometimes abstract population groups.

This last variation is especially popular in educational evaluation. The performance on standardized tests of a group receiving an instructional intervention is compared with the performance of national norms groups; for example, change in performance in mathematics from grades 4 to 5 for the group being studied is compared with the difference in average performance between the national samples of fourth- and fifth-grade pupils in the norming administrations of the test. As Horst, Tallmadge, and Wood (1975) point out, "The model rests on the assumption that the achievement status of a particular subgroup remains constant *relative to the norm group* over the pre- to posttest interval if no special treatment is provided. Empirical support for this assumption is minimal" (p. 72). The application of this model is not limited to education. Evaluation of the effectiveness of a state highway-safety program may use national accident statistics as a criterion, or the success of a community health program may be evaluated in terms of statewide incidence of disease. Such comparisons are particularly fraught with problems associated with the lack of comparability of the treatment group and the larger comparison population.

However, all nonequivalent-group designs suffer from comparability problems to some extent. In a famous paper Campbell and Erlebacher (1970) show how "regression artifacts in quasi-experimental evaluations can mistakenly make compensatory education look harmful." Gilbert and others (1975) regard most quasi-experiments as not much more than "fooling around with peo-ple" (p. 182). Nevertheless, when true experimental designs are impossible, even Campbell (1972) directs evaluators *seeking answers to certain types of questions* (and we continue to emphasize that interdependence between purpose and methodology) to "self-critical use of quasi-experimental designs" (p. 191). The key word here is *self-critical,* and the best safeguard against jumping to unwarranted conclusions from a weak design is to try to array additional evidence. To paraphrase an example we gave earlier (Anderson and others, 1975, pp. 307-310): If an evaluator of an instructional program suspects that home conditions may have as much to do with student achievement as the program itself, he should attempt to measure home influence directly and take account of it as best he can in interpreting the evaluation results. If he must use subjective ratings of program effectiveness, he should try to obtain these ratings from several different groups involved in the program (instructors, students, and administrators) and supplement them with additional (and, ideally, nonreactive) kinds of measures that would appear to bear on the same

49

process. Webb (1967) notes that "the most persuasive evidence and the strongest inference" frequently come from such a "triangulation of measurement processes" (p. 34).

Correlation Methods

Correlations have received a bad name in evaluation circles, because some hard-pressed program evaluators have been tempted to draw causal inferences about programs from simple correlational status studies (the third heading in Table 1). For example, when they obtain negative correlations between number of full-time aides in the classroom and pupil achievement, they conclude that aides are not worthwhile, without stopping to think that aides are likely to be assigned to classrooms where pupil achievement has already been determined to be low. Or they have looked at correlations between frequency of public service TV "spots" and reductions in traffic accidents and conclude that the program was effective, without taking into account the gasoline shortage that occurred during the same period. However, there are a number of positive uses of correlation methods, including regression analyses, in evaluation studies. For example, Dyer (1966) introduced a regression-analysis concept (elaborated by Dyer, Linn, and Patton, 1967) to classify schools by relative effectiveness in meeting certain objectives. The same approach can be used in ordering the effectiveness of other kinds of units delivering various kinds of health, economic, and social services. Basically the approach involves identifying variables that would seem, on empirical or philosophical grounds, to be associated with certain outcomes. These variables might be measures of previous school achievement or "hard-to-change" conditions such as socioeconomic status (SES). In the analysis, regression of actual final performance on initial performance or other variables is obtained for each of the units involved (for example, reading scores on measures of SES for sixth-grade pupils in thirty elementary schools). Discrepancy indicators based on the mean scores actually obtained and the mean scores predicted from the "independent variable" are then computed for each unit and used to identify the units performing either well above or below expectations—in graphic terms, the "outliers." This approach would seem to be particularly useful in formative (Purpose III) evaluation efforts where decision makers are seeking clues to program improvement. An intensive comparison of what the apparently more successful units are doing with what the less successful units are doing may provide such clues. (See also Burke, 1973; Trismen, Waller, and Wilder, 1973; Convey, 1975, 1976; Marco, 1974.)

A similar kind of analysis can be applied to an experimental-control group design, where the evaluator can ask whether correlations traditionally obtained are being affected by a given program. For example: Did our baseline measures for the experimental group under- or overpredict its later success relative to a comparable group of untreated people? This is a reasonable question to ask about compensatory programs, where frequently one goal is to reduce expected correlations between such characteristics as ethnic group or economic status and later performance. It is important for evaluators to remind themselves from time to time that correlation coefficients, as well as means, can be useful dependent variables in both experimental and quasi-experimental designs.

In Table 1, we suggest several other situations where correlation methods may be useful in answering questions about programs. Correlations between costs and program-effectiveness indices across several programs or program components (item IIE3) may be helpful in decisions about program continuation or modification. If the evaluator is examining the validity of selection or placement procedures for clients, staff, or administrators, then correlations between selection measures and measures of performance are as useful as they are in the personnel departments of business and industry or in the admissions offices of schools and colleges (see items IIIE1b, 2a, and 3a). Under Purpose III, evaluators studying program personnel policies might want to examine the relationships between personnel-evaluation procedures and external criteria of personnel effectiveness (items IIIE1c, 2c, and 3b).

While the results of correlational status studies will not often contribute directly to understanding basic processes (Purpose VI), they will frequently suggest hypotheses worthy of further investiga-

51

tion. Additionally, in some cases, examination of tables of intercorrelations, especially when that examination takes the form of structural analysis, will serve to clarify the meaning of certain constructs. For example, when we are considering the construct validity of a measure, we are as interested in the variables that show low correlations to that measure as we are in the variables that show high correlations. Scores on the measure should be significantly related to scores on theoretically relevant measures and should show no significant relationship to scores on theoretically unrelated measures. Patterns of relationships derived from evaluation efforts may sometimes cause us to reconsider our theoretical appraisals of what is relevant and irrelevant.

Surveys

Surveys are a major tool of evaluation efforts directed toward needs assessments (IA and IIA, Table 1), cost estimates (IC and IIE1 and 2), operational feasibility (ID1-3), program acceptability (IE, IIF, IIIA2-5, IIIB8-11, IIIC5 and 6, also aspects of IV and V), and certain program-personnel policies and public-relations activities (see items under IIID and E). These surveys may take a variety of forms: personal or telephone interviews, questionnaires, observations, content analyses of records, systematic examination of financial data. They may be either sharply focused or broadly comprehensive in content or units surveyed.

The decision to use a survey depends in the first place on the purpose of the information-gathering effort. The choice of a particular survey methodology depends in turn on that purpose and also on the nature of the units to be surveyed and the level of confidence the evaluator seeks in the results. The technical aspects actually present far fewer problems than the conceptual aspects. There are many adequate guides to constructing interviews and questionnaires (see, for example, the references listed on pp. 216–217 and 314 of Anderson and others, 1975), building rating scales (for starters, see the list on pp. 317–318), conducting observations (pp. 269–270), carrying out content analyses (p. 84), and reviewing financial data (Wixon, Kell, and Edford, 1970). In cases of interviews, questionnaires, or rating forms, the guidelines generally include appropriate admonitions to suit the level of the task to the level of the individual or group to which it is to be administered (avoid a tenth-grade reading level in a questionnaire for clients who are poor readers), to ensure the acceptability of the interviewer to the interviewee (in some situations the evaluator would be wise to send an interviewer of the same sex, race, or ethnic group as the interviewee), to avoid questions with sensitive overtones when possible (or to reword such questions so that they do not put the respondent under undue strain), and not to get carried away in asking questions that are irrelevant to the purposes of the survey (they make the task tedious, increase the likelihood of incomplete responses, and add unnecessarily to the costs of data analysis). In the case of observations, the admonitions frequently relate to making those observations as systematic yet as unobtrusive as possible.

There are also many adequate guides to survey sampling when it is not necessary to survey every unit of concern (see the references on p. 344 of Anderson and others, 1975). However, in some political contexts, the evaluator should be encouraged by the program director to include all cases even though it is not methodologically necessary. Making those who were initially negative to a program part of an effort to obtain information about it may change them to believers—or at least ensure a feeling that their views are considered.

It is the first kind of consideration—what purpose a survey is to serve—that calls for the greatest skill and judgment. One example should serve to illustrate this point—and a few other evaluation points as well. When *Man: A Course of Study* (MACOS), an elaborate and sophisticated social-studies curriculum for elementary-school children, was invented in the 1960s, evaluation of the program figured large in the effort (Bruner, 1965). Indeed, the National Science Foundation (NSF), which sponsored the development, stressed evaluation in all of the course-improvement projects it was funding. For example, in June 1963, NSF held a study conference on evaluation for curriculum developers from a variety of fields (Hastings, 1963). It is interesting to note that the conference seemed to deal almost exclusively with development, analysis, and application of tests in evaluation,

53

without focusing to any extent on the context in which the program would be presented. However, a rather comprehensive formative evaluation was carried out with MACOS. It included information about student and teacher attitudes toward the materials as well as observations and estimations about their effects (Hanley, Whitla, Moo, and Walter, 1970). Subsequent investigations included interviews with principals and other administrators as well as teachers (Cort, Henderson, and Jones, 1971). Evidently at no time did any of the evaluation teams consider the reactions of the public and parents to the curriculum, reactions which, when they surfaced, made headlines in newspapers and had repercussions in the United States Congress. MACOS and NSF suffered. As Stake (1976) sums it up: "The National Science Foundation is assiduously searching for new program review and evaluation procedures. Previous evaluation projects did not alert them to adverse reaction to the NSF curriculum 'Man: A Course of Study.' Almost none of their evaluators have been questioning whether the original funding decisions made sense, and few evaluation reports have called for negative action. NSF has a hard time explaining what it has been getting for its evaluation dollar" (p. 3).

Personnel or Client Assessment

Personnel and client assessment is, of course, used in experimental and quasi-experimental designs for obtaining information about program and component effectiveness. The category at the top of Table 1, however, refers to program or client assessment when it is out of the context of a "design" and when the information obtained from the assessment is to serve some evaluation purpose directly. We are also limiting *assessment* here to assessment of competencies, attitudes, physical and psychological conditions, and other characteristics intrinsic to the content and purposes of the program (characteristics the program might be seeking to change), as opposed to attitudes and other reactions about the program (or the concept of the program). For example, if we are conducting a needs assessment to contribute to decisions about installing a family-nutrition program, we might assess how much those we seek to serve know now about nutrition. If we find out that they know more than we suspected, we might recommend not installing a program or installing only a limited version. Or we might use the information to help design a program that will speak directly to the areas where the families' knowledge and practices are poorest.

This example relates to using client assessment as a general method in evaluation studies designed to assess needs (as in items IA and IIA, Table 1). There are some other evaluation purposes that might be served by assessment of clients and personnel (including potential clients and potential personnel). These include assessment of competencies of potential staff as a part of estimating the operational feasibility of a proposed program (ID1); assessment of the characteristics of clients being recruited for a program in order to determine whether the recruitment effort is appropriately targeted; assessment of the characteristics of clients actually participating in the program (IIIE1a and b) to determine whether the program is serving those who need it; and assessment of the characteristics of program staff and administrators, where the results might help explain the results of evaluation efforts designed to determine program impact (IIIE2a and 3a).

Table 1 also suggests that on occasion it is desirable to assess the characteristics of clients retained and not retained in a program in order to evaluate retention policies (IIIE1e). Such assessment information may also be useful in interpreting impact results. As Proper and St. Pierre (1976) observe, infrequency of attention to attrition "will inhibit the development of better evaluation technology and will obscure the identification of valuable educational and social programs" (p. 1). Yet they note, as Jurs (1970) noted earlier, that "mortality estimates are seldom given in reports of educational studies and that virtually no textbooks include attrition as a topic of interest" (p. 1). Attrition is, of course, a problem that pervades many aspects of evaluation. We do not mean to suggest here that information enabling evaluators and program directors to document it can be obtained only by assessment of clients or personnel. However, assessment results may often be useful in describing the characteristics of clients who remain in a program (or in control groups) and of those who do not and in keeping track of the characteristics of staff members who stay with a program over a period of time and of those who leave. Drop-out or turnover is seldom random, and it is very likely that a program affects—or would affect—those who stay with it and those who do not differently. It is also true that staff members responsible for initial delivery of a program may have certain attitudes about it, and investments in it, that those coming in later do not adopt.

As with survey methods, the mechanics of personnel and client assessment are better spelled out and easier to deal with than the decisions to undertake such assessment in the context of evaluation. The literature on constructing, selecting, administering, and interpreting tests and other measures of cognitive and affective characteristics and of the physical and psychological conditions of people is too voluminous for us to attempt to list even basic texts. Furthermore, each discipline (for example, education, psychology, physiology, medicine, dentistry) has its own special measurement techniques. About all we can add here is that fundamental notions of fairness, reliability, and validity must be respected whatever the assessment device. The reader might want to refer to the brief discussions of those issues—in the context of educational assessment but applicable outside that context —in our encyclopedia (Anderson and others, 1975, pp. 43-46, 325- 329, and 458-462).

Sampling, of course, can be used in personnel assessment as well as in other kinds of surveys. Special item- or matrix-sampling techniques can be used to avoid giving every member of the group(s) to be assessed all of the items or tasks in a measure and still allow good estimates of the mean and, in most cases, of the variance of the measure (Barcikowski, 1972; Lord, 1962; Shoemaker, 1973). However, as with sampling with questionnaires and interviews, there may be occasions when the efficiency derived from sampling is outweighed by practical or public-relations considerations. For example, most evaluations of educational programs take place in the real world of instructors and students, who are becoming increasingly reluctant to give their time to studies that offer nothing in return. Frequently schools are asking evaluators for feedback in the form of reliable individual test scores. So, even though evaluators might be able to get by quite nicely with group data (derived from item or matrix sampling), they may not have any groups to collect data from if they do not make concessions to the wishes of program personnel for information that is useful to them.

Systematic Expert Judgment

In the previous chapter, we deliberately defined evaluation in terms of ratiocinations as well as operations. In so doing, we are placing judgment at the heart of the evaluation process and not limiting the evaluator's role to one of data collection. We have more respect for the methods of social-science research and measurement than Stake (1976) apparently does. He said recently at an educational research conference: "The big RFPs [requests for proposals] for *evaluation* continue to expect that the evaluation methods will be those of social-survey research and experimentation even though these methods deliberately attempt to avoid subjective judgment and valuing, even though these methods are intent upon contributing to the understanding of education in general rather than to the understanding of the *particular* programs studied or to *particular* programs like them" (p. 1). Certainly the evaluator's judgment must come into play in choosing research and measurement methods, as well as in directing attention to what kinds of evaluation purposes deserve attention, to what the results imply for those purposes, and even to whether any evaluative inquiries are warranted in the situation.

In the sixth heading in Table 1, however, we are not limiting ourselves to the judgments of the evaluator or evaluation "team," although those judgments may certainly qualify as "expert" in many program settings and deserve major consideration. We are including here the judgments of other experts as well, who may be asked to comment in a systematic way on such concerns as: the initial and continuing needs for a program (items IA and IIA); the adequacy of the program conception (IB); estimations of costs and cost-effectiveness (IC) —economists and accountants may be helpful here, especially if the program directors have trouble balancing their own checkbooks; and demand and support for the program (IE and IIF), especially with respect to political, financial, and professional support. Expert panels may play key roles also in answering many of the questions important to decisions about program modification (Purpose III). For example, experts in the content of the program may be asked to estimate the validity and utility of the program objectives in meeting the needs the program is designed to serve (IIIA1) and in judging the professional and technical accuracy and acceptability of the program content, materials, and delivery system (for example, items under IIIB, C, and D). In almost all cases, the staff of the program represents an expert committee of sorts, and their judgments provide key data for decisions about program continuation and modification. Experts in the appropriate fields can also help in evaluating the personnel and public-relations policies of the program. Expert judgment can be misused, of course, by both program directors and evaluators, a topic we will go into in connection with Purposes IV and V.

Table 1 does not touch specifically on the use of experts in evaluating evaluations, but this use is important, especially if evaluations cover several program variations or settings. For example, Congress is justified in asking about the overall effects of programs funded with the taxpayers' money to provide compensatory education, parent-child centers, work-study opportunities, preventive medicine, drug-abuse centers, and so on. Yet, although the units in such groups may bear the same name, be supported under the same auspices, and supposedly function under the same set of guidelines, seldom do they operate in exactly the same way. Furthermore, even the mandated evaluations of individual programs in a group may differ in significant ways. The application of expert judgment to a complex array of programs can be illustrated with Bronfenbrenner's (1975) attempt to answer the important general question, "Is early intervention effective?" He found only seven project evaluations that met his criteria for inclusion in a combined analysis: "systematic follow-up data . . . available for at least two years after termination of intervention; similar information . . . provided for a control group matched on relevant personal characteristics . . . and background variables; and data . . . comparable from one project to another" (p. 520).

Yet in the period of interest (since the mid 1960s), there were dozens, if not hundreds, of evaluations of early-intervention projects, many sharing the same label and sponsor (for example, Head Start). Furthermore, information available across the seven projects consisted only of IQ scores and scores on standardized achievement tests. (Even the tests varied, and "equivalent" scores across them had to be estimated.) Therefore, generalizations from the analysis had to be limited to the cognitive sphere—and to a narrow subsection of that. Bronfenbrenner concluded that, in spite of the limitations in the number of projects and types of data, the available data were "not without considerable scientific and social significance" (p. 522), and he proceeded with his combined analysis. However, when he interpreted the results, he drew heavily on the results of some twenty "well-designed" *additional* researches. More important, both the interpretation and the presentation of generalized "principles of early intervention" (regarded as a milestone in the field) profited from Bronfenbrenner's judgments derived from years of experience and unparalleled familiarity with the relevant literature and practice in the field.

Guttentag (1976) gives special attention to the problems of aggregating data across social programs conducted in different sites and according to different "rules." She even points to programs such as Model Cities where the requirement of "differentness" across cities is written into the enabling legislation. Her prescriptions for evaluators faced with such variations: "Aggregate inferences rather than data" (p. 18). Guttentag recommends the application of "decision-theoretic approaches" which "permit the formal explication and prioritization of the objectives of diverse groups" and "Bayesian, rather than classical, statistics . . . to link the prioritized objectives to inferences about . . . programs." She notes further that the "Bayesian system is data-inclusive, so that it can use all of the data generated through experimental methods, as well as qualitative, archival, anecdotal, and other variegated forms of information—it is just that the diagnosticity of the data will vary" (p. 20).

We can assume that systematic expert judgments can thus be handled in the system. Furthermore, whether we go Bayesian or not, collecting systematic expert judgments or inferences about program and component effectiveness derived from a variety of evaluations of related programs has merit. Such collection may be the only means for making generalizations about the effectiveness of massive social, economic, or educational interventions and providing decision makers with guidance in such critical areas as fund allocation.

Clinical or Case Studies

"A case study is an intensive, detailed analysis and description of a single organism, institution, or phenomenon in the context of its environment" (Anderson and others, 1975, p. 46). As such, case studies are useful as the basis for hypotheses that deserve investigation in larger evaluation studies and for suggestions about variables and measures to include in those larger efforts. They are also useful as follow-ups to evaluation studies to help explain results. Earlier in this chapter we talked about the use of regression analysis to classify the relative effectiveness of schools or other program units in meeting certain objectives. Case studies of the units identified as most effective by such an analysis may point to particular characteristics of those units and the techniques they use that seem to contribute to their greater effectiveness.

Case studies may be the chief or overarching evaluation method in some situations, especially when the phenomenon to be evaluated is global. Suppose that the evaluator's task is to assess the "organizational effectiveness" of an institution or agency. No single measure, design, or analysis will determine the verdict. Rather, the evaluator is probably going to enter the organization with his own set of notions (sometimes dignified as theories) about what a strong system should be and observe and listen accordingly. For example, as Taylor and Bowers (1972) suggest, "If a natural systems analyst were to fall from the sky [to the deck of a ship] he would not first ask what the organization was trying to accomplish. Rather he would nose around the ship a lot and ask questions, perhaps about the degree of conflict among work groups, the nature of communications, the level of racial tensions, the percentage of billets that were filled by people with the appropriate level of training, what the commanding officer was trading away to get the personnel he wanted, the morale of the officers and crew, and the like" (p. 7).

This evaluator is to be contrasted with one who is more goal-oriented (although distinguishing between stated and actual operative goals presents a challenge) and who attempts to develop multiple criterion measures of how well goals (of both kinds) are being met. Even so, the more structured evaluator of operational effectiveness will probably have to adopt a clinical approach to combining the various data into a summary statement or recommendation pertaining to the overall effectiveness of the unit.

/ Bussis, Chittenden, and Amarel (1975) argue for something close to a case-study approach in evaluating elementary-education programs, especially the so-called "open-education" variety. They would, for example, focus on (a) children's capabilities rather than the objectives they are to attain, (b) facilitating environments rather than educational treatments or methods, and (c) evaluation evidence in terms of standards of quality for a wide variety of student and teacher behavior, as well as aspects of the physical environment, rather than specific behavioral criteria (p. 11). Their approach might better be labeled "phenomenological" than "case study," in the tradition of Stone (see Anderson and others, 1975, p. 191; or, as they suggest, Kelly, 1955, and Snygg and Combs, 1959). This approach is also related to what Rippey (1973) calls "transactional evaluation" and to the clinical approach proposed by Glaser and Backer (1972a and 1972b). However, we have not tried to make such fine distinctions in the categories listed at the top of Table 1. Rather, we are using "Clinical or Case Study" to refer to a wide range of methodologies that treat multiple variables and processes (either formally or informally), entail direct involvement of the evaluator (perhaps even in a participant role), and are concerned with one functioning unit at a time. In some instances, case studies may involve long-term field work in an institution or other setting. Such situations have special consequences that may be both beneficial and counterproductive for the investigator's insights (Everhart, 1977).

Of course, results from a number of clinical or case studies may

61

be aggregated to influence program decisions. For example, evidence about the intensity of individual or group need may accumulate from a number of cases (see item IA2, Table 1); estimates of operational feasibility (ID) may be based on knowledge of success or failure of a similar plan. The concern here, as with informal observation or testimony, is that if the aggregation is not systematic, any generalized decisions may be overreactions. Five cases of a serious contagious disease over a short period in a given locale may be shocking but, without more information than the fact of the five cases, the government might not be justified in setting up a massive immunization program. Similarly, we cannot often judge whether a new program will work simply from knowledge of how a similar program has worked somewhere else without much more digging into the specific and varying characteristics of both the proposed and the operating program. But we do not mean to discourage evaluators completely from case-study research or other kinds of documentary analysis. It has a place in studying the functioning of particular units. There is also an argument to be made, as Weiss and Rein (1969) suggest, for collecting qualitative information over time from a relatively small number of cases. Such data may be useful for program-improvement decisions. They may also be useful, as we indicated at the beginning of this section, in planning larger studies or deciding whether larger studies are justified.

Informal Observation or Testimony

The final general method listed at the top of Table 1 was until very recently the most prevalent form of program evaluation. How many of the textbooks that we used were adopted on the basis of anything other than testimony? Testimony was the mother of Head Start, the swine flu vaccination program, the concept of Community Mental Health Centers, and countless other massive social interventions in the last decade. Sometimes that testimony was preceded by informal observation of violent events. The Model Cities program and many other programs aimed at the victims of urban poverty were inspired far more by the drama of television newscasts than by scientific surveys or systematic expert judgment. Even after programs were funded and installed to varying degrees, formal investigations and data collection efforts have been limited largely to those required by legislative or funding bodies. And the quality of such investigations has varied directly with the force of the funding agency in monitoring evaluation efforts or in taking them into account in decisions about continuation. Furthermore, we doubt that more than a tiny percentage of program directors will ever readily welcome evaluations of the impact of their programs; a few more may be convinced that some kinds of evaluation may be helpful in program improvement. Funding agencies, for their part, seem quite ready to accept systematic help in decisions about program installation—in those instances where political or personal considerations have not already been established as the overwhelming determiners. Because of all these conflicts and pressures, testimony and informal observation will probably be around for a long time. However, in many cases program directors and sponsors, and would-be program directors and sponsors, are penalizing themselves and their constituencies by allowing major decisions to depend on powerful voices and squeaky wheels. Informal observation and testimony are not really *investigation methods,* as proclaimed at the top of Table 1, but they are certainly *likely.*

Evaluation in the Service of Purposes IV and V

The relationship of the general methods to Purposes IV and V has a slightly different meaning from the relationship between the methods and the other four purposes. The program director is likely to ask: What kinds of evidence are most likely to rally support for (or opposition to) the program? As the shaded boxes in Table 1 suggest, a professional audience would be less swayed than a lay or political and financial audience by evidence accumulated through surveys or assessments; a lay audience might be more susceptible to reports derived from informal observations or testimony than either of the other two audiences would; and the public would join professionals in respecting relatively "hard" data. The problem for the evaluator is not so much selecting the most appropriate general investigation method for the evaluation purpose but deciding whether he or she can go along with that purpose—if it has been possible to worm it out of the program director.

A naive evaluator may at least be able to begin data collection and related activities with a broad objective of discovering "truth." Of course, he may become increasingly frustrated in that search by authorities who already know what "truths" they want. The evaluator who is privy to the bias underlying the decision to commission an evaluation must deal with his own value system and the ethics of the situation at the outset: Does the evaluator have strong personal convictions about the program that are antithetical to the commissioner's interests and that may render any evaluation attempts unproductive? Or are the evaluator's personal convictions so congruent with the commissioner's that the findings are likely to have a double bias? Can the evaluator counsel the program authorities away from any requirement to ignore possible sources of contrary evidence or to bury any such evidence that may emerge? Is there another evaluator on the scene with an adversarial role?

If evaluators can satisfy themselves that they can perform legitimate functions in the face of avowed Purposes IV or V, then it is sensible for them to proceed by asking what kinds of evidence they want to present and what the best methods are for obtaining that evidence. In any evaluation report, we attempt to present data and judgments in a form that will be most meaningful to the intended audience (see Chapter Four). However, the particular methods that evaluators probably should use with caution—or avoid—in conducting investigations for Purposes IV and V are those involving "expert" judgment or testimony. Even though evidence from these sources may be highly influential in shaping the opinions of some decision makers, it is too easy to "stack the deck" in the direction desired. For example, by deliberate and apparently legitimate means we can choose expert panels that will be likely to give high or low ratings to program components. We should keep "scientific" program evaluation and practical political persuasion as distinct as possible.

Evaluation Methods

Summary of the General Methods

We have reviewed eight general investigation methods for evaluation studies and a ninth category that figures importantly in practice but can hardly be justified as a tool of the "professional" evaluator. The eight methods may be thought of as proceeding from the analytic to the enumerative to the clinical. Only the experimental and quasi-experimental studies are "analytic" in Deming's (1975) sense; that is, "The aim is to try to learn something about the cause-system . . . to be in a position to change it or leave it alone, whichever appears to be better for the future benefit of man or of his pocketbook" (p. 58). Surveys fall in the enumerative category, where "action . . . will depend purely on the estimate of the number or proportion of the people or materials . . . that have certain characteristics (sometimes on the maximum or the minimum)" (p. 57). Expert judgments form the basis of two general methods at the clinical end of the spectrum. Of course, these judgments can be aggregated over cases or situations, and, if the aggregation is systematic, we approach the definition of an enumerative study. The distinctions among analytic, enumerative, and clinical studies are not trivial, because the different categories of investigation call into play different statistical techniques and different concepts of "confidence" in interpreting the results.

We have counseled elsewhere about the imprudence of prejudging and stereotyping "hard" and "soft" evaluations: "These are extreme forms of a continuum that enmeshes design, data, and analysis. . . . But most comprehensive evaluations, of necessity, include both hard and soft components" (Anderson and others, 1975, p. 195). The important thing is to suit the method to the motive, so to speak. However, we can consider the nine general methods listed at the top of Table 1 as roughly scaled from "hard" to "soft"; there appears to be a correlation between choice of general method and the degree of specificity of the program goal or the object of investigation. Evaluators of organizational effectiveness, institutional vitality, career education, quality of school life, and so on seem more likely to wind up with case-study or phenomenological approaches, while evaluators

65

of the effectiveness of reading programs, particular drugs, or television shows seem likely to use the "harder" analytic approaches. This apparent relationship could derive directly from a correlation between the kinds of phenomena evaluators prefer to study and their predispositions to adopt certain investigatory techniques (see Chapter Six), or it could reflect the difficulties inherent in analyzing complex variables so that the parts capture the whole. Bice, Eichorn, and Klein (1975) take the latter view, noting with respect to public health programs: "As one proceeds along this continuum from evaluations of medical efficacy of specific treatments to studies of the effectiveness and efficiency of health service systems, the scope and complexity of relevant factors increase, and, in consequence, classical methods of evaluation become correspondingly less applicable" (p. 605). However, serious long-term problems for the "profession" would be generated if more sophisticated evaluation efforts came to be associated almost exclusively with relatively trivial variables and if analytical evaluators consistently avoided global phenomena altogether—or vice versa. Such associations can be avoided with a little consciousness raising, attempts at constructive interaction by evaluators in "opposite" camps, and continuing scrupulous attention to fitting the investigation methods to the problem, regardless of the evaluator's predispositions.

Four

Evidence

In the last chapter we touched on a number of special issues involved in choosing and applying evaluation methodologies. These included the orientation of evaluators toward methods or problems; attention to the context as well as the purposes of the evaluation in determining evaluation methodologies; possibilities of "contamination" from experimental groups to control groups; problems of generalizing conclusions from subjects who "volunteer" for a program or evaluation study; alternatives to random assignment of subjects to experimental and control groups; situations in which "noncomparable" comparison groups may be appropriate; fallacies in uses of correlations, gain scores, and covariance adjustments; the dependent relationship between units of study and units of analysis; "triangulation" of measurement processes; the use of correlation coefficients, as well as means and variances, as dependent variables in experimental and quasi-experimental designs; attrition problems in evaluation studies; decisions to use the whole population of interest rather than samples; possibilities for aggregating inferences, as well as data, across program units; biases and overreactions likely to be associated with some of the methods of investigation; molar versus molecular program goals and their influence on the choice of program evaluation methodologies; the central role of *judgment* in all evaluation efforts; and the basic reluctance of program officials to get involved in evaluation.

In this chapter we shall focus on the kinds of evidence that evaluators may present as the basis for conclusions intended to inform program decisions. The eight general methods of investigation initially presented in Table 1 are repeated in the left-hand column of Table 2. Each of these eight methods is augmented by examples of the types of evidence frequently offered by investigators using that method. Thus the survey method (IV) has as examples: (A) projections of manpower needs, (B) summaries of attitudes and opinions about an ongoing program among program-delivery staff, and (C) descriptions of program characteristics, operations, costs. These kinds of evidence might be assembled in the interests of decisions about installing a training program in automobile mechanics in a particular group of counties (A), the confidence of the present staff of a job-placement program for the handicapped in their ability to offer services and the desirability of additional staff training in employer and client relations (B), and extending an income-supplement program to families in other parts of the state (C). We shall give a number of other specific examples of types of evidence to aid such decisions in later parts of this chapter.

First, let us review quickly the other components of Table 2. Listed across the top are ten sources of evidence. These sources are not necessarily independent. For example, expert opinion might be obtained through questionnaire or interview, and social indicators might be taken from records. We have deliberately allowed some confounding of kind of evidence and technique used for gathering it, in order to use terms that would best communicate the essence of the sources of evidence.

Within the cross-tabulation we have associated relevant

sources of evidence with types of evidence typically presented under the general methods of investigation. The associations provide our informal definition of "appropriate" sources of data for various types of evidence. However, they are meant to be suggestive rather than prescriptive. From Table 2 it can be seen, for example, that we suggest that an investigator presenting correlations among client (for example, trainee) measures (IIID) might include the following in the matrix: test scores, data derived from questionnaires or interviews, ratings (grades), and results from clinical examination. Likewise, an investigator conducting a case study oriented toward a phenomenological analysis of institutional change (VIIB)—for example, in a human-service agency—might use information derived from logs and diaries, observations, and expert opinion.

Evidence of Program Impact

Gilbert and others (1975), in what must be one of the most significant works in the burgeoning evaluation literature, review the types of evidence offered in *experimental* (and impact) evaluations of eight social innovations and eight socio-medical programs (pp. 71–100). Ten of these programs are listed below with the types of evidence collected. All studies used randomly selected control groups even though, in the interests of economical summaries, reference to the control group is not made in each citation.

The New Jersey Graduated Work Incentive (Negative Income Tax) Experiment—reduction in number of working hours families contributed (it had been argued that a "guaranteed minimum income" would lead to a substantial decrease in work effort, perhaps to the point that people quit working altogether). Evidence was collected through interviews and questionnaires and told in favor of the program; that is, reductions in working hours were less than 10 percent for most groups. (See also Watts, 1973.)

Social Workers for Multi-Problem Families—changes in family relationships, care and training of children, social activities, household practices, health conditions, and use of community

69

Table 2. Examples of Types and Sources of Evidence Frequently Associated with the Various General Methods of Investigation[a]

■ — Likely source of evidence

	Test Scores[b]	Questionnaire or Interview Data[c]	Logs, Diaries[d]	Observations[e]	Ratings[f]	Clinical Examinations[g]	Records[h]	Social Indicators[i]	Expert Opinion	Hearsay, Chance Encounters
I. Experimental study										
A. Differences between performance of clients in the program and performance of nonclients	■			■	■	■				
B. Performance differences for clients exposed to program variations	■			■	■	■				
C. Data on differential program effects for clients with different characteristics	■	■			■	■				
II. Quasi-experimental study										
A. Changes in client performance over the time of exposure to the program	■			■	■	■				
B. Changes in client performance for different program components, variations	■			■	■	■				
C. Differential predictions of "success" for clients exposed and not exposed to the program	■			■	■		■			

III. Correlational status study

    A. Correlations between program characteristics (sometimes including costs) and client performance

    B. Correlations between client characteristics (such as race, sex) and their performance

    C. Correlations among program characteristics

    D. Correlations among client measures

IV. Survey

    A. Projections of manpower needs

    B. Summaries of attitudes and opinions about an ongoing program among program-delivery staff

    C. Descriptions of program characteristics, operations, costs

V. Personnel or client assessment

    A. Profiles of characteristics of entering, leaving, past, or prospective clients

    B. Summary descriptions of characteristics of program personnel

VI. Systematic "expert" judgment

    A. Recommendations by a commission appointed to delineate a problem and recommend possible solutions

Table 2 (continued)

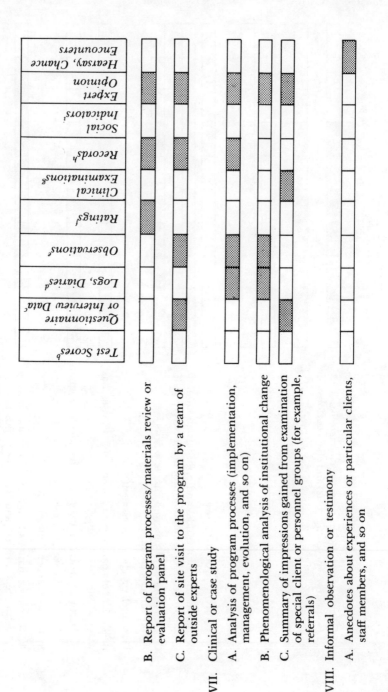

	Test Scores[b]	Questionnaire or Interview Data[c]	Logs, Diaries[d]	Observations[e]	Rating[f]	Clinical Examinations[g]	Records[h]	Social Indicators	Expert Opinion	Hearsay, Chance Encounters
B. Report of program processes/materials review or evaluation panel					■		■		■	
C. Report of site visit to the program by a team of outside experts		■		■			■		■	
VII. Clinical or case study										
A. Analysis of program processes (implementation, management, evolution, and so on)			■	■					■	
B. Phenomenological analysis of institutional change				■					■	
C. Summary of impressions gained from examination of special client or personnel groups (for example, referrals)		■				■			■	
VIII. Informal observation or testimony										
A. Anecdotes about experiences or particular clients, staff members, and so on										■

Table 2 notes

[a]See also "Table 1, Data Sources for Evaluation Efforts," in Anderson and others, 1975, p. 116. References below to same source for definitions of the sources of evidence.

[b]Tests include paper-and-pencil, situational, and performance tasks. See pp. 425–428.

[c]See pp. 214–217, 311–314.

[d]Kept by participants during the course of the program.

[e]See pp. 266–270.

[f]Including grades, supervisors' ratings, expert opinion in the form of ratings. Questionnaires and ratings are not mutually exclusive; questionnaires might include ratings as well as other types of information. See pp. 315–318.

[g]Including physiological, psychological, and psychiatric appraisals.

[h]Including personnel records, publications, financial data, program materials.

[i]Census data, crime rates, and so on. See pp. 374–377.

resources. Data were collected through observations and other methods, and on the basis of the results Gilbert and his colleagues gave the program a rating of 0 (on a scale ranging from "++" for "a very successful innovation" to "--" meaning "a definitely harmful innovation," with "0" indicating "not much if any effect in either the positive or negative direction"). (See also Wallace, 1965.)

Cottage Life Intervention Program—in-cottage behavior of boys convicted of interstate crimes, robbery, and burglary; recidivism rate; time for staying out of trouble (in comparison with boys randomly allocated to the regular training school). Records and observations were used, and, while the recidivism rate did not decrease, behavior and time out of trouble spoke well for the program. (See also Federal Bureau of Prisons, 1964.)

Manhattan Bail Project—failure to appear in court by arrested persons with "close ties to the community" and judged "suitable to be recommended for release" without bail. Evidence gathering was obviously straightforward. Only 0.7 percent failed to show up—what Gilbert and others call "a slam-bang effect." (See also Botein, 1964–1965.)

Los Angeles Sheriff's Academy—job proficiency, job satisfaction, and overall work quality of police officers trained in the academy (where collegelike training was intended to reduce the "militaristic and authoritarian aspects of the regular police training"). Records of complaints and commendations and supervisors' ratings were collected. The program evidence was convincing with respect to the worth of the program in Los Angeles. Gilbert and others caution, however, about generalizations to other sites. (See also Earle, 1973.)

Harvard Project Physics—cognitive performance of students (especially increased science-process understanding); satisfaction with the course (approach, text, and understandability without an extensive mathematics background). The investigators used tests and questionnaires to collect their data. Gilbert and his colleagues interpreted the evidence to give the course a 0 rating for cognitive performance, ++ for enthusiasm and palatability. (See also Welch and Walberg, 1972.)

Evidence

Outpatient Treatment—amount of hospitalization for one year following Blue Cross–Blue Shield coverage of outpatient treatment (it was forecast that the amount of hospitalization would go down if doctors were encouraged not to send their patients to the hospital when full hospitalization might not be required). The simple index of program effect was "percent more days in hospital" taken from hospital records. The experimental group in fact had 16 percent more days in the hospital (compared with 3 percent more for the control group), with an accompanying increase, not decrease, in overall program costs. (See also Hill and Veney, 1970.)

Operations and Education—stress (as indicated by temperature, systolic blood pressure, and pulse rate) of young tonsillectomy pateints at admission, pre- and postoperatively, and at discharge; other postoperative signs (for example, vomiting, time of first void, amount of fluid drunk); reports of mothers one week after surgery about children's progress and their own stress during the total process. The treatment, directed at the mothers, was informational in nature and was based on the assumption that "if mothers knew in more detail . . . what their child would be undergoing . . . they would provide emotional support and information to the child that would reduce his or her postoperative distress." The evidence was collected through clinical procedures, nurses' observations, and questionnaires completed by the mothers. The program was rated a ++ success. (See also Skipper and Leonard, 1968.)

Probation for Drunk Arrests—number of rearrests and time before first rearrest of chronic drunk offenders fined $25, given thirty-day suspended sentences, and assigned to specialized treatments (alcoholic clinic or Alcoholics Anonymous). Control group comprised offenders also fined and given suspended sentences but not assigned to a specialized treatment. Records indicated that the no-treatment group did as well as or better than the forced-treatment groups, evidence not supportive of the program. (See also Ditman and others, 1967.)

Rehabilitation of Nursing-Home Patients—improvement in the abilities of nursing-home patients to function in such ways as locomotion, feeding, dressing, and washing as a result of special training in self-care; reduction in hospitalization and mortality (the last two kinds of evidence fall in the category of possible side effects). Evidence was based on observations by visiting testing teams; rating, 0. (See also Kelman, 1962.)

Two points are striking about the varied examples that Gilbert and his colleagues (1975) found of the application of true experimental methods to evaluation of education and human services programs. First, there were so few such experiments. This is unfortunate, for anything less than random assignment of subjects and meticulous care in data collection (for example, "blind" collection of data by the testing team in the study of Rehabilitation of Nursing-Home Patients) lowers one's ability to draw firm conclusions about the efficacy of important (and frequently expensive) interventions. Even with the relatively careful controls in the sixteen evaluations of social and socio-medical programs analyzed by Gilbert and others, only four produced evidence leading to a ++ rating for the program. There were four + ratings, seven 0 ratings, and one – rating; two of these programs actually received mixed ratings.

It should be noted that Boruch (1974) had a little better luck than Gilbert and his colleagues in locating examples of randomized field experiments for program planning and evaluation. In response to a challenge by Campbell (see Salasin, 1973), Boruch listed references to fifteen randomized experimental tests of social rehabilitation programs for juvenile and criminal offenders (including the Cottage Life Intervention Program); seven experimental tests of law-related and law-enforcement procedures (including the Manhattan Bail Project, the Los Angeles Sheriff's Academy, and Probation for Drunk Arrests); eighteen experimental tests of rehabilitation in mental health; thirty-seven randomized experimental assessments of training and education programs; fifteen socio-medical and fertility-control experiments (including the Rehabilitation of Nursing-Home Patients); six experimental tests of communications methods and media effects and effectiveness; twenty experimental tests of methods for assuring reliability, validity, completeness, and data utility in information collection, transmission, and retrieval; two experiments on research utilization; three economic experiments; one research effort on surgical (and social) rehabilitation of criminal offenders (seven references); and eleven experimental tests of the effects of welfare services on children and adults. However, even these sums are minuscule compared with the number of social and educational interventions that were spawned in the last fifteen years or so.

The second striking point was that the program effects were usually small. As Gilbert and his colleagues point out, those who install new social programs are frequently "dreamy" about large effects—raising IQ twenty to thirty points, advancing education four additional months per year, cutting the highway death rate 50 percent, and so on. "These optimistic forecasts often play a crucial role in the political process that leads to a program being tried. These dreams lead people to suggest that if one has a first-class social program it will speak for itself. . . . One cannot argue with this position, given its assumptions; such programs will indeed be beacons in the night. In the cold light of day, however, such slam-bang effects are few. . . . For this reason we suggest that evaluations of these new social programs should be designed to document even modest effects, if they occur, so that new programs may be built upon these gains" (pp. 52–53).

The second general method of investigation listed in Table 2 is quasi-experimental study. Again we turn to Gilbert and others for examples of types of evidence submitted in such studies, and again these studies were designed primarily to serve summary decisions about program effectiveness. Gilbert and others describe several non-randomized studies of field innovations using the kinds of evidence listed below (pp. 116–126):

The Baltimore Housing Study—evidence on physical morbidity, social-psychological adjustment, and children's school performance (for example, achievement, attendance, promotion rate) for families accepted in improved housing; plus, expected benefits of improved shelter, cooking, and toilet facilities. The housing treatment appeared to have some positive effects, but possible biases in the processes used to select the families accepted for the improved housing affected the validity of the conclusions. (See also Wilner and others, 1962.)

Nutrition Delivery in the Philippines—reduction in the death rate from beriberi resulting from substituting fortified rice for white rice in the diet of families in the Bataan Peninsula. For families in the experimental area of the peninsula, the incidence of beriberi dropped from 14.3 percent to 1.5 percent; in the control area, it rose from 6.7 percent to 8.7 percent. There was also indication that the new rice would be accepted in the rice trade. These results were "positively convincing," but the possibility existed that some other innovations in the peninsula might have contributed to the effects and even that the availability of the fortified rice did not mean that it was incorporated uniformly in the diets of the experimental families. (See also Salcedo, 1954.)

Head Start Planned Variation—academic achievement, general cognitive development, and response styles in coping with tasks (as measured by various tests and observation schemes) of children exposed to eleven specially sponsored Head Start curricula, of children in regular nonsponsored Head Start centers, and of children not enrolled in any preschool program; mother-child interaction styles (measured through a Hess-Shipman, 1965, performance task); parental attitudes and involvement in the programs (measured by a questionnaire). Although some differences among sponsors were noted, there were no large differences between the sponsored centers and the nonsponsored centers. Because of uncontrolled variations among the groups, the results were generally so hard to interpret that Gilbert and others conclude the investigation is best viewed as "a sort of pilot study of implementing new curricula." (See also Bissell, 1971.)

Performance Contracting—achievement (especially reading) of children taught by outside firms "contracting" to get results that the public schools were having particular trouble producing. The study was so poorly designed and implemented that the minimal evidence produced in favor of the contractors could be handily rejected by those already politically inclined to do so. (See also Gramlich and Koshel, 1975.)

It is unfortunate that nonrandomized control groups appear to be the chief strategy adopted by evaluators in the name of quasi-experimental investigation when more powerful approaches to situations where randomization is prohibited or prohibitive are available. For example, the Baltimore Housing investigators might have produced less equivocal results with a regression-discontinuity design; the Performance Contracting studies would have benefitted in any case from more time and even without randomization that might have provided an opportunity for comparing time-series analyses across sites.

Increasingly, funding agencies and public interest groups call for evidence of the long-term effects of social, educational, or economic interventions into the lives of people. In Chapter Two, we reviewed some of the difficulties evaluators encounter in trying to provide such evidence: feasibility of measuring the ultimate criterion of program effectiveness, the logistics of tracing clients, problems in maintaining privacy of records, and premature demands for early evaluation results (sometimes from the very agencies that are also demanding evidence of long-term effects). Several more difficulties arise as well. Some programs are designed to promote such subtle effects that picking them up later is almost doomed to failure; others offer such slight competition with all the other activities and influences that fill people's lives that they could not be expected to show major impact over time. We remember seeing Donald Campbell go to the blackboard at an OEO meeting some years ago and draw a diagram (shown at top of next page). The hatched box represents the total Head Start experience in the child's first nine years. "How," he asked, "could you expect such a small input to have discernible impact on children when they are nine years old?" Furthermore, as the time between treatment and estimation of effect lengthens, so too does the number of intervening events, thus weakening any inferences about the program as cause of the effects (Gilbert and others, 1975, p. 145). There are also development and design problems attending attempts to obtain evidence of long-term project effects. For example, it may not be possible to give comparable measures to, say, five-year-olds and ten-year-olds; or, even if superficially comparable measures can be given, they may not assess the same dimensions at the two age levels. And it is difficult to decide how many measures to apply over the period of interest. As the number of measures increases,

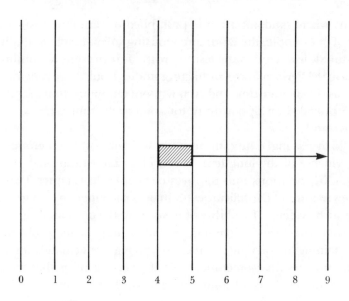

greater sensitization effects can be expected, to the point where responses may result more from previous measurement experience than from the treatment per se. For all of these reasons, Nunnally (1975) suggests that evaluators conducting program evaluation research covering more than three years may be out of their minds!

There are also situations where the long-term effects a program is designed to promote may differ from, or conflict with, the short-term effects. For example, desirable immediate behaviors of program clients (for example, skills demonstrated at the end of training) may later prove maladaptive (for example, in relationship to supervisors on the job). In the area of school learning, Maehr (1976) proposes continuing motivation (CM) as an important but "seldom considered" educational outcome. He has evidence (Maehr and Stallings, 1972) that treatments (in this case, pupil-control techniques) contributing to desirable classroom behavior may do so at the price of negative long-term effects on CM. It is quite a responsibility for program evaluators to detect and document such discontinuities.

Program sponsors and directors also have problems to deal with while long-term follow-ups of program impact are underway.

Evidence

What should be done with the program in the meantime? Should it be allowed to continue during the years it will take to follow up clients to a point where long-term effects can be evaluated? Or is it discontinued—held in suspense, so to speak—with the risk that, even if long-term effects exceed its promoters' expectations, the impetus for starting it again will be gone or the program will be out of date? This is an awkward position for program directors, even though programs owing their existence to claims for long-term effectiveness deserve to have those claims validated.

One possible set of decision rules might be as follows: If short-term effects of the program are positive, continuation and even expansion should be seriously considered even while the probe for long-term effects is going on. If short-term effects are equivocal, retract the program to a pilot effort and await the long-term findings. If short-term effects are negative, cancel both the program and plans for a longer-term follow-up. Of course, these rules do not take care of the rare case where a program might claim no immediate effects but only long-range ones.

Standards figure as prominently in evaluating program impact as they do in determining the need for a program (see Chapter Two). What level of performance can be taken as evidence that a program had an impact? Most human-service programs involve interventions into the lives of those judged to be deficient or unlikely to function in a desirable way without special help: the poor, sick, antisocial, unskilled, or just careless or unaware. And most judgments about what constitutes "deficiency" or "desirable functioning" are relative. A family is poor if their income is in the lower 20 percent of the national distribution; a fifth-grader is a low achiever if he performs in the bottom third of the class; a manager needs awareness training if he has smaller percentages of women or blacks in his department than other managers have.

Current practices of assigning students to compensatory education under Title I of the Elementary and Secondary Education Act use relative criteria based on scores on educational measures. Cut-off scores determining eligibility for compensation are then set according to the funds available. For example, one school district might be able to accommodate the lowest 20 percent, another the lowest 25 percent. The current guide for evaluating the effectiveness of these Title I programs (Tallmadge and Wood, 1976) provides for the use of one of three kinds of expectancies—all relative—in a pretest-posttest design: (1) expected posttest performance defined in terms of same rank as pretest performance on national norms; (2) expected posttest performance defined in terms of posttest performance of an untreated but otherwise comparable "control" group; (3) expected posttest performance defined in terms of the regression of posttest on pretest performance for a group systematically eliminated from Title I because of higher scores on the selection instrument (in this case, the same as the pretest). In all instances, evidence on the effectiveness of Title I would be the degree to which actual posttest performance of the Title I students exceeded expectations.

Programs are rarely conceptualized in absolute terms. For example, few reading-instruction efforts are formulated in terms of the types of reading the trainees will need to handle for personal satisfaction or economic survival, regardless of how their reading skills compare with others. And few nutrition programs are launched with a clear definition of a "nutrition threshold" in mind. How many court judges—what is more, program directors—know what the "right" mix is of Anglos and others, men and women in certain job or educational settings?

Yet with only relative standards, program planners trying to improve the lot of "have-not" groups must also contend with what happens to the "haves," and program evaluators must contend with what evidence of impact on the "have-nots" makes sense. Consider that many social-service programs have as their objective bringing the treated group up to the level of the population judged not to need treatment. The "difficulty" in evaluation lies in getting the unneedy group to stand still. Poor children may learn much from a special educational program, but rich children may also learn plenty over the same period of time (from the same program or other sources, depending on the amount of "contamination" present in the situation). In fact, although both groups improve, the gap may be even wider than before. Similarly, while special programs appear to be improving the nutritional habits of poverty groups, people who become interested in nutrition on their own are also improving their food-buying and eating behavior without benefit of the program. Standards anchored to the general population are constantly changing; once we bring everyone "up to the mean," the mean moves up! The so-called "criterion-referenced measures" were invented partly to handle this phenomenon. Although many such measures are mislabeled, misused, and misunderstood (see Anderson and others, 1975, pp. 100–104), criterion referencing is a sound idea for evaluators trying to collect evidence about the effects of social-action programs on those at the lower ends of scales of characteristics judged desirable. The important issue is not so much how these program recipients compare with their more "privileged" peers but whether they have reached some standard of adequate performance or receipt of service.

Intervention programs aimed at reducing undesirable characteristics or events do not suffer from the same psychological, philosophical, and political problems as do many oriented toward raising performance. Almost everyone rejoiced over the evidence that smallpox and poliomyelitis had nearly vanished (but see Chapter Five). It is unlikely that anyone would complain if the number of criminals in all social classes was reduced. However, in these situations, too, the evaluator frequently must define expectations and standards for program impact in operational terms.

How broadly should the program evaluator range in the specification of data to be collected and evidence to be presented on program impact? Two related issues arise here. The first pertains to the search for possible side effects (unintended outcomes) as well as effects specified or implied by the program objectives. In Chapter Two, we emphasized the importance of such searches. For example, in assessing a training program directed toward changing negative attitudes of police trainees toward black people, evaluators might also look for any spillover to attitudes toward other minority groups with whom the trainees may come into contact. Or a study of effects of a rehabilitation program on delinquent youth might be extended to include a survey of reactions of the families of the target group. From a practical standpoint, evaluators can hardly assess all possible side effects, so they tend to tread a course somewhere between limiting their attention only to the outcomes specified by the program directors and extending their inquiry to a large number of possible side effects. Or they may first try to determine if major intended outcomes are being met and then address the possibility of side effects in a second, smaller study.

The second issue pertains to diffusion of effects (whether the effects are intended or unintended). Some program planners and evaluators maintain that the only program effects worth looking at are those on the clients or subjects submitting directly to the treatment. We reject this point of view. Improvements in the surrounding business economy may be a noteworthy effect of a new welfare payment plan; increases in teachers' understanding of mathematics may be an important long-term outcome of a new math curriculum for elementary-school pupils; reduced demands for other services may be the chief benefit to the local government of a particular new service. Furthermore, in some cases a program may be directed toward one audience (for example, parents) when the ultimate target is a group that audience is expected to influence (for example, the preschool children of those parents). Consideration of such wider-reaching or secondary effects strengthens program planning; including evidence on such effects enhances the meaning and usefulness of evaluation reports. However, evaluators concerned with ethics should be alert to situations where program directors press for assessment of distal effects less from conviction than from a vain hope of saving a program in trouble. And program directors concerned with economy should keep an eye out for evaluators who embark on mere fishing expeditions in the name of searching for secondary or side effects.

As a final point, we must acknowledge the unpleasant possibility that evaluators may be asked to assemble evidence of program impact after the program has been completed and clients have gone on to other things. Almost all evaluators who have been in business for any length of time have received such requests. The famous (or infamous, depending on point of view) Westinghouse Learning Corporation–Ohio University (1969) study of Head Start provides an example. The investigators were asked to produce evidence on whether preschool Head Start experiences had made a difference for children who were then in the primary grades. Furthermore, the investigators were faced with inadequate records about which children had gone to Head Start and about the period, purpose, and auspices of their attendance. A number of critics (for example, Smith and Bissell, 1970) pointed to major flaws in the conduct of the study and the interpretation of the results. Even if evaluators can work with a very large pool of subjects and have access to preprogram records on those subjects, offering the opportunity for ex post facto "matching" of experimental and control groups through sophisticated multiple covariate analysis of covariance, the chances are that the results will not give a reliable indication of program effects. We are inclined to say that most ex post facto studies lack any redeeming value in answering the questions typically posed (Anderson and others, 1975, pp. 159–160) and to advise evaluators to eschew them because they offer little opportunity to satisfy clients' needs or to provide any useful new insights into the field. An exception might be made in the case of situations where good and reliable social indicators are available over a period of time before and after the introduction of the intervention of interest. In such a case, some inferences about program effectiveness might be drawn from time-series analyses, subject, of course, to the usual attention to plausible rival explanations of any apparent program effects.

Evidence Related to Other Evaluation Questions

So far, we have dwelled on Purpose II (see Table 1) evaluations using experimental and quasi-experimental designs and on the kinds of evidence produced as background for decisions about program continuation, expansion, or "certification." However, other kinds of evaluation decisions with associated methods for producing evidence are useful for those decisions. Even the much maligned correlational status study—maligned if it is used for a purpose it cannot serve—can provide evidence for certain program actions. For example, if no relationship is found between the costs of job-training programs in different sites and trainee performance at the end of those programs, the overall program coordinator might want to review the management strategies used in the less costly programs with an eye to transferring those strategies to the more costly programs (see IIIA, Table 1).

Correlations between background characteristics of clients and their characteristics after exposure to a program (IIIB, Table 2) may suggest that the program is differentially effective and that either client-selection or program-delivery procedures may need to be modified. For example, a formative evaluator of a new program for teaching English to adult immigrants might report a negative correlation between number of months in the United States and performance on the English proficiency measure given at the end of the course. Such a correlation allows more than one interpretation, of course—the immigrants least motivated to learn English might also be the slowest to sign up for the adult course. But the results still suggest that the course seems to work better for new immigrants than for those who have been in the States for some time, with attendant implications for course content and sectioning. (The wise evaluator might well use this type of evidence to press for further study of the reasons why recent immigrants perform better.)

Correlations among program characteristics may also provide useful guidance for program modification (IIIC, Table 2). Consider, for example, correlations among degree of structure observed in group counseling sessions, group size, and percentage of males in the group. If degree of structure is significantly related to the other variables, a program director committed to relatively unstructured approaches might want to try different group configurations to see whether they, rather than such variables as predispositions of the counselors, contribute to the unwanted style of some sessions. Surveys are useful in securing evidence about program needs (actual or perceived); attitudes and opinions of program staff, participants, and other interested groups; management-related variables (for example, available manpower for program staffing, proximity of alternate program centers to public transportation, and costs of various materials-production techniques); program audiences (if they are remote from the delivery source); and a number of other areas important to decisions about program installation and implementation and, sometimes, appraisal of effectiveness. As Table 2 suggests, the methodologies most closely associated with surveys are questionnaires, interviews, observations, and content analyses. The chief requirement for survey evidence is representativeness or lack of bias. Unless program decision makers are patently biased in the type of evidence they are prepared to receive and the evaluator's survey evidence conforms to those biases, the evaluator should be prepared to defend the exact nature of the population or sample used in the data he puts forward.

Personnel or client assessment (V, Table 2) at the end of a program can seldom in itself provide data attesting to the effectiveness of that program. To know, for example, that trainees scored at such-and-such level on a performance test following specific training begs the question of what their scores might have been without training. There are occasional exceptions; for example, when it is generally understood that students knew no Russian at the beginning of the program or could not type a single word. However, personnel or client assessment data can provide excellent evidence of effectiveness if they are interpreted within the context of a reasonably controlled study.

An aside: Frequently, standardized tests are used in evaluations of educational or training programs. As Coulson (1976) says of federal programs, "The evidence that Congress is likely to understand and appreciate will probably be normative—for example, do students in the program learn more than students did before the program was introduced, or better than they might have been expected to perform based on national norms?" He points out, however, that useful program feedback can be provided by reporting not just total scores on standardized tests but also performance on the subset of items "selected by the local program staff as most representative of their project's top priority goals" (p. 6). Chapter Five treats the relationship between the evidence presented and the audience for that evidence in more detail.

Finally, some evidence on program functioning can be obtained from assessment data alone. For example, assessment data can provide evidence concerning such program-related questions as:

Are we getting students of the type for whom the instructional program was originally intended (for example, students reading below a certain level)? Are the knowledge and skills of people completing the program comparable to those of clients in previous years? Does the program staff possess the cognitive competencies important for effective program delivery? Do we have enough people in this geographical area with knowledge or skills deficiencies to warrant offering the program? Of course, a related question, if program participation is to be voluntary, is "Are enough people in this area willing to avail themselves of the program if it is offered?" Evidence on this question can be obtained through survey techniques.

Expert judgment (VI, Table 2) is avoided by some evaluators simply because they are aware that with lay groups it can be highly persuasive and that it can be badly misused. The problem of using expert judgment arises chiefly in viewing expert judgment as a substitute for actual program-performance data. Systematic assembly of expert judgments is most useful and effective when coordinated with recommendations about program installation or improvement. For example, we are familiar with an elaborate television instruction series on "parenting" that proceeded through scripting, casting, and production without review by experts in child development and clinical psychology. The resulting tapes were fraught with technical errors and with philosophical stances that bucked the tide of current thinking in the area. It would not have been a productive use of an evaluator's time to pursue formal study of the effects of the program on the target audience. A great strength of some of the curriculum-development programs of the 1960s was the involvement of outstanding scholars in the curriculum conceptualizations. By and large, the programs lacking such involvement have long since disappeared from catalogs and shelves. For local programs, the identification of local experts to make recommendations about needs, content, and delivery can be invaluable in getting the program off the ground and later accepted. That experts can serve a political as well as a program quality-control function should not dissuade evaluators from encouraging program directors to avail themselves of this resource or prompt evaluators themselves to eschew evidence derived from expert opinion.

Evidence

That would be very foolish indeed. *Expert* can, of course, vary in meaning with the situation. Foremen may be experts about the appropriate training of employees who will work in their shops; admissions officers may be experts about the characteristics of entering freshmen who will succeed in their colleges; Nobel-prize mathematicians and physicists may be needed in decisions about a new space program.

Case studies (VII, Table 2) are the darling of the phenomenologists, and, as indicated in the previous chapter, especially useful in accumulating evidence about additional evidence that might be accumulated. We suspect, however, that when case studies are provided as the only evidence of program need or effectiveness, the credence given to that evidence is due more to the verbal facility of the person writing the case study than to the actual content of the case. The limitations of case studies for impact evaluation were pointedly singled out in a review of the inadequacies of evaluations of the massive federal manpower-training programs of recent years. These programs cost billions and ostensibly trained millions; yet, in spite of almost $2 million invested in evaluation, "little is known about the educational or economic effects" (National Academy of Sciences, 1974, p. 1). "The report goes on to document the methodological inadequacies of the evaluations, *primarily case studies,* involving nonrandom samples with data collected retrospectively" (Gilbert and others, 1975, p. 161, italics ours).

However, case studies do have some value in the evaluator's methodological kit, as discussed in the preceding chapter. A case study gives the evaluator opportunity for immersion in, and understanding of, the kind of program he or she is asked to address. Case studies also provide an excellent opportunity to explore existing sources of information (records and personnel) and to try out information-collection procedures (questionnaires, interviews, and so on).

As we indicated in the previous chapter, informal observation or testimony (VIII, Table 2) really has no place as evaluation evidence. It can be useful as a source of ideas for more studied investigations. However, we must continue to remind ourselves of realities. More decisions about more educational and social programs have probably been made on the basis of hearsay, chance encounters, strong personal or political convictions, and "squeaky wheels" than on any combination of evidence secured from experimental or quasi-experimental designs, correlational studies, carefully conducted surveys or assessments, panels of experts, or case studies. The program of early school dismissal on Wednesdays was canceled because of three irate phone calls from three influential parents who did not want their kids home early. Head Start and WIN were launched when they were because Mrs. Johnson and President Ford, respectively, got behind them. The computerized program monitoring system was installed because the computer was there and had considerable down time. The family service counseling program was discontinued in the wake of one family's threat to sue for invasion of privacy. The list is endless. And evaluators, even as they decry such tendencies, must be aware of them.

Summary

Many evaluation methods and kinds and sources of evidence may be brought forward to support or discourage decisions about installing, continuing, and changing programs. Table 2 is presented to evaluators or persons commissioning or monitoring evaluations to give more definition to the general methods of investigation listed in Table 1 and discussed in Chapter Three, to remind them of the varieties of evidence that might be used in a particular study, and to focus attention on compatibilities between types of evidence and the sources of information on which they are based.

Five

Dissemination, Communication, and Utilization

"Behold a sower went forth to sow; And when he sowed, some seeds fell by the wayside, and the fowls came and devoured them up: Some fell upon stony places, where they had not much earth: and forthwith they sprung up, because they had no deepness of earth: And when the sun was up, they were scorched; and because they had no root, they withered away. And some fell among thorns; and the thorns sprung up, and choked them: But others fell into good ground, and brought forth fruit, some an hundredfold, some sixtyfold, some thirtyfold" (Matt. 13:3–8).

Too often evaluations of educational and human-service programs are like seed sown in thin soil or among thorns, their results undisseminated or confined to a select few, with little in the way of follow-up or utilization.* The evaluator is responsible to those who foot the bill for the evaluation and for the program under study and, ultimately, to the public. This form of public responsibility has been prominent in recent years, ranging from exposure of cost overruns on military aircraft to allegations about inadequate safety regulations at nuclear generating plants. These issues have engaged national attention through the media, resulted in endeavors to suppress the controversy, and led sometimes to resignations and hardships for those most earnestly concerned. While it is unlikely that such publicity and drama will usually attend the evaluator's attempts to disseminate results, the social and professional responsibility still exists. Indeed, as we shall argue, the responsibility covers the dissemination not only of results but also of plans and procedures.

Dissemination can be effectively executed only if the broader issue of communication has been adequately handled. Communication channels have to be established and maintained if dissemination (which is but one element in the communication complex) is to be effective. Of course, dissemination can take place without communication. We all know of instances where plans or results are disseminated but no one pays attention. But this is not effective dissemination.

Similarly, utilization of evaluation results is related to communication and dissemination. If communication and dissemination have been ineffective, utilization is unlikely. All three can be made more effective if the relationships among them are understood. Although we shall discuss each in turn, they are in fact interdependent.

---

*"Utilization" and "utilize" are words we would prefer not to use (or utilize). The reason is that we prefer the simpler words "use" or "usage." However, the literature abounds in such phrases as "utilization of results" (rather than "use of results") so we bow, happy word, to usage.

Dissemination, Communication, and Utilization

Communication

It is rather obvious that program evaluations cannot be carried out without some communication among the agents in the process—funding organization, program director, program participants, evaluation staff, and the communities and institutions within which the program is being developed or assessed. Within this communication network, the evaluator has an opportunity to facilitate the evaluation, inform and even excite various audiences, and eventually move decision makers to utilize the evaluation findings. Unfortunately, the evaluator has an equal opportunity to abort the evaluation, alienate the various audiences, and ensure that decision makers ignore or repudiate the information generated by the evaluation effort. Which of these eventualities will occur depends on the evaluator's skills in identifying and opening communication channels, using them in timely and appropriate fashion, and above all making sure that messages are understood at both ends. Understanding is the essential feature of communication.

What are some of the components of an adequate communication network? First, we should identify the communicators, the agents in the process who need to receive or provide information or opinion. The major agents are presented in Figure 2. This figure also indicates the major lines of communication among the agents for both program-related and evaluation-related needs. However, we will comment here only upon the communication lines pertaining primarily to evaluation.

Arrows at both ends of the communication lines emphasize the need for communication to be bidirectional. We do not presume to dictate the leadership styles of evaluators. Some are doubtless more democratic than others; some, more authoritarian. But irrespective of the leadership style, there is little doubt that a one-way communication flow is an unproductive path to follow. (Interestingly, dissemination is one-way communication. Thus, we argue that if dissemination is the only major kind of communication, then the evaluation can be in serious trouble.) Even in an evaluation led by an authoritar-

93

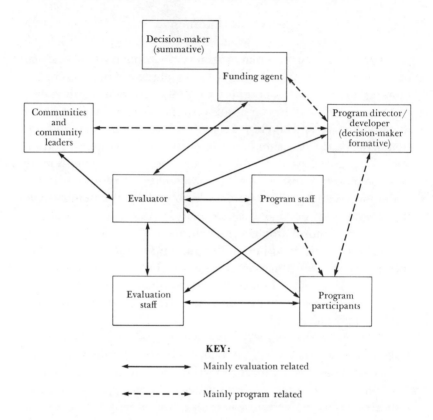

KEY:

◄────────────► Mainly evaluation related

◄─ ─ ─ ─ ─ ► Mainly program related

Figure 2. Major Lines of Communication in Program Evaluation

ian, the need for feedback between leaders and followers is so great that it would be absurd to ignore it. For example, data collectors have experiences in the field that evaluation directors should hear about. And the evaluator had better listen to community and institutional representatives if the evaluation is to be relatively trouble-free and properly sensitive to the program context.

We turn now to an intensive examination of the boxes in Figure 2, beginning with the funding agent. The funding agent may be some government or foundation officer or an executive from the same organization that is developing or providing the program. The funding agent frequently has the chief decision-making role from authorizing the evaluation to utilizing the results. At the outset, the funding agent needs to inform the evaluator of the kinds of evaluation information required. Realistically, and not necessarily unfortunately, the funding agent may need help conceptualizing and articulating these requirements; for example, the wisdom of looking for negative unintended outcomes. Often the evaluator has to help determine what kinds of information the evaluation will attempt to provide. The funding agent may be politically sophisticated but may not be sophisticated in the world of evaluation. As the evaluation moves toward a conclusion, the communication flow between funding agent and evaluator is likely to reverse direction. Now it is the evaluator who does most of the communicating to the funding agent. Again, however, it is not a one-way street. It is the funding agent's duty at least to point out to the evaluator any inadequacies in the reporting style. For example, some funding agents may want a simple report so that the lay public can understand the evaluation message. And we have even heard of funding agents who wanted a complex report to ensure that the evaluation message was *not* understood. (Obviously, such a situation would introduce severe ethical problems for the evaluator.)

Sometimes the funding agent is less likely to be the decision maker of major immediate concern than is the program director or developer. For example, a formative evaluator (Purpose III) would need initial briefings from the program developer for whom, typically, the evaluation will be conducted. Subsequently, discourse should be frequent, as the evaluator reports various findings and the program developer presents to the evaluator emerging information needs to help guide program development and installation. We should note that the program director or developer will often feel more certain than the funding agent of the kinds of information required of the evaluator. Sometimes, however, it is helpful for the evaluator to remind the program person that evaluation services can be more comprehensive than initially conceived. That is, many program people tend to think of formative evaluation as solely a matter of testing materials or procedures after development but before integration into a final program (or product). They may not consider that formative evaluation can encompass surveys of target clients or research on program processes such as pacing and organization.

The evaluator may also need to communicate to the community and its leaders. By *community* we mean the social context of the program and the evaluation. It may be a community in an urban slum with some compensatory education programs; a hospital community (doctors, administrators, nurses, medical technicians, maintenance staff, patients, and relatives and friends of patients) in certain health-care programs; or a nursing-home community (professionals, other staff, volunteers, patients, relatives and friends of patients) in particular gerontological programs. There are as many kinds of communities as there are programs, and this chapter cannot adequately deal with the specific communication duties of the evaluator vis-à-vis all communities. We can provide a few more illustrations of communities that may have considerable interest in, and influence on, certain evaluation studies: teachers unions, parent advisory councils, prison wardens associations, community action agencies, medical groups, parent-teacher associations, and local chapters of the NAACP. We urge the evaluator to take the time to identify communities relevant to the evaluation and to consider how best to set up channels of communication to them. Fortunately, though the details may differ, the principles do not. The evaluator must make it a prime task to confer with such relevant groups. Somehow the evaluator must explain what the evaluation is all about (a dissemination task), attempt to elicit formally or informally the views and reactions of the community (adjusting the evaluation plans if necessary), and maintain this relationship, based on mutual respect, throughout the evaluation. The reasons for this stance should be obvious. Not only will it facilitate the evaluation and its dissemination, but it also responds to the fact that community groups have rights just as program sponsors, developers, and even evaluators do. Further, all of these groups have responsibilities to their constituents. The best way of considering and adjusting to the rights and responsibilities of groups lies in open communication. In addition, the views of community groups are themselves valuable data. No program can hope to succeed over the long haul without the support of such groups.

We well remember an event in the late 1960s when we were conducting large-scale evaluations of programs aimed in part at educating disadvantaged children. We attended an evening meeting of a parent advisory group running preschool programs in an economically disadvantaged area of a large northeastern city. That night, three research and evaluation proposals were discussed. Two proposals were accompanied solely by letters of transmittal that assumed the parent group would accede to the already fully planned studies involving their preschool children. The parent group did not accede. The third proposal was ours. Since we were attending the meeting, the parents could raise questions, and we could explain what the evaluation study was about. We were questioned sharply but properly: How would the children benefit? Who would be employed in the evaluation effort? Would we simply be trying to show that disadvantaged kids cannot learn well? Would there be any cost to the community? Some of our answers turned away possible hostility. Other questions proved troublesome: Why use minority college students as testers? Why not use mothers on welfare? The important point was that, when adjustments were made (we instituted special training so mothers could become testers) and explanations given, the evaluation had solid community support. We had communicated effectively.

Some readers will protest that small evaluations or routine program-monitoring efforts need no such palaver. Indeed they do not. Sometimes there is no money, time, or necessity to do more than a straightforward, technical program evaluation, and some such evaluations are efficient and useful. However, it is quite unprofessional for evaluators to ignore context completely. If the context involves groups with strong interests in the program, then the evaluator fails to communicate at the risk of an inadequate evaluation or no evaluation at all. We said above that the evaluator has the opportunity to abort the evaluation. It is well to remember that, to some extent, this privilege—or power, if you will—may also rest with community groups.

Finally, Figure 2 indicates communication lines among evaluator, evaluation staff, program staff, and program participants.

There are six possible pairings among these four groups, all but one of which are major evaluation communication channels. Clearly, the evaluator must maintain open lines of communication with each of the other three groups. Again we stress two-way communication. When the size of the staff allows conferences, such meetings should be held regularly. Staff morale will rise if the feeling that staff experiences and opinions are welcomed, listened to, and used is widespread. And the evaluation will probably benefit from such feedback.

Less obvious but perhaps as important is the communication between the evaluator and the program staff and program participants. Some of this communication may be mandated by the data-collection procedures; the evaluator may have to interview staff and program participants. But that is not the major kind of contact we refer to here. Rather, it is the evaluator's duty to maintain a dialogue with program staff and program participants in order to keep them appropriately informed of what the evaluation is about. The key word is *appropriately*. It would be unfortunate if the evaluation goals and procedures were made so explicit that invalidities due to overcooperation by program staff and participants were added to the results. However, the informed consent of the participants may be required. That informing might well include the notion that program evaluation is being conducted, and it should also provide for introducing the evaluation staff to the program staff. The evaluator should allay fears ("I'm here to evaluate the program—not you"); motivate cooperation ("We all want to provide the best possible program—each of us in his or her own way"); and provide sufficient information to allow the program staff to understand what is happening ("Now every Tuesday morning, Bob and Jane—stand up, good—will be coming around with these forms"). However, it would be wrong to provide information detailed enough to destroy the validity of the evaluation ("We'll be dropping by to listen to your conversations with clients. We'll be looking for the number of encouraging comments you make, how close you position yourself to your client, whether you provide specific, behavioral advice or just general ideas . . .").

A final note and a difficult one to deal with: We have observed that many evaluators who pay lip service to the ideal of comprehensive, two-way communication have difficulty putting the ideal into practice. It is as though some fundamental personality trait gets in the way, and, whether through shyness, distrust of others, need for personal aggrandizement, or anxiety, they hold themselves aloof. Staff members and others, feeling that there would be no point in coming to these evaluators with ideas and experiences, do not come. And aloof evaluators seem not to reward those who crash through the personality barriers and talk to them anyway; these brave ones go away feeling they have wasted their time. The problem is seemingly intractable; we know of no easy way to change personality. It might be argued that those with such characteristics should not be entrusted with evaluations of educational and human-service programs, but that might be too drastic a solution. Perhaps the best thing to do is to suggest that all evaluators specifically plan the communication to be carried out routinely during the evaluation. The plan might be based on Figure 2 and address such questions as these asked of each important communication channel: Have I made initial contact? Have I incorporated any suggestions from this person or group into the evaluation? Have I checked with this person or group this month? Have I informed this person or group of the changes made as a result of their suggestions? Have I thanked this person or group for their cooperation now that the evaluation is coming to an end? We may not be able to change personality but perhaps we can change practice.

Effective communication is a sine qua non for a healthy evaluation. And a healthy evaluation is one that evaluators can take pride in presenting—or disseminating.

Dissemination

The major justification for program evaluation is the help it may provide decision makers in making wise, or at least informed, decisions about program installation, the delivery system, program continuation and expansion (or contraction), and perhaps accreditation or certification. So it is not surprising that most writers on the topic have emphasized the need to disseminate the findings of evaluation efforts. Furthermore—and this point is not trivial—dissemination of the results of good evaluation work serves the evaluator's important professional needs for reward and closure. However, dissemination is more than something tacked on to the end of program evaluation like some shiny chrome molding on the exhaust pipe of a fancy car. With that conception, dissemination will most certainly be nonfunctional. Dissemination, therefore, involves more than simply telling the world (or some subsection of it) the conclusions of the evaluation. Dissemination should take place throughout evaluation. At a minimum, it should involve informing others about the evaluation plans and procedures as well as the eventual findings.

In considering the dissemination process we should bear in mind the multiple purposes of program evaluation. For example, the requirements for dissemination in summative evaluations (Purpose II) differ from those in formative studies (Purpose III). The dissemination task in the latter case is less clear than in the former. Some formative evaluation studies do not warrant wide dissemination; they are conducted for a very specific purpose in the development of a specific program. Apart from the program developer, no one else cares much about the results. However, this is not always the case. Consider, for example, the formative work paid for by the Fund for the Improvement of Post-Secondary Education and carried out under the aegis of National Project II, a consortium of four-year and junior colleges with programs for the underprepared college student. This was a highly experimental area for which colleges were singularly not ready—or, to extend the jargon, we had colleges underprepared for underprepared students. Each of the members of the National Project II consortium developed programs for these students, and each program had a formative evaluation component. Here is an example of formative evaluation results with real value for those not directly concerned with the particular programs examined but interested in other efforts to meet similar needs. Another example is the Children's Television Workshop, producers of "Sesame Street" and "The Electric Company," which has received hundreds of inquiries about its formative evaluation techniques and results from groups around the world who are attempting to produce their own educational television programs. No standard clearinghouse and no readily available journal provide dissemination of information about formative efforts even when the demand for such dissemination exists. Perhaps this situation will change as the information industry continues its apparently inexorable expansion. In the meantime, however, the dissemination of formative evaluation results will probably remain more specialized and more difficult than the dissemination of summative results.

This leads us to inquire into the question of the audience for dissemination. In formative evaluation, as we have noted, the audience is usually a specific program developer and, less often, others developing similar programs. A comparable situation obtains with Purpose I efforts, those directed toward decisions about program installation. But in summative evaluation the question of the audience for dissemination is more complex. We certainly disseminate to one audience: the funding agency. However, the plans, procedures, and findings of summative evaluation studies are frequently of value and interest to more than just the agency funding the program or the evaluation. In considering how to disseminate, our first criterion is that if the evaluation is worth doing, other groups have some interest, perhaps strong, in finding out more about it. Responsible—or responsive—evaluations specify these audiences and analyze their information needs early in the process (Stake, 1975, p. 29). A second premise is that, given different audiences, a single medium of dissemination will probably be insufficient and inappropriate. The medium must fit the audience. Technical reports frustrate lay audiences; nontechnical reports frustrate technically sophisticated audiences.

To facilitate the evaluator's consideration of potential audiences for dissemination and of means for communicating plans, procedures, or results, we have provided Table 3. The table lists fifteen classes of audiences for evaluation findings (left-hand column) and ten media for disseminating results (see the column headings). Shaded boxes indicate particularly compatible relationships between audiences and media. For example, the funding agency should certainly be given all technical reports and executive summaries (short,

Table 3. Dissemination of Evaluation Plans, Procedures, and Results

Likely communication form

Potential Audience	Technical Report	Executive Summary	Technical Professional Paper	Popular Article	News Release	Press Conference	Media Appearance	Public Meeting	Staff Seminar, Workshop	Other (film, filmstrip, book, and so on)
Funding agencies for program or evaluation	▓	▓								
Program administrators	▓	▓	▓	▓	▓				▓	
Other relevant management-level staff		▓		▓						
Board members, trustees		▓		▓						
Technical advisory committees	▓	▓	▓							
Relevant political bodies (for example, legislatures, city councils)				▓						
Interested community groups				▓				▓		
Current clients (guardians where appropriate)				▓				▓		
Prospective clients				▓			▓			

Providers of program service (for example, instructors, counselors, distributors)

Professional colleagues of evaluator(s)

Organizations or professions concerned with program content

Local, state, regional media

National media

Other

intelligible presentations of the major plans or the principal findings, with a minimum of jargon). Relevant political groups might receive executive summaries and any popular articles concerning the evaluation. Local, state, or regional media will usually not want technical reports but may be interested in receiving news releases, attending press conferences, or covering public meetings. This kind of matching of media and audiences not only will result in dissemination but also should contribute to communication and comprehension.

Table 3, by intent, goes beyond what a program evaluator probably can do in any one evaluation. Even so we could add to it. We could add evaluation staff to the potential audiences, for example, or we could include the lowly memo among the media. However, we do not want the scope of Table 3 to intimidate the evaluator. Rather there are two purposes of Table 3: to suggest the communication forms most appropriate for specific audiences, and, more important, to emphasize the need for evaluators to list consciously and systematically the potential audiences for their work and to broaden their consideration of useful forms of communication.

We return now to a point made at the outset. The best-laid dissemination plans can go awry. We refer here not so much to their execution; rather, to the problem illustrated by a nightingale's song falling on deaf ears. To help ensure that dissemination is not simply an elaborate waste of energy (well executed and ignored), the evaluator should establish good relationships with potential audiences and set up effective two-way communication. Ultimately, however, the evaluator may begin to disseminate news that such audiences as the program people, community, or funding agency dread hearing—the program is having negative effects. That some of the audiences then stop listening is understandable though regrettable. We assume that not all the audiences will quickly develop diplomatic auditory insufficiency; and we suggest that the evaluator continue to fill the important dissemination function anyway.

Utilization

"Once the evaluation is completed, the logical expectation is that decision makers will use the results to make rational decisions. ... With all the money, time, effort, skill, and irritation that went into the acquisition of information, why does it generally have so little impact?" (Weiss, 1972, pp. 25-26).

Let us assume that dissemination was adequately carried out, an assumption which, in turn, assumes that communication channels were developed and used properly during the evaluation. Under these conditions, the chance is greatest that the results will be utilized. However, as we all know, even the best planning does not ensure utilization. We repeat the question Weiss poses: Why so little impact?

Weiss (1971) suggests a number of possible reasons, which she groups under two major categories: the organizational systems expected to use the evaluation results, and the current state of evaluation practice. The organizational category includes such factors as organizational conservatism, inertia, and fear of the consequences of change. Decision makers may be more influenced by de facto pressures to maintain organizational status quo than by the need for change to which they publicly pledge allegiance. Thus, when an evaluation, which they themselves sought, indicates a need for change, they opt for the more primitive demands of survival and reject the findings.

Longood and Simmel (1972) elaborate on this theme. They argue that a basic goal of any organization is to perpetuate itself. As an illustration, they point to the National Foundation for Infantile Paralysis, which when confronted with the positive outcomes of the Salk polio vaccine sought strenuously to maintain itself even though its ostensible goals had been met. Clearly an evaluator who recommends that an ineffective program be discontinued will probably see serious objections raised by the program's parent organization, whose existence might thus be threatened. Ward and Kassebaum (1972) report on an extensive evaluation of their own, which confirmed previous evaluations by others. They found that, with recidivism as a criterion, group counseling does not work with prison populations. Decision makers, who had a vested interest in such programs reacted by *expanding* group counseling programs, suggesting new criteria for success, and impeding the dissemination of the results of the evaluation studies. In short, the very nature of organizations is sometimes inimical to the utilization of program evaluation results.

The second of Weiss's categories refers to the poverty of much evaluation practice. (Of course, she was writing some years ago, based on a speech some five years earlier still!) It is true that a few evaluations are palpably absurd. However, even well-conducted evaluations are open to criticism, and sometimes this criticism is sufficient to immobilize the decision maker. We can argue that, if the decision maker and evaluator have communicated closely throughout the evaluation process, the worst of this post hoc carping can be avoided. Nonetheless, especially in the face of built-in antipathies to institutional change, some evaluations are too fragile to support strong movement for change.

Still other factors have been suggested as working against the utilization of evaluation results. For example, Riecken and Boruch (1974) point to the possibility that the organization might be receptive and the evaluation technically adequate, but the relationship between the evaluation results and possible subsequent action may be unclear. As they claim: "At least one quarter of the field experiments we have examined in preparing this volume are characterized by a good deal of ambiguity in the relation" (p. 241).

We have one more reason why results are not utilized: Decision makers have to listen to many people besides evaluators. There are program advocates and program detractors drawn from many sectors including the public at large with its myriad, politically conscious pressure groups. There may also be economic considerations unknown to the evaluator. Perhaps in such circumstances evaluators should feel fortunate if their results are simply attended to. Yet somehow that reasonable, relatively humble outlook is unsatisfying. Certainly we want our results attended to, but we also want to see them utilized. And we should be outraged if Myers's (1970) cynical comments remain true: "I have yet to see an instance where a researcher has been asked to provide information for a decision. . . . If the researcher is not asked to provide information for a decision, what is he asked to do? Well, he is asked to provide information about things for which decisions have already been made. In short, he is asked to justify the administrator's decisions" (p. 372). This abuse does occur, but Myers's charge is too gross. Certainly now, almost a decade after

Myers's conclusions, there are many examples of evaluation and research information being used to make decisions about programs. And the question we ask here is, How do we maximize the possibility of evaluation payoff?

We can point to earlier comments and suggest that utilization is most likely if communication channels were opened early in the planning of the evaluation and kept open thereafter and if dissemination media appropriate for the audiences of concern were chosen. In other words, utilization should be a prominent question from the outset. "All the experiments we have examined suggest that experimental results are more likely to be used if clear and acceptable strategies are developed beforehand to facilitate the use of negative as well as positive findings" (Riecken and Boruch, 1974, p. 242).

Weiss (1971) enumerates four ways the evaluator can optimize utilization. Three of these suggestions have been discussed at some length already. They are identifying potential users of information early, promoting their involvement in evaluation planning, and ensuring the effective dissemination of results. To these three Weiss adds the eminently practical injunction that the evaluator complete the evaluation promptly and release the results quickly. It is a good point. We recall an eminent researcher, noted for the great care with which he massaged his data (one study stood more than four years of data analysis), who took great pains to remind us of all the work that had not been done when the first-year evaluation of the "Sesame Street" program was released (Ball and Bogatz, 1970). To what degree could the outcome variables be reduced to a smaller number of factors? Had we thought of conducting a factor analysis separately for each of the three age levels and comparing the factor structures? Well, yes, we had—but as an interesting scientific exercise to be conducted after the major results were disseminated.

In similar vein, Berke (1976) suggests, in a paper on how to make evaluation research relevant to policy, that style in evaluation and in report writing is an important factor. He lists as elements:

• Brevity and clarity. Critical findings should be summarized clearly and simply at the outset.

- Timeliness. To be useful and utilized, results must be reported according to other people's schedules and not by an evaluator's research clock.
- Interim products and reports. These help prepare decision makers for the impact of larger, later evaluation reports. Besides, they can allow preliminary planning for utilization even before the final report is available.
- Responsivity. He notes here that traditional researchers tend to make questions more interesting, designs more elegant, analyses more comprehensive, and utilization recommendations more guarded than necessary!

As the reader can see, these ideas return again and again to communication and dissemination.

Finally, we commend a statement by Longood and Simmel (1972). They were concerned with public-health programs and the role of social science, but their statement has merit for all areas of applied social research and evaluation:

> We believe that both the public-health physician and the social scientist need not less engagement, but more. For an effective partnership, they must confront each other both as professionals and as full-blown human beings, arguing differences on their merits and working toward synthesis. It is not academic atmosphere that will help social scientists who range into the field of application, but engagement with the organizational ferment. . . . Our quarrel is with the social scientists who do no more than tentatively flirt with the field of application in which they are working. If one strongly identifies with professional standards, maintains some contact with one's professional reference group, and exposes oneself to its criticisms, one's scientific objectivity will not be undone by lively personal involvement in the organization whose practical problems are the social scientist's intellectual problems. But we go one step further. If these problems are no more than distant intellectual problems for the social scientist, he will discover that he and his findings are ignored. If he is not willing to share in the responsibility of his organization, he him-

Dissemination, Communication, and Utilization

self becomes the principal source of resistance to the innovations which his research may suggest [p. 317].

In short, program evaluators have to be advocates of their results—active in bringing them to the attention of others, and willing to identify publicly any policy and practical implications. Such dedication to communication and dissemination cannot but promote utilization.

Six

Values, Predispositions, and Preferences of Evaluators

There is the old and popular notion that science is value-free. The scientist labors only to understand the processes and products under investigation. The scientist cares not what others do with this knowledge. Thus, goes the notion, scientists develop information about atomic energy; politicians and statesmen decide to use it for peace or war. There is, of course, a division of labor in our society, and we know that scientists are generally not responsible for political decisions. But to assume on that basis that science goes its own way outside the realm of values is to be guilty of a gross misunderstanding.

In the words of an important scientific theorist: "The controlling factor in any science is the way it views and states its problems.

110

Values, Predispositions, and Preferences of Evaluators

Once stated, a problem can yield no further insights than are allowed by the constructing frame of its original formulation" (Lynd, 1939, p. 202). And the way we view and state problems is influenced by our values. These thoughts are echoed and elaborated by Kelman (1968) as he reflects on the social sciences: "There is a close and continuing relationship between social science and social values. On the one hand social research has a potentially important impact on the values that are held and achieved within the society. . . . On the other hand values have an important impact on social research. . . . [It] is impossible to carry out social research, particularly on social research issues, that is unaffected by the values of the investigator and the groups to which he belongs. The choice of problem, the approach to it, and the interpretation of the findings inevitably reflect the value assumptions and preferences that the investigator brings to his research" (pp. 110–111).

Now if this is true of science in general and of the social sciences in particular, it is even more clearly true of program evaluation, where the evaluator frequently works in a highly value-charged setting. Yet most books on program evaluation neglect the topic of the evaluator's values. This pervasive and basic element in all program evaluations is also the most camouflaged and the hardest to detect. The values, predispositions, and preferences of the evaluator play a prominent role in determining the design of the evaluation effort, the measures, the kinds of analysis, and the interpretation. Let us consider the evaluator's task and then see how values become involved.

We can conceptualize the evaluator's task as providing decision makers with descriptions and judgments (Stake, 1967). Descriptions may be of the program itself, of the backgrounds of the trainees or clients, of the changes that are noted among the trainees or clients over time, of the perceptions of the staff or program administrators or clients about the program, of the costs of implementing the program, and so on. (See Table 1 for more examples of what could be described in an evaluation.) Even opinion data can be used for descriptive purposes. Thus, the evaluator might indicate in a report that five experts endorsed the goals of the program or that 83 percent of the trainees judged the multimedia materials to be "moderately helpful" on a scale of helpfulness.

111

The Profession and Practice of Program Evaluation

The descriptive element in a program evaluation is usually not a matter for dispute unless, of course, someone doubts the technical accuracy of the work (for example, were attendance records properly kept?). It can be shown that 347 clients did receive medical benefits or that 73 percent of trainees in a job-skills program did complete the course. In the words of the old television detective series, "Just the facts, ma'am, just the facts." And the actual evidence could be placed before even a dubious observer. The facts, as described, are a matter of record; and the evaluator, as describer, is simply collecting those records and presenting them in a technically responsible fashion. On the surface, therefore, description does not involve the evaluator's values, predispositions, and preferences. However, that surface impression is an illusion. Values, predispositions, and preferences are actually very much involved, for they determine what the evaluator looks at and for, the methodologies used, and the ways the facts are displayed.

The second element in program evaluation—judgment—is explicitly involved when the evaluator interprets the descriptions. Here are some examples of judgments that might appear in final evaluation reports:

- The changes in behavior of the clients resulted directly from the program. Disadvantaged mothers now seek medical attention for their infants faster and more confidently than they did before because of their experiences in the Community Health Program.
- Increased time spent on teaching this skill has a positive impact in terms of the program's goals. The more time students spent in the metalwork shop, the more adept they were at oxy-welding.
- Overall, this program was most cost-effective. It provided the greatest gains in the most important goal areas for the least cost per adult trainee.

Note that we are no longer dealing, as we were with the descriptive element, with facts that, if properly gathered, are not matters of dispute. Rather, we are dealing with the evaluator's judgments, which are clearly fallible and disputable. In short, evaluator judgments carry the predispositions, preferences, and values of the evalu-

112

ator. One evaluator might judge that the results of a quasi-experimental study do not provide adequate evidence of a program's causal impact. That evaluator is predisposed to the belief that a true experiment providing statistically significant results would provide worthy evidence of causation but less rigorous designs provide less than valid evidence.

We can see that judgment, virtually by definition, involves the evaluator's values, predispositions, and preferences. Thus, some argue that all the evaluator should do is describe and leave interpretation to decision makers. For example, the evaluator might describe the program in operation, indicate the perceptions of the participants, and lay out the pretest and posttest scores. But interpreting the gains and the perceptions and arriving at conclusions about the program would not be the evaluator's role. There are two problems with this argument. Many decision makers lack the technical skills to make the interpretations. But even when the decision maker can make adequate interpretations of the descriptive information without help from the evaluator, the evaluator would still not escape heavy involvement in values—because, as we pointed out earlier, values permeate the descriptive process too. They may be implicit, but they are there nonetheless.

Even a cursory examination of the values issue leads to the realization that we are dealing with a layered phenomenon. At the deepest level is ideology, the basic set of values concerning society and morality. These values usually influence the evaluator's work implicitly. Since most evaluators share the same ideologies, such values do not seem to discernibly influence their evaluations. Virtually all evaluators agree that health services or better education for handicapped children are worthy. The provision of such services fits their ideology. Thus, ideology does not differentially affect their evaluation plans in these areas. However, the provision of some services is controversial, sometimes splitting evaluators in terms of their ideologies, and, as a result, affecting the evaluation plans they would develop if they had a free hand. (Frequently, of course, evaluators do not have a free hand in deciding the kind of evaluation they will conduct.) Consider a number of evaluators, each given freedom to plan an evaluation of a program to provide free abortions to teenagers. Evaluators with one ideology would show how the death rate for teenagers obtaining free abortions is much lower than the death rate from illegal abortions among teenage girls in the same community in the years preceding the establishment of the clinic. These evaluators might conduct a survey of teenagers to see whether they favor the program, and they might also compare the cost to society of supporting a mother and her unwanted child on welfare with the cost of the abortion program. Another group of evaluators with a different ideology might obtain information on the number of abortions performed (unborn children "murdered"), the cost of subsequent mental-health support to teenagers traumatized by the experience, the number of teenagers left sterile by complications after surgery, and the cost to the economy of a lower birth rate and the resulting stagnant market—in the short run for such products as baby foods and cribs and in the long run for a complete range of goods and services. Different ideologies, therefore, lead to different evidence.

Some writers on program evaluation, who are perhaps less accepting of present mainstream ideologies or values than the majority of evaluators, show clearly that their ideologies influence their ideas on how to conduct program evaluation (House, 1972, 1976; MacDonald, 1974). House, for example, argues that evaluation is a social mechanism for the distribution of resources; that is, it helps determine what gets funded. Therefore, the evaluator should ensure that the evaluation not only is "true" but also is "just"—a proposition based on the social theories of Rawls (1971) and Nozick (1974). By *just*, House means that the total net satisfaction in our society is maximized, not just the satisfaction of an elite. Suppose, for example, that a program for verbally gifted children were developed and evaluated. The evaluator should not only find out the direct and indirect impact of the program on the participants and their associates but also should consider the program in relation to the least advantaged members of the society. Few children from this disadvantaged societal segment are likely to participate in the program; yet the program uses resources that might otherwise be used to alleviate their disadvantage. Therefore, the views of the disadvantaged must also be obtained and

114

considered in an evaluation of the program for the gifted. In short, according to such thinkers, a "just" evaluation requires the inclusion of questions challenging the nature of the program and the societal values on which the program is based.

As a second illustration consider the argument presented by Bowles and Gintis (1976), two "radical" economists. In their view, one of the major purposes of education in our society is to maintain economic inequality. Education accomplishes this purpose, they argue, by socializing children to accept certain power relations and to adopt expectations consonant with their status in our hierarchical society. Bowles and Gintis may be mistaking correlation with causation; indeed, we rather wish that education could sometimes be as purposeful, powerful, and efficient as they say it is. But neither their values nor our opinions are at issue here. Rather, we are simply arguing that a program evaluator with their values studying an educational, economic, social, or medical program would have to include in the evaluation various nontraditional procedures, perhaps even the judgments of groups not normally considered.

The obvious questions arise: Given the effect of ideology on evaluation, what is the evaluator's professional obligation? What should the evaluator do to inform or, perhaps, protect the program director and the other audiences for the evaluation? Our answer to these questions is revealed in detail later in this chapter. However, at this point, we would emphasize two principles—the evaluator cannot become a Spock-like emotionless Vulcan, and it is worthwhile for the evaluator to make explicit, in as honest and open a way as possible, the values he holds. If simply a matter of conservative versus radical ideologies, the explication of values would not be so difficult. However, other layers of values also need attention and complicate the issue. We turn to those layers now.

Personal and Professional Values

Each evaluator has a set of values or predispositions that are focused more on the evaluation process itself than on our social, moral, and economic contexts. Each evaluator comes to a given evalu-

115

ation from different disciplinary backgrounds, each with its own built-in values and predispositions on how to proceed. We call these *professional values.* Thus, a sociologist might be more concerned with contextual descriptions and impacts, while a psychologist might be more interested in individual or group growth resulting from a particular treatment. And even within a discipline there are marked divisions. A clinical psychologist trained in the Rogerian tradition would perhaps plan for a case-study approach emphasizing affective changes, while a cognitive-developmental psychologist would plan for a longitudinal study emphasizing changes in cognitive functioning. Professional values will vary a great deal even among those who belong to a subdiscipline such as cognitive-developmental psychology. Some members will place great value on theoretical constructs; others will be far more practical and pragmatic in outlook and will value applied research and programs over discussions of theory and tight laboratory experiments to test theoretical postulates.

In addition to professional values, the evaluator has a host of affective reactions to a program and its evaluation based on personal values. These values derive from experiences outside the professional training and experiences of the evaluator. They may be values learned during childhood and adolescence, or they may derive from experiences as an adult. Such values could include, for example:

- It is good to treat the disadvantaged with respect.
- It is bad for the government to pay any form of welfare to people who can work.
- Policemen are good and helpful.
- There is nothing more important in life than helping handicapped children.

Within each of us, professional and personal values will usually not be in particular conflict. But they may not overlap a great deal either. An evaluator's professional values may lead to a preference for factor analysis as an analytic technique in contrast to the more descriptive and less analytic display of the intercorrela-

tion matrix. Personal values may not intrude at all in such preferences.

The distinction between professional and personal values is
worthwhile. An evaluation can be carried out without any overriding
concern for personal values because we can assume some degree of
integrity in the evaluator, who will attempt to overcome personal
biases. Consider an evaluator who is a parent of a handicapped preschooler. The worthiness of helping such children may be a prominent personal value for the evaluator, but we would expect him to
evaluate a program for the handicapped with great care to ensure personal values do not bias the work. In this instance, personal values
would probably reinforce professional values in guaranteeing a carefully conducted evaluation. Nonetheless, there may be some impact
on how the evaluation is conducted—the perceptions of the children
themselves and the parents would perhaps be more likely to be
included as relevant data than if another evaluator were handling the
study. But we doubt that personal values are a major problem for
most evaluators. As a general rule, if there seems to be a danger that
personal values might be a salient influence on the evaluation, evaluators should disqualify themselves. In our experience, such occasions
arise very rarely.

A major instance when personal values can become worrisome
occurs when the evaluator makes personal, subjective judgments or
perceptions in a phenomenological evaluation. Selective perception
can be a major problem. We recall spending a few days consulting
with a formative evaluation group for a children's television show.
The young evaluator showed us the process by which decisions were
made. First, the evaluator viewed a film sequence to develop familiarity with it and to derive some open-ended questions to ask of the audience. Then the evaluator went to some schools and showed the
sequence to small groups of children, observing their reactions and
asking questions afterwards. On the day we came, the evaluator had
in hand a sequence that he assured us was "really great," an evaluation based on the evaluator's personal values about what constituted
greatness in children's television. But quite a few children watching
the film looked bored, turned away from the screen, and talked to

117

other children about unrelated events. Subsequently, however, we noticed that the evaluator had checked on the observation form a "5" for "rapt visual attention." The evaluator had seen what the evaluator had wanted to see. (Or maybe the evaluator was correct in his perceptions, and our perceptions were biased by our distaste for such a subjective procedure.) The point is that, whoever was perceiving selectively, certain technical procedures can be used to check that the personal values of the evaluator and the evaluator's staff do not intrude on the evaluation. One can vary staff and obtain interjudgmental reliabilities, for example. Unfortunately, this safeguard does not hold true for the evaluator's professional values. There are no clear checks or balances to combat their influence. It is virtually impossible to disentangle and dissociate the evaluator's professional values from the phenomena chosen for study and from the methods selected for investigation.

Messick (1975, pp. 959–960) discusses the impact of these professional values in an excellent paper. He points out that values pervade not only our decisions on where to look but also our conclusions about what we have seen. And he presents an illustration that is better left in his words than paraphrased in ours (lest our values distort his meaning!):

> Consider the evaluation of "Sesame Street" as a case in point: Ball and Bogatz (1970) evaluated the educational effectiveness of this television series by analyzing gains in test performance on measures of each of the show's major curriculum goals, which included classification skills, relational terms, puzzles, knowledge of body parts, letters, forms, and numbers. They found the program to be generally effective in that those children who watched the show more learned more in each goal area, and that finding held for all types of children who watched: boys and girls, three-year-olds and four-year-olds, urban and rural, and advantaged and disadvantaged.
>
> This evaluation was then subjected to review by Cook, Appleton, Conner, Shaffer, Tomkin, and Weber (1972) in what turned out to be part metaevaluation (Scriven, 1972) and part reevaluation. Cook and others' conclusions were negative: Since more middle-class children than poor children

watched the show, the program should no longer be continued in its present form because it widened the gap between the
advantaged and the disadvantaged. Cook and others were
looking selectively at different aspects of the data than did Ball
and Bogatz (1970) and from the perspective of a different value
premise. Ball and Bogatz started with the curriculum goals of
the show and with its general objective to stimulate the
growth of all children. Cook and others started with a dis-
tinctly different perspective: [In the statement of objectives for
"Sesame Street"] the reference to stimulating 'the growth of
all children, *particularly disadvantaged preschoolers'* is
ambiguous. It does not make clear whether the objective of
"Sesame Street" is to make the economically disadvantaged a
special target group for receiving "Sesame Street" as an input;
whether a special outcome has to be that those children will
learn and grow because of "Sesame Street"; or whether these
children are to develop more than their economically advantaged counterparts because of "Sesame Street." We have chosen the latter interpretation (Cook and others, quoted in
Lesser, 1974, p. 186).

Cook and his colleagues looked at different parts of
the data, sometimes by means of different analyses, but they
suffered a disadvantage in that they could not at this point
undertake to collect new data that might shed direct light on
their position.

This intellectual 'square-off' illustrates the pervasive
intrusion of values into social research and evaluation. Two
sets of investigators, beginning with different value perspectives, filter different aspects of the data in different ways and
derive different conclusions. These different value premises
engender limitations in both studies, leaving each incomplete
and reflective of selective viewpoints. This is a general phenomenon, because all of us apply 'systems of intuitive meaning' to lend shape to our data, and these intutitions mirror
ideologies (Hudson, 1972). The ubiquity of this state of affairs
has led Hudson (1972) to formulate a law of selective attention
to data, which holds 'that the greater the ideological relevance of research, the greater the likelihood that the research
worker doing it will pay selective attention to the evidence he
collects.' Furthermore, the research is 'relevant inasmuch as
it illuminates men's ideologies. It is relevant, in other words,
to the extent that it examines the nature and tests the validity

of the assumptions we use in making sense of the world about us' (p. 160).

So the question is repeated: How can the professional evaluator best handle this crucial problem of professional values influencing the evaluation? Myrdal (1944) argues: "There is no other device for excluding biases in social sciences than to face the evaluation and to introduce them as explicitly stated, specific, and sufficiently concretized value premises" (p. 1043). Unfortunately, as we shall see, that is easier said than done.

Churchman (1968, 1971) adds another idea for clarifying values and making obvious their impact on evaluations. He calls for a kind of advocacy-adversary model of evaluation (Levine, 1973). The idea is to uncover the evaluator's values and predispositions by developing a reasonable and attractive opposing viewpoint. While Churchman points out that this can be done at the end of an evaluation, it could also be done at the planning stage. The adversary, who need not oppose every plan or interpretation, becomes the "deadly enemy" of the evaluator's original approach, a role that should provoke serious questioning of plans (if done early in the evaluation process) or of interpretations (if done late in the evaluation process).

There are, of course, problems with this approach. Should the original evaluator be his own "deadly enemy"? If values permeate our choice of design, measures, analyses, and interpretations, can we act as our own "deadly enemies"? Perhaps, as in the Catholic Church when sainthood is at issue, another evaluator should be chosen to argue in adversary fashion as a "devil's advocate." Such an arrangement would raise the cost of the evaluation, and it might also confuse the decision makers for whom the evaluation is undertaken and the other audiences who have an interest in the results. We think Churchman's ideas are potentially very useful but insufficiently tried out. They also add complexities to the already complex procedures the evaluator has to handle.

We will now summarize our views on values and propose a relatively simple procedure for examining one aspect of the values problem in evaluation.

Values, Predispositions, and Preferences of Evaluators

Explicating Professional Values

There is no way to remove the evaluator's values, predispositions, preferences, and training from the evaluation process. After all, the word *evaluation* puts values at the heart of the matter. Thus it is important, if not essential, that the evaluator explicitly present for the inspection of those commissioning the evaluation (and later for the various audiences for the evaluation) what the values, predispositions, and preferences of the evaluator are. It is also important for the evaluator to show how these values may have influenced the design, measurement procedures, analyses, and interpretations of the evaluation.

Up to now, evaluators have been little pressured by their clients or potential clients to make their values explicit. Occasionally theorists have called for such action. But there is no convenient means for making values explicit. An enlightened evaluator with time to spare (a rare occasion?) might consider underlying values, predispositions, and preferences in a preface to the evaluation proposal or to the final report. But that would be time consuming. Where would the evaluator begin? What areas should be explored? Is anything important missing?

Table 4 presents a preliminary, tentative scheme by which an evaluator can indicate values, predispositions, and preferences. It does not pretend to deal with the issue of the evaluator's personal preferences toward the objectives, content, or operations of a specific program. Rather, an attempt has been made to describe seven bipolar dimensions that seem to be central to the evaluator's professional values and that are not necessarily highly correlated. Of course, our choice of seven dimensions almost certainly does not cover all possible value areas comprehensively, and we would appreciate concerned readers' suggestions for expansion of this list and comments or reports by those who try to use the table (or some variant). Further, we cannot be sure that a given dimension in fact relates to the choices an evaluator makes. That is an area ripe for research, but we have to start somewhere.

Each of our seven bipolar dimensions is labeled; for example,

**Table 4. Predispositions and Preferences of Evaluators
(Including Examples of Design, Measurement, Analysis, and Interpretation
Preferences Associated with the Principal Dimensions)**

● ——— ● ——— ● ——— ● ——— ●

	Phenomenological	*Behavioristic*
Design	Clinical or case study	Experimental or quasi-experimental design
Measurement	Subjective measurement methods, content analyses, self-reports	Objective measurement methods, tests, systematic observations
Analysis	Descriptive statistics and nonparametric techniques	Inferential statistics
Interpretation	Judgmental, value-laden	Nonjudgmental

● ——— ● ——— ● ——— ● ——— ●

	Absolutist	*Comparative*
Design	One-group design	Experimental or quasi-experimental design with comparison group(s)
Analysis	Within-group analysis	Between-group analysis
Interpretation	Standard-referenced	Comparison-group referenced

● ——— ● ——— ● ——— ● ——— ●

	Independent	*Dependent*
Measurement	Goal-free measures	Measures tailored to program goals
Interpretation	Nonclient-oriented	Goal-referenced, client-oriented

● ——— ● ——— ● ——— ● ——— ●

	Pragmatic	*Theoretical*
Design	Widely varying	Experimental or quasi-experimental design (hypothesis testing)
Measurement	Ad hoc measures, records	Established measures, construct validity emphasized
Analysis	Widely varying	Inferential statistics
Interpretation	Program-specific conclusions, little generalization (ideographic)	Hypothesis confirmation, generalization (nomothetic)

Table 4 (continued)

• —— • —— • —— • —— •

	Narrow Scope	Broad Scope
Measurement	Few and specific measures	Many and global measures
Analysis	Univariate contrasts	Multivariate analyses
Interpretation	Oriented toward component functioning	Oriented toward system functioning

• —— • —— • —— • —— •

	High Intensive	Low Intensive
Design	Repeated measurement occasions (longitudinal)	Infrequent measurement occasions (perhaps cross-sectional)
Measurement	Multitrait, multimethod (triangulation)	Survey tests
Analysis	Multivariate analyses, including factor analyses	Univariate analyses, descriptive statistics
Interpretation	Generalization	Description

• —— • —— • —— • —— •

	Process	Product
Design	Repeated measurement occasions	Experimental or quasi-experimental design, infrequent measurement occasions
Measurement	Observations, logs, interviews	Tests
Analysis	Descriptive statistics	Inferential statistics
Interpretation	Recommendations for program improvement	Recommendations for program continuation, expansion, "accreditation"

absolutist-comparative. We have also provided examples of the kind of design, measurement, analysis, and interpretation preferences that might be associated with the poles of those dimensions; for example, within-group analysis as opposed to between-group analysis. The examples might also be thought of as "symptoms." If an evaluator prefers clinical or case studies to experimental or quasi-experimental designs, it is more likely the evaluator has a predilection for a phenomenological over a behavioristic approach. (It should go without

123

saying that we do not intend to make value judgments about the dimensions themselves; phenomenological is not "good" nor behavioristic "bad," or vice versa.)

Consider an example: One evaluator might characterize himself as leaning more toward Behavioristic (than Phenomenological), Comparative (than Absolutist), Independent (than Dependent), Pragmatic (than Theoretical), Broad Scope (than Narrow Scope), High Intensive (than Low Intensive), and Process (than Product). Another evaluator might characterize himself as different on two of these dimensions, describing himself more as Dependent and Narrow Scope. Other things being equal, we would expect the second evaluator to develop an evaluation plan different from the first evaluator's, with measures tailored specifically to the program or client's goals, fewer and less global measures, and more emphasis on the functioning of program components. The scheme provided in Table 4 may contribute to explicit predictions of such outcomes on the basis of the evaluator's predispositions and preferences. It should also offer evaluators the salutary experience of trying to analyze their own professional values and disentangle them from their conclusions.

This leaves us with the undeniable fact that evaluators with different basic social, moral, and economic values, different predispositions, and different preferences will perform different evaluations. Unless the audiences for the evaluations are informed about these underlying influences misconceptions are likely to arise.

We once had the experience of going to an engineering research and development company to explore the prospect of a joint venture in educational technology—they would produce the hardware, a university group would produce the courseware, and we would produce the evaluations. The head of the engineering firm made us wince as he launched into an attack on evaluators. Evaluators are dispensable, he assured us. Each evaluator produces a different evaluation. With such subjectivity, why have any evaluation at all? Then he made his fellow engineers wince as he also argued that engineers, on the other hand, presented with an engineering problem and the appropriate parameters, would all come up with a similar solution. A river of given size, a given amount of water flow, a given kind of geologic structure would lead to a given type of dam by any one of a given set of engineers. In our view, and in the view of most engineers, it is not true that engineers are so constrained and so lacking in individuality; but it is true that different kinds of evaluators produce different kinds of evaluations. As we have seen, such difference is inevitable.

The solution then is not to dispense with evaluation services. Rather, the solution begins with the evaluator's self-examination of values. Perhaps Table 4 (or some variation of it) will be a useful mirror to help the evaluator see his professional values and the ways they influence evaluation design, measurement, analysis and interpretation. However achieved, self-awareness is certainly an important early step in at least mitigating these problems. A second step is to try to inform the commissioner of the evaluation of the professional values that may influence planning. Similarly, to the extent possible and without creating intolerable confusion, the evaluator should inform audiences for the evaluation results how those results are based upon a particular evaluation approach. We have seen how an advocacy-adversary model might be useful in this respect. However, the evaluator will generally have to depend on a simple accounting of what decisions were made during the evaluation, why those decisions were made, and what the major alternatives were. This is the honest and open approach. Given our values, we recommend it!

Seven

Internal and External Relationships in Evaluation

The evaluator's values influence evaluation, but they are not the only source of bias, as we shall see in this chapter. The selection of evaluation purposes and methods and the decisions concerning the presentation of evidence occur within a political-economic context that also introduces bias.

Who are the principal actors in the political-economic context of program evaluation? There are the funding agent, the program director (or program developer), and the evaluator.* Of course,

*Riecken and Boruch (1974) argue for six major roles: initiator, sponsor, designer-researcher, treatment administrator, program developer, and

groups may play the role of one or more of the actors (for example, a funding consortium or a program development committee), and actors can take more than one role (for example, the program director may also be the funding agent). In this chapter, we shall focus on the evaluator's relationships with the other actors. We shall see how these relationships can become a source of bias in program evaluation. In addition, although ethics is the topic of the following chapter, a number of ethical issues are closely related to the evaluator's relationships to the funding authority and to program personnel and need to be addressed here. For example:

- What are the evaluator's obligations to the disciplines related to the evaluation, to the evaluation profession, and to an "employer" who may have a proprietary or other vested interest in the program being evaluated?
- What are the evaluator's obligations when ill-conceived evaluation requirements are specified by a funding agent (as, for example, in a badly written Request for Proposal)?
- Under what conditions and to what degree should an evaluator maintain personal detachment from the program being evaluated?

Clearly, the answers to these ethical questions rest in part on the way we structure the program-evaluator-funder relationships. However, an analysis of the evaluator's internal and external relationships with funder and program personnel has practical relevance in its own right. These relationships help determine how well the evaluation proceeds, and they influence the morale of the evaluation staff and the program staff. That is, they affect not only such principled and abstract topics as bias and ethics, but also such bread-and-butter issues as the evaluator's mood on Friday afternoon after a week of either repeated friction or relative harmony with program personnel.

---

the audience-user. In our treatment, *funding agent* includes both *initiator* and *sponsor*, *evaluator* corresponds to *designer-researcher*, and *program director/developer* includes *treatment administrator* and *program developer*. We treat the audience question separately in Chapter Five.

The Profession and Practice of Program Evaluation

Basic Relationships

As a first step let us examine some of the basic relationships between the evaluator and the program director/developer. (Hereafter the term *program director* indicates the person who directs either an ongoing program or the development of a new program.) Of most concern here is the position of the evaluator, who can be dependent upon, related to, or independent of the program director. Dependency has two major aspects: administrative and financial. The evaluator is administratively dependent upon the program director when he is required to report to the program director in some institutionalized way. He is financially dependent on the program director when the program director controls the funds available for the evaluation. The evaluator is administratively independent when he reports to an external authority (perhaps some governmental, professional, or foundation group) and financially independent when funds for the evaluation are allocated directly to him by an agency that has no other connection with the program.

"Relatedness" occurs either when the evaluator and program director report to the same administrative authority (for example, a board of education, company vice-president, or economic development council) or when funds for program operation or development and for the evaluation stem from the same agency (for example, a large corporation, foundation, or government source).

These relationships are graphically represented in Figure 3 and are determined by the answers to two simple questions:

	Financially dependent	Financially related	Financially independent
Administratively dependent	1	2	3
Administratively related	4	5	6
Administratively independent	7	8	9

Figure 3. Dependence-Independence of the Evaluator

Internal and External Relationships in Evaluation

- Whom does the evaluator report to?
    - The program director (administratively dependent)
    - The same authority as the program director (administratively related)
    - An independent authority (administratively independent)
- Where do the funds for the evaluation come from?
    - The program director (financially dependent)
    - The same funding source as the program (financially related)
    - An independent funding source (financially independent)

On the surface, it might seem that the more independent the evaluator, the better the evaluation. Further consideration shows that this is not necessarily true. Each of the categories of relationship has its own advantages and disadvantages, depending on the purpose of the evaluation.

Pros and Cons of Different Relationships

Dependent relationships may promote the evaluator's responsivity to particular program needs. This can be worthwhile when the purpose of the evaluation is to improve the program (III, Table 1). However, dependence can be counterproductive when the purpose of the evaluation is to provide a credible, global assessment of the program's impact (Scriven, 1967). Skeptics will certainly question positive evaluation results produced by a dependent evaluator.

There are instances when it is very desirable for the agency that funds the program to fund the evaluation as well. Indeed, this has frequently been the case with large federally funded intervention programs or major curriculum projects paid for by foundations. Again, the advantage is the evaluator's responsivity, this time to the expectations of the funding agency. However, the judgments of such agencies can become warped. Having committed themselves heavily to a new program, they may become increasingly reluctant to hear anything negative about it. They may even reach the point where, on receiving a negative report, they tend to fault the evaluator rather than the program, a reaction akin to the ancient custom of beheading the bearer of bad news.

The Profession and Practice of Program Evaluation

Just as there are problems in dependence and problems in relatedness, independence has its problems. These problems were demonstrated empirically by Bernstein and Freeman (1975), who found that the quality of evaluation studies (as measured by expert judgments) decreased as the independence of the evaluation effort increased. Independence can also be related to the potential impact of evaluation results. At the extreme, independent evaluations could produce results that have no bearing on the decision needs of program directors or generate valuable information that never even reaches the program directors.

We shall return to these general arguments as we discuss evaluator relationships in the context of bias, ethics, and specific evaluation processes.

Relationships and Bias

Scriven (1976a), in a typically provocative paper, specifically addresses the question of evaluator relationships and bias in evaluation: "The simplest instance of bias in program evaluation is the case of the evaluator who is part of the program staff and loses objectivity because of social and economic bonds to the development staff compounded by the cumulative effect of repeated acceptance (or rejection) of evaluative suggestions. The resulting situation of quasi-coauthorship (or frustrated coauthorship) naturally destroys the external credibility of the evaluation and often the validity of the evaluative judgments" (p. 120). Pace (1972) takes the same line as Scriven. Writing about the relationship between evaluator and program administrator, he argues: "I personally think it is advisable to maintain a firm independence of the two—and that evaluation should not be defined in a way that makes independence difficult to attain" (p. 4). Thus both Scriven and Pace worry about the evaluator being influenced or co-opted in some way by the program people.

Scriven suggests two "remedies." One is to add external evaluators as consultants to keep internal evaluators on track. This, of course, increases costs and conceivably sets up another set of frictions. Besides, the problem of whom the consultant works for remains. The second remedy is suitable for large organizations such as states and major corporations. It involves the systematic rotation of evaluation staff from project to project "to avoid the effects of excessive loyalty or hostility" (Scriven, 1976a, pp. 120–121). We have problems with this idea, too. If the evaluators are involved in a developing program, then rotating staff makes an evaluational contribution difficult. If the evaluators are carrying out a summative evaluation of any length, then rotating staff could mean that the people who plan the evaluation would be different from those who carry it out who would be different in turn from those who analyze and report it. And if the rotations were carried out only infrequently, they would hardly be effective in Scriven's terms.

We do not deny that evaluators who work directly for program directors are likely to be co-opted or to become otherwise ego-involved in the program. But does that need remedy? Let us first examine Purpose I and III evaluations. In these it could be worthwhile for evaluation and program personnel to be related closely. Consider:

- Since some program personnel distrust evaluators and, therefore, reject their results, it may be a step forward to achieve a close relationship.
- Formative and front-end evaluations require of the evaluator a great sensitivity to program goals and to program personnel and their needs. This sensitivity can best be developed by working close to them.
- The formative evaluator and the program developer have a common goal, which is to produce the best possible program. The evaluator's ego-involvement in this effort should hardly be seen as retrogressive. A mark of positive, successful formative evaluation is a successful program.

Of course, a close relationship between formative or front-end evaluator and program developer carries with it a problem. What if the evaluator and developer are both involved in self-deception, developing a bad program with blithe optimism that it is actually terrific? Well, that problem is always with us; stupidity and self-deception will occasionally foul the best constructed nest. The important question is whether such close administrative and organizational relationships will systematically develop self-deception. We think not, because there are at least two important checks. First, later summative evaluation will probably uncover poorly developed and poorly operating programs. At least in theory, this should be the case and, il it is not, then summative evaluation capability should be improved. A second check is that the program will have to prove itself eventually in some marketplace. For every program there is a consumer. In the commercial world, for example, a program for preschoolers, declared needed by and pleasing to its pint-sized clientele, could become a profit-maker's nightmare if in fact the preschoolers hated the program. And the errant evaluator is unlikely to survive the wrath of management. In the world of government, a program instituted to provide health care for the children of rural migrant workers (but which had egregious flaws, say, in its delivery system) would sooner or later come under attack from militant leaders among the migrants. It is not very likely that the government, faced with political attacks and evidence that target children are still not receiving treatment, would respond, "But our formative evaluator in the state demonstration said the delivery system is viable." A more likely response is to ensure that the formative evaluator never deludes himself (and the government) again—by promoting the person to some supervisory post.

Formative evaluators know that in the long run their work will be evaluated in terms of the success of the programs they helped formulate. The formative evaluators of "Sesame Street" were still writing about their successes (Palmer, 1971; Palmer, 1976) long after the program was put on the air. The formative evaluators of the health show (generally unsuccessful despite revision) developed by the same organization, Children's Television Workshop, have not been nearly as well known for their formative evaluative work. (However, their academic reputation is as high as it was before the show was televised.) Formative evaluators get their fame by contributing to the development of successful programs. Thus, there are built-in sanctions against formative evaluators who delude themselves and the program developer. These sanctions allow us to consider the full range of possible relationships between evaluators and program developers without necessarily rejecting a close relationship out of hand. The options in Figure 3 range from cells 1, 2, 4, or 5 (if a close relationship is wanted) to cells 6, 8, or 9 (for a distant relationship).

Scriven (1976, pp. 125–126) illustrates two possible administrative relationships with a simple diagram, which can be abstracted in the following way:

The "segregated" model (close to our "related")
Director (developer)
Production unit   Evaluation unit

The "integrated" model (close to our "dependent")
Director (developer)
Production unit No. 1   Production unit No. 2
(writers, designers,   (writers, designers,
and evaluators)   and evaluators)

We strongly prefer one of these arrangements over complete independence for formative evaluators. The important factor to consider is how best to ensure that the program developers listen to the formative evaluator. Either an administratively related or a dependent position meets this requirement. We prefer the related position because it gives the formative evaluator extra status by making him at least equal to the production unit and it may make for direct access to the chief of development. It also provides a distinctive status so that the evaluator's time is not as likely to be preempted by nonevaluation activities, and it allows a working relationship close enough that the evaluator can be quite sensitive to program needs.

Let us assume, then, that the formative evaluator is administratively dependent or related to the program developer. What about the financial relationship? It would seem that this would have to be consonant with the administrative relationship, or friction is likely. Imagine a formative evaluator with independent funding working directly under the supervision of a program developer:

Developer: I want you to get me some quick feedback
on whether our welfare mothers would be
willing to come to the clinic twice a
month. No money for babysitters.

Evaluator: No way. We know it won't fly. Tried it out
on a project two years ago in Boston. Terrible response.

Developer: I don't care what happened in Boston.
Everyone knows Boston is Boston. This is
Philadelphia. Now get me some feedback.

Evaluator: Sorry, chief. No funds for that little study.
What else would you like done?

The drama is overdrawn; the point is not.

Let us now consider relationships in summative evaluation. Here the need for independence by the evaluator is clear. Wholey and others (1972) point out: "It makes obvious sense to place the responsibility for evaluation at a level appropriate to the decisions which the evaluation is to assist. No program manager should be expected to evaluate the worth of his program, for example, nor should a member of the manager's staff be put in the position of having to criticize his boss" (p. 23). In short, the summative evaluator should be external to the program and independent—cell 9 in Figure 3. This, of course, does not mean that the evaluator should be insensitive to and uninformed about the program.

Renzulli (1972) indicates why it is important to use an objective definition of *evaluator independence:* "Institutions stand to gain such benefits as continued funding and prominence from a successful program, and the persons operating these programs stand to gain job security, prestige, and power in the form of decision-making authority. With these stakes consciously or unconsciously in mind, the administrators of programs and projects seek personnel who are euphemistically dubbed 'independent external evaluators' " (p. 299). Renzulli argues that as long as the program people select the evaluator and pay for the evaluator's work, the notion of independence is a mockery.

134

Internal and External Relationships in Evaluation

Scriven (1976) proposes a few ideas (or "morals") to lower evaluator bias caused by evaluator-program relationships. Evaluation funding must not come through the program budget. The agent funding the program should not fund the evaluation. (Scriven rules out even the "related" role.) A general-purpose evaluation office should be set up, like the U.S. General Accounting Office, to call for and fund evaluations of programs—at least public programs. (However, Renzulli (1972) warns: "If we were able to create a completely independent cadre of external evaluators, . . . would we not also widen the gap between the evaluator and the people whose honesty, trust, and cooperation are needed to mount an effective evaluation?" (p. 307).) And, finally, if such an overseer proves impractical, then the agency that funds the program and the evaluation should ensure that the personnel monitoring the program are different from the personnel monitoring the evaluation. Indeed, it is preferable that they come from different divisions of the agency.

Two points conclude this discussion. First, the summative evaluator has a professional reputation to uphold. If that reputation suffers, if the evaluator's professional colleagues see the evaluator as an accessory conniving with program directors to make programs look good, then that evaluator loses credibility. It is especially true that large and prestigious firms involved in evaluation (such as Rand and American Institutes for Research) can hardly want to lose professional respectability. This is an important check on irresponsible behavior in summative evaluations.

A second idea we learned to respect through personal experience: An evaluation advisory board serves as a buffer between program director and evaluator. The board can adjudicate disputes, assign responsibilities, and serve as a resource to the program and the evaluation. Scriven (1976) points to the "Sesame Street" evaluation as an example of the working of such a board. The board was needed because the developers themselves funded the summative evaluation; the evaluator was fiscally dependent. However, the evaluators worked for a private, independent organization, so the administrative relationship was independent. (Actually, in the first year, the U.S. Office of Education monitored the evaluation and approved its funding as a

135

proxy for the major funding consortium that was the "angel" for "Sesame Street." In the second year of the evaluation, the program people did take over that funding role.) We were the summative evaluators and we therefore personally experienced working with administrative independence (for ETS) but with fiscal dependence. A useful organizational buffer proved to be the prestigious and powerful research advisory panel whose members did not work for CTW ("Sesame Street" producers) or for the evaluator. The panelists had impeccable credentials. When final decisions on design had to be approved, or when evaluators and program personnel disagreed occasionally, the panel was there to listen, approve, or adjudicate. CTW could hardly go on record as countermanding major suggestions of the advisory board. Thus, despite fiscal dependence, the evaluator was protected from possible program pressures. Nonetheless, we do not quarrel with our colleagues who argue that summative evaluators should be both administratively and fiscally independent if possible.

Ethical Considerations

The first ethical question posed early in this chapter concerned evaluators' duties to their profession as opposed to their duty to those with vested or personal interests in the program being evaluated. It is not only good ethical policy to stand on one's professional rights and refuse to carry out biased designs or to condone misleading interpretations; it is also sound practice. In the short run a willingness to be unprofessional might bring in a few extra evaluation contracts, but in the long run even shady program developers will not want the work of a tarnished evaluator.

The second question concerned the evaluator's response to ill-conceived requests by a funding agency. The principled response would be to oppose such requests by being nonresponsive. If possible, the evaluator should also point out clearly why he is being nonresponsive and, if the evaluator wishes to be constructive, what would constitute an adequate proposal. When working for a large research and evaluation group, it is relatively easy to be principled and refuse to bid on ill-conceived projects. When working for a small organization struggling to exist, the temptation to succumb is stronger. It may be the best practice, even for struggling groups, to be nonresponsive and to provide the funder with a little education about the inadequacies of the request. Who knows? This approach might influence the funder to see the nonresponsive group as helpful, amend the request, and later even give the group a contract.

The third ethical question—the degree of involvement or detachment desirable between program evaluator and the other two major actors—has already been treated at length. Our response was quite scientific; we argued that it depends! It depends primarily on the purpose of the evaluation whether you maximize sensitivity to program needs or maximize objectivity regarding program impact. The ethical evaluator fills the legitimate role of helping the decision maker. Different decision makers need different kinds of help.

Practical Considerations

We turn now to issues less abstract than bias and ethics but nonetheless part and parcel of the evaluator's formal relationships with the program director and with the funding agent. These relationships help form the evaluation context. The importance of that context is shown by Weiss (1973) in a survey she conducted for the National Institute for Mental Health to investigate in considerable detail ten studies with evaluation components. She writes: "The context within which evaluation proceeds has enormous consequences for the kind and quality of the results produced. In most of our cases, evaluation was subordinate to the administrator; he controlled the evaluation funds and the researcher was dependent upon him for approval of major decisions and often minor ones as well. . . . Several [evaluators] felt that administrators should have less control over decisions . . . when these affect research design, measures . . . and so forth. In their view administrators had made some decisions that severely hampered evaluation, not so much out of defensiveness of their program as out of sheer ignorance. . . . They believed that fiscal control would have strengthened their hand" (p. 51).

It is comforting to discover that this set of evaluators found their respective program directors relatively lacking in defensiveness. We are not sure of the universality of that phenomenon. Indeed, it is reasonable to expect that the program director will feel some commitment to preserving the program and defending it against attack. On the other hand, the program evaluator is likely to have change and not stability on his mind. Some evaluators, given negative results, may recommend the program's termination. Given potentially different commitments, it is no wonder that the program director and the evaluator might not always have a harmonious relationship.

Caro (1971) argues that if the evaluator and the program director are working in the same organization and if the evaluator wants to have an effective and influential relationship vis-à-vis the program director, he should have a prestigious position with high status. If the evaluator is an outsider, it is helpful to have strong professional credentials and strong organizational backing. If the outside evaluator also has the backing of a high-status insider, so much the better. Warren (1963) adds that the evaluator should give administrators the impression of technical competence, understanding of and sensitivity toward the program, and personal integrity. In short, the evaluator's effectiveness can be enhanced, irrespective of the formal relationship with the program director, if certain personal characteristics and professional status qualities are displayed.

Writers have also drawn attention to a number of factors contributing to friction in the working relationship between evaluator and program director (Weiss, 1973; Rodman and Kolodny, 1964; Argyris, 1958). The personalities of the two incumbents are often mentioned. Evaluators tend to be more logical, and program people more emotional—or so goes the legend. All cynicism aside, it would not be surprising to find the evaluator putting his faith in the conclusions of a formative study, and the program director putting his faith in the intuitive judgments of the best and most creative writer on the program development team. The program people tend to be "believers"; they identify with their program. And, as with good salesmen, this belief in the program often leads to excellent outcomes—high morale and increased productivity, for example. The evaluator on the other hand tends to doubt rather than believe. "Do not get too involved," he says to himself. "Retain a degree of detachment." Splendid advice for the program evaluator, but less than splendid advice for the program director. A possible remedy to such problems is to have program directors and program evaluators receive similar kinds of training (or at least some overlap). However, given that even evaluators among themselves cannot claim much overlap in their training (see Chapter Nine), it is unlikely that this remedy will soon become universal. Nor is it likely that we can have much effect on basic personality differences. However, we can influence certain emotional states (anxiety, for example) with sensible practices. Defining the responsibilities and roles of evaluation and program personnel clearly and explicitly at the outset is one obvious point. Institutionalizing regular meetings is another.

Gurel (1975) provides a useful discussion of the human problems aspect of program evaluation. Focusing on relationships between program director and evaluator, he looks at personality stereotypes of the two and includes not only believer versus skeptic (see above) but also adds, in some detail, bureaucrat versus scientist. The major point is simple enough. Whichever social-psychological theory we espouse—personality types self-select roles, or role taking determines personality—the program director and evaluator still have different roles and goals. What are Gurel's solutions? "If left to their own devices, I am confident that managers [directors] and evaluators would slowly learn to be more accommodating to one another and would eventually learn to work more productively together" (p. 27). Indeed Weiss's (1973) survey shows just that. However, the laissez-faire approach may be insufficient. We recommend developing formal institutional relationships of relatedness (or dependence) for front-end and formative (Purpose I and III) evaluations and of independence for summative (Purpose II) evaluations. We also suggest that both program director and evaluator indulge in a little consciousness-raising. At the outset they should consider and discuss together the potential problems of their relationship (so, too, should the funding agent vis-à-vis these two) and work out rules for accom-

139

modation. The director must come to understand that program goals have to be made explicit or the evaluator's role will be miserably frustrating. The evaluator may have to be reminded that the program exists for purposes other than evaluation. Perhaps the actors in our funder–program-director–evaluator drama may need some common experiences to provide a basis for discussion. They could even use the reading of this chapter as a common experience.

Eight

Ethical Responsibilities in Evaluation

Ethics deals with what is good and bad and with moral duty and obligation. When focused on the profession of program evaluation, ethics comprises the principles of conduct governing an individual or a group. It is, therefore, appropriate to place this chapter on ethics after the chapter on values. Values provide a basis for ethics, and the ethical responsibilities of the evaluator cannot be properly understood without firm agreement on the value system in which the evaluator is working. For example, consider the situation where one evaluator subscribes to the thesis that evaluation is a political activity, while another argues instead that it is a scientific activity. The former evaluator will consider it a duty to be, at a minimum, knowledgeable about the political context of the evaluation. The latter evaluator may decide that the evaluator has no ethical responsibility to be concerned with the program's political context—though it may be a relevant variable to study.

Please note the wording of our chapter heading; it was chosen carefully. We mean to write about ethical responsibilities *in* evaluation—not just the ethical responsibilities of the program evaluator. The program-evaluation drama involves a range of players, each with ethical responsibilities. In this chapter, we shall be discussing the evaluator, the person or agency commissioning the evaluation, the various participants in the program being evaluated, the public receiving the evaluation report (and ultimately providing the authority for the whole evaluation process), and any secondary evaluators who may reanalyze the data and perhaps reinterpret the results.

Special note should be taken of the need for a clear statement on ethical responsibilities. Weiss (1970) points to the increasing politicization of program evaluation: "Researchers who undertake the evaluation of social-action programs are engaged in an enterprise fraught with hazards. They are beset by conceptual and methodological problems, problems of relationship, status, and function, practical problems, and problems of career and reward. To add to the perils of the evaluation career, evaluation is now becoming increasingly political" (p. 57). This politicization is also a publicization, and it means that consideration of ethical problems is magnified by the increasing number of eyes looking at evaluation processes and products. Despite the growing need for a clear statement on ethical responsibilities, relevant professional organizations have only just begun to set up groups to consider the topic in detail (see Chapter Eleven for specifics). Some of the many authors of books and articles on program evaluation have indeed delved into ethical issues—almost always pointing a concerned finger at the evaluator. Our professional relatives are somewhat better off. The American Psychological Association has a detailed statement, including nineteen principles, on ethical standards for psychologists (APA, 1977). Medical and legal boards of ethics can readily point to accepted ethical standards in their professions. A number of books and articles on ethics in biomedical research have appeared (Shaw and Chalmers, 1970; Zeisel, 1970; Barber and others, 1973), and a clear statement of professional standards for test developers has been prepared by a joint committee of the American Psychological Association, American Educational Research Association, and the National Council on Measurement in Education (1974). This standards statement, while omitting many important issues, at least tells test developers what professional steps they ought to take in developing tests, and tells test users their responsibilities. School psychologists have ethical codes and models (Bersoff, 1973; Trachtman, 1972), which have even been scrutinized from a legal viewpoint (Cardon, 1975).

We can find useful advice by looking at such sources and, indeed, it is to be expected the relevant standards will be met. But there is more to the ethics of program evaluation than can be found in reading about the ethics and standards of clinical psychologists, medical doctors and lawyers, test developers and users, school psychologists, and other well-established professional groups. Certain ethical questions are unique to program evaluation.

We have noted that ethical considerations depend on our value structures; that ethical responsibilities in program evaluation involve more than just the program evaluator; and that although individual authors have pointed to a need for a set of ethical standards, no such set has yet been developed. An extensive examination of the literature on ethics in program evaluation reveals a wide scattering of more or less uncoordinated caveats, fiats, injunctions, and, occasionally, individual indictments. The topic is an inherently difficult one.

One of the best treatments of ethical responsibilities in program evaluation is provided by Riecken and Boruch (1974). In a chapter on human values and social experimentation, they draw attention to ethical issues of two kinds. First are ethical problems associated generally with sound experimentation and evaluation. They here point to ethical problems that some would argue belong to program developers and program evaluators in particular. Examples include:

• Harmful program side effects that doom programs in the long run and that should have been foreseen; for example, the Pruitt-Igoe low-income housing project in St. Louis, Missouri. It cost over $30 million to construct the high-rise buildings, which became crime-ridden, and it cost many more millions later to pull them down.

• Damaging treatments or failures to provide needed treatments, violating the rights of program participants. An example is the biomedical research study among prison groups of the long-range effects of venereal disease, in which, to ensure a control group, some prisoners were denied medical treatment. Another example is provided by the study of the effects of protein supplements given to pregnant women in Central America on the mental development of their offspring. Women in control villages received a soft drink with no protein value. The value of protein for those on a protein-deficient diet was already well known. Yet the study was so designed that some pregnant women were knowingly denied a source of protein that would have helped them whether it was important for infant mental development or not.

With respect to summative evaluations, Riecken and Boruch argue that program evaluators must first satisfy themselves that the program to be evaluated is potentially beneficial—perhaps by obtaining a review of the program by appropriate authorities. Further they must ensure that the evaluation design does not itself violate the rights of those for whom the treatment is potentially available. In this regard they provide a number of useful remedies or conscience-salving positions:

• If the treatment is not clearly beneficial, including no-treatment groups in the evaluation design is not an ethical problem.
• If the treatment is clearly beneficial, there is little need for an evaluation involving no-treatment groups. In fact, there is little need for evaluation!
• If the value of the treatment is in question (the typical instance) but we find from the evaluation that the treatment is worthwhile, then the no-treatment groups can be provided the treatment later (unless, for example, the disease being treated is fatal).

If resources are limited, the evaluator can use a randomization technique (the evaluator's lottery) to decide who will receive the limited resources. An example here is a study of the effects of an income-maintenance program. A population of families below some specific

144

floor income can be found, but the funds for extra-income payments are enough to bring only a small number of the families to the floor level. Random allocation of the treatment will mean a boon to some families and continued poverty for others. But at least the basis for the decision was fair; all had an equal opportunity to be in the fortunate treatment group.

The second major ethical area that Riecken and Boruch draw attention to is encompassed by such words as *informed consent, deception, privacy,* and *confidentiality.* Again their discussion is forthright and relevant. Informed consent of the participants in an evaluation is now virtually a necessity if government funds are involved or if publication of the work in a responsible journal is desired. However, there remain grey areas. What if it is necessary to have a placebo group (or to control for Hawthorne effect)? Riecken and Boruch see no problem in the minor deception involved in sug-gesting to subjects that they are all in a treatment group. Letting all subjects think they are in the treatment group is not irresponsible if proper safeguards and later debriefings are also arranged. (However, the subjects' belief that they are in the "treated" group may be suffi-cient treatment, and the evaluation design and analysis should take account of this possibility.)

Privacy and confidentiality are very much current concerns. Evaluators have a strict moral and professional obligation to protect the privacy of evaluation participants and to keep individual data confidential unless participants have given informed consent to release those data. We realize there will be problems in all this. Sup-pose, for example, that in a study of a program for young mothers we wish to videotape some training sessions, but we want mothers to behave as "naturally" as possible during those sessions. Suppose we obtain the mothers' consent at the start of the program. Do we need to keep on reminding them that when they are at the program center, they may be videotaped? If we keep reminding them, there is a clear risk that we will be obtrusive and that the mothers will behave unnaturally as a result. We would probably consider the initial agree-ment sufficient and would not insist on repeated reminders. There may also be legal problems. Researchers and evaluators have had their data subpoenaed by courts on occasion to discover, for example, if welfare mothers earn extra income (Walsh, 1969). When journalists of the *Fresno Bee* newspaper refused to divulge the source of their information for a story (an ethical stance for journalists), they were jailed for contempt of court. Evaluators should probably be prepared to take a similar stand even if they suffer similar punishment. Since opinions about both consent and privacy may well differ, we recommend, as Riecken and Boruch do in a different context, that the concerned evaluator establish some kind of external review of confidentiality and privacy procedures.

Guba (1975), in discussing difficulties in utilizing evaluation results, focuses intensively on the evaluator's ethics. He sees three forms of "evaluation corruptibility" (p. 51):

- Evaluators willing to twist the truth and produce findings that appear to be advantageous. (We do not doubt such evaluators exist; some program developers indeed look for them. The problem is not restricted to evaluators. Some physicians tell patients what they want to hear, and some car salesmen also bend the truth if it means increasing profits. However, we do not agree with the generalization encapsulated in a quotation from a director of a federal program and reported by Guba: "Evaluation is a whore." There is, by and large, not that much money in program evaluation.)
- Evaluators who sometimes unknowingly brighten the information produced by the evaluation. (We are sure this occurs. Perhaps the evaluator thinks that the program provides many benefits but most of the objective data show no significant differences between treatment and control groups. The evaluation report then highlights the few differences favorable to the program and quickly dismisses the nonsignificant areas by saying that no negative program effects were found there.)
- Evaluators who shade the evaluation results into a negative tone, perhaps in order to show their tough-mindedness. (Again, reality has been perverted for less than ethical reasons.)

In his article Guba does not solve the problem of the corrupt evaluator. Corruption is probably inevitable and cannot be eliminated, but there are ways of minimizing it. A code of ethics for evaluators established by a multidisciplinary board of eminent researchers and evaluators could provide standards that might positively influence the behavior of those commissioning and conducting evaluations. We strongly support the establishment of a code. A second proposal is to establish a board of review or appeal composed of people similar to those who develop the ethics code. Such a board might then be able to impose sanctions on (or draw attention to) unethical behavior by evaluators or program personnel. This second proposal is tentative, because many related issues remain to be resolved.

Perloff and others (1976) discuss still a different ethical issue for evaluators—what to do when positive results do not appear for a program with good intentions (for example, minimizing inequalities of opportunity, diminishing criminal recidivism, improving health care). The modest evaluator must always wonder whether the failure is due to inadequate design, measurement, or sampling in the evaluation rather than poor performance of the program. But what if the evaluator decides that indeed the program rather than the evaluation is at fault? Should this result be disseminated at the risk that the public will consider all possible programs in this area worthless (convicts will always be criminals, addicts cannot be helped). As Caplan and Nelson (1973) and Wortman (1975) point out, evaluators should balance the need for the dissemination of the truth, as they see it, against the possible political consequences of dissemination, such as misinterpretation of results and the resultant loss of funds for all such programs. Our view is that evaluators should indeed be sensitive to the possible political impact (including illogical political decisions) of their evaluation publications. However, refusing to publish results is no remedy. That would be like women deciding never to be friendly to men because of the possibility that some man, sometime, would perniciously misinterpret the intent of their friendliness. The responsibility of the evaluator is to anticipate misinterpretations and overgeneralizations and to warn explicitly against them in evaluation reports. If that is done and if the evaluator is also willing to speak out assertively against misinterpretations of the evaluation, the responsibility has been met.

A number of ethical issues arise out of the role relationships of the evaluator vis-à-vis the program developer and the funding agency (see Chapter Seven). Renzulli (1972), in his "Confessions of a Frustrated Evaluator," points out that we would be deluding ourselves if we failed to see that a program developer or administrator usually wants positive evaluations. He wants to avoid negative evaluations because they imply that he is incompetent. As Renzulli says, "Please remember that this is the same project director that hired the evaluator, squired him through several three-martini lunches, and suggested that he publish the results of his evaluation in a professional journal." Renzulli concludes: "As long as factors such as funding, prestige, and power are involved, the political relationship between the evaluator and those being evaluated will not be an easy problem to solve" (p. 299). The same observation holds true for the ethical relationship as well.

As discussed in Chapter Seven, the evaluator's role depends on whether the evaluation service is primarily formative/developmental (the evaluator might well work directly for the program director) or summative (where the evaluator is independent of the program). In the former case the evaluator must try not to be forced into unprofessional behavior by the threat of economic sanctions such as loss of employment. Of course, even the case of an independent evaluator with a legal contract guarantees no freedom from indirect or implied threat ("You'll never get another evaluation contract from me"). It is a situation that cannot be avoided entirely in our society, and it is here that a board of review or appeal composed of eminent evaluators, other social scientists, and legal experts might be able to alleviate the problem. Therefore, a board or committee within the profession of program evaluation whose purpose it is to publicize improper threats and to stand behind evaluators who might otherwise be victimized may well be needed.

Some general conclusions about ethics can be drawn from the writings of others and from our discussion:

• The evaluator's responsibility transcends simple competence in the work of evaluation. It includes not promising too much at the outset, ensuring that role relationships are proper and secure before work begins, and insisting on appropriate warnings about the limitations of the evaluation in all reports of the results.

- The evaluator must assume loyalties other than those to the program. These include loyalties to the profession of program evaluation and to the public, which ultimately provides the authority for both program and evaluation. Thus, the evaluator has the responsibility to refuse to perform any evaluation services demanded by a program director or funding agent that he deems unethical.

- Evaluations should be as open as possible, within the constraints of the privacy of the participants, the confidentiality of individual data, the contractual obligations, and the smooth working of program and evaluation. When the evaluation is open, germs like suspected evaluator bias and undue program pressure do not thrive as readily.

These generalizations are unlikely to raise much counterargument. But they are generalizations, and, as such, they lack operational specification for those involved in program evaluation. Trying to specify those responsibilities is our next difficult task.

A Draft Statement of Ethical Responsibilities

We have pointed out that the evaluator works in a value-laden, often politically volatile, pressure-filled area. Evaluation conclusions are potentially powerful—programs called for by some highly vocal group may not be undertaken because of a needs-assessment study; programs under development may be drastically changed because of the results of formative studies; operating programs may be eliminated (or local programs may go national) as the result of summative studies. Until a coherent statement of the ethical responsibilities of those involved in the evaluation process comes from the appropriate professional organizations, we hope that the statements presented in Table 5 will serve as a guide to ethical behavior in evaluation and as a starting point for subsequent standard-setting activities by profes-

149

Table 5. Ethical Responsibilities in Program Evaluation

Evaluator to Commissioner of the Evaluation (COE), Participants, Public, and Profession	*Commissioner of the Evaluation (COE), Participants, and Secondary Evaluator to Evaluator*
1. To acquaint the potential COE with those values and orientations of the evaluator that may bear on the proposed evaluation effort.	COE: To provide the potential evaluator with as complete information as possible about the program (or proposed program), the COE's expectations for the evaluation, and the proposed conditions and resources for carrying it out.
2. To work toward a contract or "agreement" with the COE that is ethically, legally, and professionally sound.	COE: To work toward a contract or "agreement" with the evaluator that is ethically, legally, and professionally sound.
3. To refuse to perform work until such a contract or "agreement" is reached.	COE: To refrain from insisting that work be performed before such an "agreement" is reached.
4. To fulfill the terms of the contract or "agreement" to the best of the evaluator's ability.	COE: To cooperate with the evaluator and to fulfill to the best of the COE's ability any commitments or obligations called for in the contract or "agreement."
5. To acquaint the COE promptly with problems arising in fulfilling such terms and attempt to work out a solution.	COE: To acquaint the evaluator promptly with problems associated with the program that may affect the evaluation effort; to work with the evaluator in attempting to solve any mutual problems that arise.
6. To adhere to relevant professional and legal standards and ethics in the conduct of the evaluation, including appropriate provisions for privacy and informed consent of participants and confidentiality of data.	COE: To support the evaluator's adherence to relevant professional and legal standards and ethics in the conduct of the evaluation.
7. To carry out data collection and other evaluation activities with as little interference as practicable with the operation of the program.	COE: To encourage full and honest cooperation by program participants in supplying data needed for the evaluation effort. Participants: To cooperate in the data-collection effort associated with the evaluation and to provide accurate information in response to legitimate requests.

150

Table 5 (continued)

Evaluator to Commissioner of the Evaluation (COE), Participants, Public, and Profession	*Commissioner of the Evaluation (COE), Participants, and Secondary Evaluator to Evaluator*
8. To acquaint the COE with any aspects of program philosophy or operation that do not appear to be ethically, legally, or professionally sound or physically safe but are observed by the evaluator, even if such observation is not part of the evaluator's specific charge; in addition, to inform the appropriate authority if the evaluator obtains evidence of legal misconduct by the COE.	COE: To recognize the evaluator's "amicus" role in noting ethical, legal, safety, or professional problems associated with the program; to seriously consider the evaluator's observations in this area.
9. To acquaint the COE, in advance of any response, with requests received by the evaluator from superordinate agencies for information (testimony, and so forth) about the program or evaluation; to ascertain with the COE whether such requests are valid; if so, to acquaint the COE fully with the nature of the response.	COE: To advise the evaluator on the validity of requests for information from superordinate agencies.
10. To present a "balanced" report of results to the COE in timely fashion and in a form usable to the COE; to spell out limitations of the investigation, along with the evaluator's values and orientations, that may bear on the conclusions.	COE: To discourage misinterpretation and misuse of the evaluation results.
11. To reserve the right to publish rejoinders to any misinterpretation or misuse of the evaluation results by the COE.	
12. To identify other groups with a legitimate concern for the results of the evaluation and to make the results available to them.	COE: To advise the evaluator about groups that, to the COE's knowledge, have a legitimate interest in the results of the evaluation; to encourage dissemination of results to such groups.

151

Table 5 (continued)

Evaluator to Commissioner of the Evaluation (COE), Participants, Public, and Profession	Commissioner of the Evaluation (COE), Participants, and Secondary Evaluator to Evaluator
13. To allow interested professionals to examine the data produced by the evaluation, within the limitations of accepted standards for privacy, confidentiality, and informed consent related to the purposes for which the data were collected.	Secondary evaluator: To specify, at the time when permission is sought to review the evaluation data, the purposes of the secondary evaluation effort; to maintain professional and ethical standards in conducting the secondary evaluation, including honoring any relevant commitments to those who supplied the original data; to report in a professionally sound manner on the results of the secondary evaluation.
14. To reserve the right to publish rejoinders to any misinterpretations or misuse by the secondary evaluator of the original evaluation data or results.	
15. To share with professional colleagues and relevant agencies and institutions knowledge about basic processes (educational, psychological, social, and so forth) derived from evaluation studies.	

Definitions used in the presentation:

Program—institution, organization, activities, or materials with an interventionist function in improving human welfare.

Evaluator—person(s) or agency with major responsibility for planning, carrying out, and reporting evaluation activities (see Table 1). May be independent or dependent (see Figure 3).

Commissioner of the Evaluation (COE)—person(s) or agency with major responsibility for securing the services of an evaluator.

Participants—administrators, staff, program recipients, and other persons with a role in the program being evaluated.

Secondary evaluator—person(s) or agency engaging in critical review of evaluation activities. May include reanalysis of previously collected data.

sional organizations. Table 5 does not pertain to the evaluation of programs with proprietary or national-security interest. In such cases different provisions may apply; for example, the results of the evaluation may not be available for general public scrutiny.

Ethical Considerations in Evaluation

Table 5 is divided into two columns: The first lists some of the evaluator's principal responsibilities to the commissioner of the evaluation, program participants, the public, and the profession. The second column lists some of the responsibilities of the commissioner of the evaluation, of program participants, and of the secondary evaluator to the evaluator. Every statement in Table 5 could be discussed—and debated—at great length. However, we shall content ourselves with providing only brief comments and some examples, not necessarily hypothetical, of compliance or noncompliance with the "code."

At the Outset. (Responsibility 1 from Table 5, in which the evaluator presents his values and orientations and the commissioner of the evaluation [COE] presents the program or proposed program, expectations of the evaluation, and conditions and resources for carrying it out.)

We have discussed the evaluator's responsibility for presenting values and orientations in the previous chapter. However, the COE's role has been less comprehensively discussed. We did present Riecken and Boruch's (1974) suggestion that the evaluator must obtain at the outset a description of the program or proposed program in order to make an independent assessment of its potential value. Their point was that if the program clearly would not provide benefits or would have injurious side effects, then the evaluator should not proceed. The evaluation deal would not be consummated—a form of evaluation birth control. This approach has problems stemming from the fact that the question of whether a program is helpful or injurious is usually empirical. Rarely does an evaluator have convincing evidence in advance. A second problem is that the evaluator should not be the only one to judge whether the program is harmful. If the question were raised before a board of review, unanimous agreement prior to formal evaluation that the program is clearly harmful would be surprising.

A perhaps better reason for the initial briefing is to ensure that the evaluator knows what the evaluation expectations are. The evaluator can then be sure that there is a meeting of minds on what is to be accomplished. This seems a rather simple and obvious responsibility of the COE to the evaluator and of the evaluator to the

COE; yet surprisingly often it is not carried out adequately.

Such neglect can have interesting repercussions. A program evaluator is called in to conduct an impact evaluation of a drug-information program designed to reduce drug abuse in a city's high schools. The COE explains what the program is all about and what the expectations are for the program evaluation. The evaluator responds by pointing out that since the program is new and has never been tried on a high-school population before, it would be better to introduce the program into only a few schools and to conduct a small series of formative studies. These studies would aim to find out whether students comprehend the written units, whether the film sequences excite curiosity more than they lower interest in drugs, whether the biology teachers who are to implement the program have constructive ideas for integrating it into the total school program, and whether the parents also need some education in order to ensure their understanding of the program. The evaluator points out that if this is done and the program is subsequently modified and implemented, then and only then would it be time to consider a summative evaluation. The COE is impressed by that logic and agrees to radically change the expectations for program evaluation in the coming year.

However, one can hardly expect that ethical behavior will always result in such beneficial outcomes. Consider the true case of the school board of a predominately white middle-class suburban district. The board was conservative and was under siege by the liberal part of its constituency. "We ought to bus in minority students from inner-city areas," claimed the liberal parents. So, with some craftiness, the board decided to run a small experimental program and have it evaluated. The real intent was to have the evaluator provide evidence against the experimental busing program (Purpose V). The board hoped that the evaluator would come up with findings of increased school disruptions, lowered achievement levels in the predominantly white schools, and no offsetting benefit for the minority children who were bused in. Unfortunately for the school board (the COE in this case), these expectations were not made clear to the respectable evaluation firm the board called in. Had they been made clear, this particular firm would have refused to carry out the work. Then, we presume, the board would have changed its expectations or else have found one of those corruptible evaluators referred to earlier in this chapter. But the evaluation was carried out and the first run of the data analysis was explained to a board representative. That run showed that the program had no discernible effects on the white suburban schools with respect to discipline or achievement and markedly benefited the achievement of the minority children who were bused in. Before the results could be checked and published, the board voted to close down the program. The board was furious with the evaluator (and even more so when the evaluator made the evaluation findings public). The liberal voters in the district were furious with the board, as was the evaluator who found his integrity under attack by some of the conservative board members.

Of course, this illustrates that if the board had been ethical in admitting its scientifically inappropriate and unethical expectations, it might have succeeded in its plan. The responsible evaluator would have left the scene and an unethical one might have been found. That is, a greater disservice to education might have occurred if the board had carried out its unethical plan in an ethically responsible way. However, we would then hope that the first evaluation firm would have made public its reasons for declining to carry out the board's work.

Developing the Contract. (Responsibilities 2 and 3 from Table 5, in which the evaluator is enjoined to develop a contract that is ethically, legally, and professionally sound and not to work until such a contract is developed; the COE is similarly advised.)

For major evaluation efforts, a formal, legal contract should be negotiated; not to have one would be foolish for both parties. In smaller evaluation efforts, a formal contract might be unnecessary, but even then a letter of agreement signed by the evaluator and by the COE makes excellent sense. In either case, the agreement should spell out not only the financial arrangements but also the main elements and requirements of the planned evaluation.

Now for a parable: A young assistant professor was once asked by the state director of rehabilitation training to evaluate a rehabilitation program in a nearby state prison. Funds for the evaluation were not great but they did enable the evaluator to spend 20 percent of her time in the evaluation. She agreed, completing the arrangements in a manner that used to be called "a gentleman's agreement"—a firm handshake. Over the next six months, she spent about five days developing instruments, another few days interviewing staff and inmates, several days analyzing data, and a few more days writing her report, which was not very positive. The prison officials were irate. How could she expect to do a decent job when she spent fewer than ten days in the prison? How could she get a feel for the program with such a limited investment of time? The state director waffled quickly. "Of course, of course," he nodded. "I'm surprised she only spent such a short period of time at state prison. I expected she'd have been there at least a day a week observing." "I had no time for that," our assistant professor protested. "You know I only had one day a week to run this evaluation from start to finish." But there was no proposal for her to point to, no formal letter of agreement that detailed the number of days nor how she was to spend those days on the project. And she was bad-mouthed for many years thereafter. The moral: As Samuel Goldwyn used to say, oral agreements aren't worth the paper they're written on.

Young assistant professors are not the only ones who can be hurt by beginning an evaluation before the detailed agreement is in place. We know of an instance where a large evaluation organization, assured that a contract would be forthcoming, began work on a large-scale evaluation. Unfortunately, there was a palace revolution in the government agency funding the evaluation and the study was never actually commissioned. The big evaluation organization was left with sizeable unpaid costs.

Fulfilling the agreement. (Responsibilities 4, 5, 6, and 7 from Table 5, in which the evaluator works sincerely at the task, maintains communication with the COE, adheres to established standards of conduct, and interferes with the program as little as possible; the COE, in turn, cooperates by supporting the evaluator as outlined in their agreement and encourages program staff cooperation; the participants [administrators, staff, and clients] also cooperate fully in the data collection.)

These codes may appear labored in their presentation and obvious in their content. However, in practice, much of the "obvious" content proves less than apparent. Consider this list of readily recognizable transgressions by evaluator, COE, and participants:

• An evaluator, given responsibility for a particular project, turns over most of the work to far less experienced and less well-trained evaluation personnel. Little wonder, because in addition to having more than 150 percent of his time allocated to various evaluation projects, the evaluator teaches a course at a local university, writes a column for a professional magazine, attends five conferences a year to the tune of four days apiece, consults privately four days a month, and is heavily involved in writing a chapter in a social-psychology book (on delegating authority in small- and large-scale evaluations).

• A professor, well-known for his work in psychometrics (especially in the use of factor analysis), is persuaded by a jovial colleague from a different branch of psychology to conduct a lucrative evaluation of a program designed to improve the reading comprehension of third- and fourth-grade disadvantaged children. He conducts the study but the report is six months overdue, mainly because the professor spent so much time working out different ways of factor analyzing the pretest scores. The time was not spent in vain either. He published a paper on this work in *Psychometrika,* something he could never have done had it not been for the released time and the data-analysis funds provided by the evaluation study of reading comprehension.

• A large evaluation group is conducting a three-year longitudinal study of the impact of a rehabilitation program for young convicts on their subsequent behavior after their release. Because data were badly coded and banked in the initial year of the study, it is impossible to retrieve a great deal of the pretest data. The evaluators neglect to tell this to the federal agency until another twelve months have elapsed. "Why didn't you tell us?" asks the federal project moni-

157

tor concerned that an extra $200 thousand had been wasted. "We hoped we could fix it up," explains the evaluation director. "And we didn't want to worry you unnecessarily."

• An expert in evaluation is asked by the school board to develop an accountability plan, which is then implemented. The plan involves having teachers specify behavioral objectives and criterion levels for each of five areas in reading, four areas in mathematics, and three areas in social studies. Every Friday each class takes a two-and-a-half hour test to assess whether the criterion levels were attained. The teachers object that their nonteaching school time is almost completely taken up in writing objectives, tests, and criteria. The parents of some of the children protest that testing consumes the whole of Friday morning. The evaluation expert scoffs at such traditional objections. "Taking tests can be a good experience," he tells his critics. "Besides, the teachers don't have to mark the tests. I take them away, have them keypunched, verified, the data tapes cleaned of error, and the scores run, analyzed by child and by class. Indeed, the teachers and children get feedback on their work on the average within three weeks. Now that's good turnaround."

• A first-grade teacher is thought to be going through some neurotic episode. Each morning this week, in defiance of the school authorities, he lets the children into the classroom, locks and bolts the classroom door, turns on the fluorescent lights, and pulls down the shades of all the windows. He also makes strange noises when he meets the Title I Evaluation Team Classroom Interaction Observers in the hallway. No one knows why. Every day for the previous six weeks he has happily allowed members of the team into the room to videotape lessons and make audio tapes. He has also allowed the evaluation director to lead groups of graduate students who are studying the evaluation process into the room at unscheduled times to observe classroom social relationships.

• The remedial-reading teacher has agreed to cooperate fully with the college evaluation team that is designing an evaluation of the school's remedial-reading program. This teacher is no fool. He knows he is the only remedial-reading teacher in the school. Any evaluation of the program, he reasons, is an evaluation of him. None-

158

theless, he agrees to cooperate. First, the evaluators tell him, he must pretest all his students during October when the program gets underway. In November he is to send them the completed tests. At the end of November he receives a phone call. "Where are the tests?" "On the way," he assures them. Early in December, twenty tests (rather than the forty promised) arrive at the evaluation headquarters. This time, a visit. "I know I should have finished the testing in October," he explains, "but I individually tested as you said and some of the kids are often absent. You know how it is in school these days. Interruptions for this and that." The evaluator has an idea. "It's too late to pretest in December. The program is already two months underway. It only lasts another five months, so this can't be pretest data any more. We'll use a posttest-only design. Posttest the remedial reading students in May. Send us those tests. Right?" "Right! I'll cooperate all the way," asserts the remedial-reading teacher. In May the evaluator calls. "Remember?" "Sure I do," the teacher says. "Starting tomorrow." On the last day of school, the evaluator receives a parcel of tests—twenty of them. Enraged, he calls the teacher. "Why only half the tests?" "What do you mean, half the tests? I tested twenty kids in October. I tested the other twenty in May. By the way, is there anything else I can do for you?"

The point surely is that a tremendous range of tensions and pressures can occur in the process of fulfilling the evaluation agreement. If we have made light of some of the problems, it is partly because we tend to laugh at horror stories. But they remain horror stories. Ethical responsibilities are hard to uphold during data collection. Many evaluators find planning and reporting fun. Data collection can become dreary. Participants during data collection suddenly realize whom the evaluation pressure is really squeezing— themselves! So, Responsibilities 4 through 7 in Table 5 may seem obvious, but that makes them no less warranted.

Extracontractual Relationships. (Responsibilities 8 and 9 from Table 5, in which the evaluator, irrespective of his designated role, is urged to tell the COE about aspects of the program that seem unsound, to tell relevant authorities of legal misconduct, and to keep the COE informed of requests received from and responses made to superordinate agencies; the COE, in turn, is urged to recognize these evaluation prerogatives and to advise the evaluator on the validity of evaluation information requests.)

Fortunately, most evaluators usually are not asked by superordinate agencies to provide more information than the agreement or contract with the COE calls for. It is also fortunately rare for an evaluator to come across evidence of illegal activity by the client. However, just as physicians should be prepared to recognize and treat relatively rare disorders, so too evaluators should know how to respond to unusual requests and situations. We know of at least one instance where an evaluator discovered larcenous behavior by a program staff member. Since it is a crime to know about such behavior and not report it (an accessory after the fact) and since legal penalties are proscribed for such failure, it was ethical, legal, prosocial, and practical for the evaluator concerned to report his findings to the appropriate authorities.

Illegal behavior is not confined to program personnel. We also know of an evaluator who spent part of his on-the-job time conducting a random survey, all on his own, of the sex habits of women whose names appeared in the phone directory. The questionnaire was apparently well-constructed but the behavior constituted a "nuisance"—one especially unethical because the COE for a different kind of survey was being called on to pay the phone bills. Of course, this must be an unusual kind of unethical behavior. Somewhat more frequently one comes across evaluation staff who steal equipment, make up fictitious data, and otherwise misuse the trust the evaluator has placed in them. There is no wonder drug for this kind of malaise. Careful selection and close supervision of staff and assiduous quality-control of data are essential antidotes, however.

The issue raised in Responsibility 9 relates to special requests for information about the program or evaluation. The evaluator may be asked to provide opinions about the trainers or wardens or hospital aides—people who figure in the evaluation but who are not, themselves, being evaluated. This is especially troubling when the request is for opinions quite beyond the limits of any data. On occasion an evaluator is asked to comment on the quality of a program even before the pretest data have been collected. The following is a true story. A government official recently contacted an evaluator friend of ours and asked whether he was evaluating a certain TV series. "I am," said the evaluator. He felt somewhat mystified because he was working under contract to the TV producer (who was getting government funds) and not directly for the government.

"What do you think of the series?" asked the official. The evaluator explained that he was conducting an impact study. The design called for pretests and posttests involving a certain target audience. And the pretest data were only now being collected.

Now it was the official's turn to sound mystified. "You mean you've designed a pretest instrument without even looking at the series?"

"Of course, I looked at the series. I believe it is essential to review the program before developing the assessment instruments," said the evaluator, testily.

"Then what do you think of the program? I am being asked for funds for a second-year series, and I need your current opinion about the first-year series."

There followed an unusual conversation in which the evaluator pointed out that he was not a TV critic, the government official wondered aloud how an educational psychologist could view an educational TV series without forming some judgments, and the evaluator philosophized about the wisdom of a system that funds a second series before finding out about the impact of the first. In the end, the evaluator decided to inform the COE of the government official's request. He followed that up with a lengthy memo to all concerned detailing the conversation and presenting his criticisms of the series along with appropriate disclaimers about his expertise as a critic. The government official subsequently decided to re-fund the project but primarily in order that extensive formative work be conducted on the first-year series. We generally approve the evaluator's behavior. It illustrates a problem (and a possible ethical resolution) that can befall the evaluator when loyalties and contractual terms conflict.

Ethical Problems in Dissemination. (Responsibilities 10, 11, and 12 from Table 5, in which the evaluator's and the COE's

161

major responsibilities concerning dissemination are spelled out.)

Many ethical questions concern dissemination. The typical dissemination effort is to write a report and file it. That level of effort is probably unethically low. (See Chapter Five for a discussion of what we consider to be a reasonable level of effort.) The typical client resists the dissemination of negative findings and encourages the dissemination of positive results. A balanced report is not what some COEs want; they want it glowing. That preference may be human nature, but it is nothing the evaluator should condone. Rather, the evaluator must communicate to a variety of audiences in intellectually honest ways what the findings of the evaluation are. That is the minimal effort consonant with an ethical stance.

Secondary Evaluations. (Responsibilities 13, 14, and 15 from Table 5, in which ethical behavior involved in secondary evaluation is made explicit.)

It is a heartening development in program evaluation that interest in secondary evaluation is increasing. There was a time, not so long ago, when even primary evaluation was not given much consideration. Now there are people of good humor who have even presented thoughts on tertiary evaluation and beyond. But, joking aside, secondary evaluation is with us, and the ethical issues should be considered. The responsibilities regarding secondary evaluation listed in Table 5 seem to be self-evident. The evaluator should encourage, or at least be responsive to, requests from secondary evaluators for data. Those data should be provided in such a way as to protect the privacy and confidentiality of both individuals and institutions. This openness by the primary evaluator is the best way to minimize the grossest charges that the evaluator has fudged. Besides, primary evaluators do not normally have the time or resources to polish their data as brightly as they would wish. Ideally, then, a secondary evaluator can provide a very welcome extra examination of the data.

For their part, secondary evaluators should be prepared to specify why they want data. Mere fishing expeditions, without full consultation with the primary evaluators, can be a cause for concern for the following reasons:

- The secondary evaluator might unwittingly violate promises to evaluation participants. Suppose, for example, that the primary evaluator, in obtaining inner-city community support for data collection, promises *not* to compare the urban children's status with the status of suburban middle-class children. (This promise is a partial response to the charge, "You just want to come here and collect your data, exploit our families, and then tell everybody we have dumb kids.") Then, later, along comes a secondary evaluator who is ignorant of the promise and is attached to comparative measures.

• The primary evaluator, having collected the data, should know best what its strengths and limitations are. The secondary evaluator who simply goes away and runs new analyses may make inappropriate interpretations if full consultation with the primary evaluator is not part of the secondary evaluation process. Consider the case where a number of subscales and subtests are included among the scores provided to the secondary evaluator. Suppose the secondary evaluator assumes that the name of the subtest or scale provides all the understanding required of what is being measured. (It's called the Letters Test, so it must be a test of simple knowledge of the letters of the alphabet. But, in fact, the test includes an assessment of the ability of the respondent to classify and sort on the basis of letter shapes, sounds, and alphabetic position.) The primary evaluator could readily save the secondary evaluator the embarrassment of professional error if he has the opportunity to review the secondary evaluator's planned analyses and the rationale for them.

• The primary evaluation involves a design and instrumentation to provide certain kinds of evidence. It is not a simple matter to take the same data and use them to answer different questions or provide evidence on different issues. Thus, a problem arises when a secondary evaluator takes evidence collected for one purpose and tries to put it to some other use. The problem worsens when the secondary evaluator finds that evidence provided by the primary evaluator does not answer the secondary evaluator's questions and proceeds to criticize the primary evaluation for poor design. It may not be obvious to some secondary evaluators that a car designed for a superhighway is not the vehicle of choice for the cobbled lanes of an old village. While we do not advocate that the primary evaluator refuse to share data, everyone's ethical goals are best served if the secondary evaluator, who is bent on using data for purposes not intended when the data were initially collected, is forced to justify his work and is given good argument over any deficiencies.

For these reasons, we would look askance at the routine establishment of data banks from important primary evaluations if those banks were open to any or all secondary evaluators without proper and built-in safeguards against misuse. Secondary evaluation is an important new development in program evaluation. But the ethical problems associated with it need to be addressed conscientiously and specifically by government agencies, evaluators, and concerned professional groups.

Nine

Training Evaluators and Evaluating Their Competencies

Training program evaluators is an educational enterprise of rather recent vintage. Until recently, evaluators were drawn into the profession by the work to be done—or by the lack of work in related fields. Psychologists, educators, operations researchers, sociologists, economists, medical and health professionals, anthropologists, and MBAs have all done stints in the field. Some have written a critical note here or a how-to-do-it chapter there and then returned to the haven of

Note: We are indebted to William I. Sauser, Jr., for assistance on the survey described in this chapter. A preliminary report was presented at the twenty-second annual meeting of the Southeastern Psychological Association, 1976.

their basic discipline. Others have stayed, some to try to invent new programs to train evaluators.

The nature of these inventions varies from those designed to train program evaluators directly to those designed to train them inductively or by osmosis; from those emphasizing the area in which evaluation is to be conducted (for example, mental health) to those emphasizing methodologies that might be applied to the evaluation of programs in a variety of areas (for example, social, medical, or educational programs); from those that require a major in a specific discipline (such as social psychology) to deliberately multidisciplinary approaches.

Growing out of psychology, for example, are several new kinds of Ph.D. programs that specifically recognize the requirement for some of their graduates to engage in program evaluation. The Wright Institute in Berkeley, California, offers a program in social-clinical psychology that includes training for students with "an interest in working in social agencies or community programs or in social action or evaluation positions" (Freedman, 1976, p. 183). The experience of the Michigan State "Ph.D. Program Aimed at Survival Issues" has been that "the majority of . . . students have gone to nonacademic positions, often as program evaluators at the state or local agency level," even though the authors of the program are not optimistic that the world is ready for the broader ecological psychology they would prefer to foster (Tornatzky, 1976, p. 191). At Pennsylvania State a graduate program designed to prepare students for public-affairs careers includes substantial work in "research methods and quantitative skills"; one of the outcome objectives is "ability to design studies that will empirically reflect the probable concurrent and long-term consequences of putting policy-oriented programs into effect" (Vallance, 1976, p. 197). The doctoral program at Northwestern is cited as one which is "helping to shape the emerging multidiscipline of program evaluation"; Northwestern also has a postdoctoral program in program evaluation (Perloff and others, 1976, p. 573). The environmental-psychology program at City University of New York (Proshansky, 1976) and the public-affairs program at Claremont (Brayfield, 1976) represent other reactions to such conten-

166

tions as those made by M. Brewster Smith, George Fairweather, and Albee and Loeffler: "Our graduate training, heavily focused on the methodology of laboratory experimentation and its accompanying statistics, is seriously out of date in equipping the coming generations of psychologists for new roles in evaluation and policy research" (Smith, 1973, p. 465). "Most psychologists were, and are, largely inept in field methodology and had virtually no skills to bring to bear on policy-related research" (Fairweather cited in Tornatzky, 1976, p. 189). "Separate professional training schools for psychology must be established, following the historically evolving model provided by other professions, to eliminate role conflicts and make clear the essential division of labor between the psychologist as a scientist and the psychologist as a professional" (Albee and Loeffler cited in Perloff and others, 1976, p. 589).

Phi Delta Kappa has prepared a list of seventy-seven training programs in educational evaluation, including information on degrees offered, number of required credits and semesters, admission requirements, faculty members in the speciality, and costs. The list is available through the Evaluation Network (see Chapter Eleven). The National Institute of Mental Health also has a list of about thirty training programs for evaluators in health or other areas leading to undergraduate, master's, or doctoral degrees, some of them mentioned at the beginning of this chapter. (See Scriven and Ward, 1977, pp. 19–21.)

It should also be noted that there is a growing trend toward continuing education and self-study in program evaluation for concerned lay persons and for those who may have received their Ph.D.s long before program evaluation became popular. For example, there is hardly a meeting of the American Educational Research Association that does not include a training "presession" in program evaluation; the University of Massachusetts holds an annual summer institute in evaluation research (Wright, 1977); Sechrest and Campbell (1975) developed a summer training program in health-care research methodology, and the ETS Programs of Continuing Education regularly include components on evaluation. Instructional materials intended to be largely self-explanatory include Scriven's (1971) cassette, which makes introductory evaluation skills as available to the automobile commuter as foreign phrases are; *A Procedure for Assessing the Performance of a Particular School,* also by Scriven (1976b); *The Evaluation Improvement Program,* developed by the California Department of Education (1977) and distributed by Educational Testing Service to "lead" school district personnel "through the steps required to develop and carry out a comprehensive plan of evaluation"; *Citizen Evaluation of Mental Health Services* (MacMurray and others, 1976) aimed at helping citizens assure themselves of adequate community health care; *Program Evaluation in the State Mental Health Agency,* a manual prepared by the Southern Regional Education Board (1975) and designed to assist administrators in evaluating mental-health programs; and *Resource Materials for Community Mental Health Program Evaluation,* a five-volume set of educational materials produced by the Langley Porter Institute (1974).

The variety of modes of training in evaluation reflects some of the controversies in the field:

- Should evaluation be perceived as a discipline or profession, as opposed to a job? (The latter perception seems to be associated with some bias against formal training and with advocacy of "internship" or "in-service" experiences.)
- Does training in social or educational research per se qualify a program evaluator? (After apparently enormous success in World War II, experimental psychologists were inclined to proclaim that their brand of training was sufficient preparation for work on any problem involving human performance.)
- Do some of the popular terms in the field represent real substance rather than jargon, and thus do future evaluators need to become acquainted with them? (Some of the "models" of evaluation are cited as examples: "CIPP," "Discrepancy," "Goal-free"—see Stufflebeam and others, 1971; Provus, 1971; and Scriven, 1974.)

As other sections of this book suggest, we are inclined to view program evaluation as a profession. We do not hold that training in social or educational research alone is sufficient to prepare people for all of the exigencies associated with evaluation of real-world programs. We favor highlighting the conceptual underpinnings of evaluation rather than the favorite terms of particular people.

However, regardless of the merits of our positions, the first task in a rational approach to specifying a productive training program for evaluators is to define what the important evaluation competencies are, no matter how they are obtained or whether they are applied full- or part-time.

Evaluation Competencies

A panel meeting held in Princeton, New Jersey, in late 1974 (see the Preface) served as the stimulus for an initial listing of important knowledge and skills we might expect of the competent evaluator. We modified that list somewhat in an Office of Naval Research report the following fall (Ball and Anderson, 1975b, Table 6). Then in the spring of 1976 we submitted the list to a larger group of experts for reaction. Since the knowledge and skills evaluators need are a matter of opinion, *whose* opinion takes on considerable importance. We sought counsel from our colleagues, searched the indexes of books in the field, and relied heavily on Stake's unpublished "Partial List of Persons Who Can Give Valuable Counsel on Curriculum Evaluation." The result was a list of sixty-four people whose opinions we would value and which would seem to carry weight in the field: Marvin Alkin, Gilbert Austin, Bernard Bass, Thomas Bice, Urie Bronfenbrenner, Donald Campbell, John Campbell, Hugh Cline, William Coffman, Jacob Cohen, Thomas Cook, William Cooley, Richard Cox, Lee Cronbach, Joel Davitz, Henry Dyer, Robert Ebel, Albert Erlebacher, John Feldhusen, James Gallagher, Eric Gardner, William Gephart, Robert Glaser, Gene Glass, Irwin Goldstein, Egon Guba, Marcia Guttentag, Robert Heath, Gerald Helmstadter, Wells Hiveley, Ernest House, Paul Kelley, Nadine Lambert, Henry Levin, Edward Loveland, Daniel Lyons, George Madaus, Thomas Maguire, Jack Merwin, Jason Millman, Jum Nunnally, Ellis Page, David Payne, Robert Perloff, Robert Rippey, Seymour Sarason, Michael

Scriven, Marvin Sontag, Charles Spielberger, Robert Stake, William Stallings, Julian Stanley, Howard Stoker, James Stone, Elmer Struening, Daniel Stufflebeam, Robert Thorndike, Melvin Tumin, Herbert Walberg, Henry Walbesser, Carol Weiss, Frank Womer, Blaine Worthen, and Albert Yee.*

Since we have been accused in the past of taking too behavioristic a view of program evaluation (behavioristic = objective, psychometric, experimental, mechanistic, rigid, or hard, depending on who makes the charge), we made a deliberate effort to include some people whose positions might be characterized as more phenomenological (phenomenological = subjective, case-study, nonexperimental, comprehensive, responsive, or soft, again depending on the labeler). We also tried to include some professionals who were identified more with evaluation of health and social-action programs than with evaluation of education and training programs (with which we are more familiar).

Although we are less concerned with the etiology of evaluation competencies than with whether those competencies exist, we thought that it would be informative for purposes of this exposition also to ask the experts for their opinions about the best ways to obtain initial levels of competence and information about programs and prospects for training evaluators in their institutions. Opinions and information were sought through a questionnaire. The first part consisted of a list of thirty-two "content areas" and "special skills and sensitivities." Responders were asked to rate the importance of each (essential, desirable, not very important) and suggest the best source of initial competency in each area (formal instruction, independent study or application, supervised field experience, other). Comments and additional listings were invited. The second part of the questionnaire contained questions about training in evaluation for graduate students in the responder's institution. Replies were received from forty-eight, or three fourths, of the group on the mailing list—a fair

*We hope that it is not a violation of professional ethics to list these names here. The listing is the only way we can adequately describe the expert sample whose views we sought. The names will not be identified with responses or nonresponses.

record for an undertaking of this kind. But then social scientists—and especially those who get mixed up in program evaluation—probably have a peculiar appreciation of the difficulties posed by nonresponse.

However, of the forty-eight who replied, four did not complete the questionnaire. Three said they could not cope with it for one reason or another:

> I found the questionnaire impossible to answer. All items are essential for some applications. Some are very essential but require no training—just smarts and/or effort. Others may not generally be essential but require training.

> I am sorry to have to return your questionnaire this way because I believe professionals should try to be helpful. However, . . . I can't possibly make a decision between instruction, independent study, and field experience. We believe that all three go together and that is the way we train our students. . . . Also, for the importance issue, they are all important. If one is more important than others, it can only be determined by the particular problem.

> The questionnaire presupposes an orientation to evaluation, and therefore the training of evaluators, which I do not fully subscribe to. Therefore, I'm afraid my answers would be misleading.

One person who did not fill out the questionnaire returned a comprehensive paper he had written in the general area. And one responder who completed parts of the questionnaire still had some pretty scathing things to say about it—but expressed an important, and not entirely idiosyncratic, view about evaluation: "That was terrible. Such a mindless approach to talking about professional competence. I am ashamed of you for being associated with it. What I mean is that skills are important to situations. There is no standard evaluation situation and hopefully there will not be one. We should be encouraging educators and others to think of how *they* can increase their understanding of the value of a program rather than suggesting that specialists can find out and tell them. There should not be an edu-

171

cational specialty, only educators who can observe, think, judge, and so on."

Somewhat chastened, we present Table 6 showing the numbers of responders assigning each of the importance ratings to the "content areas" and "special skills and sensitivities" listed on the questionnaire. The content areas that seemed to appeal to the greatest number as "basics" were in the category of statistics, analysis, and design. Even a couple of people who usually avoid formal designs and analyses in their own evaluation work nevertheless labeled knowledge in these areas as at least a desirable part of the armamentarium of the competent evaluator. Perhaps they also think it is important for abstract painters to know how to draw.

Less than one fourth of the respondents thought that expertise in case-study methodology or job analysis was essential for the pro-

Table 6. Importance of Content Areas and Skills
(Rated by Number of Persons Responding to Each; N = 44)

	Importance			
	Essential	Desirable	Not Very Important	No Response
Content Area				
Descriptive statistics	38	6	0	0
Inferential statistics	38	6	0	0
Statistical analysis	35	9	0	0
Quasi-experimental design	35	9	0	0
Experimental design	34	10	0	0
Data preparation and reduction	33	11	0	0
Correlation and regression methods	33	10	1	0
Survey methods	32	12	0	0
Major literature and reference sources useful for evaluators	32	11	0	1
Method of controlling quality of data collection and analysis	32	10	1	1
Sampling	31	11	2	0
Application of interviews, questionnaires, ratings	31	11	1	1

172

Table 6 (continued)

	Essential	Desirable	Not Very Important	No Response
		Importance		
Alternative models for program evaluation	31	9	4	0
Psychometrics (reliability, validity, scaling, equating, and so on)	30	12	1	1
Applications of tests (paper-and-pencil, situational, performance, and so on)	27	14	2	1
Application of observation techniques, unobtrusive measures	23	20	0	1
Techniques of setting goals and performance standards	23	16	4	1
Reactive concerns in measurement and evaluation	21	16	3	4
Field operations	21	15	1	7
Major constructs in education and the social sciences	20	16	3	5
Cost-benefits analysis	19	20	4	1
Contracts and proposals	17	20	5	2
Legal and professional standards for empirical studies	15	24	4	1
Content analysis	14	24	3	3
Case-study methodology	11	29	4	0
Job analysis	7	22	15	0

Skills

	Essential	Desirable	Not Very Important	No Response
Professional and ethical sensitivity	37	4	1	2
Expository skills (speaking and writing)	32	10	0	2
Sensitivity to concerns of all interested parties	31	5	0	8
Interpersonal skills	28	12	3	1
Public-relations skills	17	20	6	1
Management skills	14	26	3	1

gram evaluator, and fifteen relegated job analysis to the "not very important" column. Some of the "no responses" tabulated in Table 6 were asterisked by a responder to indicate "areas which might be of greater or lesser importance, depending upon the nature of the evaluation task. In some situations these items may be of *no* importance." Such comments reinforce the situational nature of evaluation, which is a continuing theme in this book.

In terms of the number of endorsements, professional and ethical sensitivity is as important for evaluators as knowledge of statistics, analysis, and design. Public-relations and management skills were judged less important than the other skills areas listed, but one responder noted that the "need for managerial skills would vary with the size of the project." However, the whole skills area met with enthusiasm or was singled out for special comment by several of the responders. For example:

> The importance of such sensitivities cannot be underestimated! Your "skills areas"—and cost analysis—are very important but often neglected areas of training.

> We do a relatively good job of teaching the evaluator-to-be what he needs to know in the technical role (statistics, measurement, and research design). BUT we are failing in the interpersonal-skills area, in the recognition that research and evaluation serve different purposes, in the ability to identify the decisions on which an evaluation is to focus, in recognition that decision makers, our clients, process information in different ways than we as evaluators do, and in the role and importance of the affective domain in evaluation.

> All essential skills will not generally be found in any one person. Consequently, an evaluation team with complementary skills will generally be required for program evaluation.

Other competency areas listed by respondents as important are given in Table 7. Some of the suggestions overlap somewhat with the tabulated categories, but they are repeated here because some expert

Table 7. Other Suggested Competency Areas
(Numbers in Parentheses Indicate Number of Responders Choosing
Each Area)

Preparing reports, papers, and articles (5)
Decision theory and the decision-making process (4)
Knowledge of evaluation politics and political acumen (4)
Substantive knowledge of the content of the program to be evaluated
    (3)
Bayesian statistics, residual analysis and transformations, trend analysis,
    etc. (2)
History of evaluation, with special attention to the impact or absence of
    impact (2)
Philosophy of science, including limitations of the scientific method
    (1)
Similarities and differences between research and evaluation (1)
Group planning of evaluation (1)
Negotiating the scope and focus of evaluations (1)
Evaluation of evaluability—determining which evaluations are worth
    doing (1)
Budgeting of evaluations (1)
Identifying goals to be investigated (1)
Cost-benefits judgment regarding trade-offs in design (1)
Cost-benefits judgments in choice of instruments, techniques, and indicators
    for data collection (1)
Phenomenological procedures: historiography, diaries, logs, etc. (1)
Matrix sampling (1)
Theories of change (1)
Problem solving (1)
Relations with subject individuals and communities (1)
Specifying and delineating values of groups (1)
Interpreting technical results to lay audiences (1)
Listening skills (1)
Social psychology (1)
Organizational psychology (1)
Planning skills (1)
Grantsmanship: how to get money (1)
Wisdom (1)
Judgment, insight, and originality (1)
Understanding of role conflicts and latent objectives (1)
Needs assessment (1)
Systems-analysis skills (1)
Computer skills—included under data preparation and reduction (1)
Picking up side effects—included in design (1)

or experts called specific attention to them. They range from the theoretical (for example, philosophy of science, including limitations on the scientific method) to the very practical (how to get money) and from the very general (wisdom) to the specific (preparing an evaluation budget).

While this chapter focuses on a list of evaluation competencies stimulated by a particular panel discussion, modified by the authors, and supplemented by the responses of the distinguished group we surveyed, it is important to add that other lists of evaluation competencies have been produced by other groups, notably a task force of the American Educational Research Association (Glass and Worthen, 1970; Worthen and Gagné, 1969; Worthen, 1975). The Worthen synthesis of the AERA work, based on a logical analysis of research and evaluation tasks, groups competencies under the twenty-five headings paraphrased below:

1. Obtaining information about phenomenon to be evaluated
2. Drawing implications from prior research and practice
3. Defining object of evaluation
4. Selecting appropriate inquiry strategy
5. Formulating hypotheses or questions to be answered
6. Specifying data or evidence necessary for rigorous tests of hypotheses and unequivocal answers to questions
7. Selecting appropriate designs to collect data to test hypotheses or answer questions
8. Identifying population to which results should be generalized and selecting sample
9. Applying design and recognizing or controlling threats to validity
10. Identifying program goals at appropriate levels of generality
11. Assessing value and feasibility of program goals
12. Identifying standards and norms for judging worth of phenomenon to be evaluated
13. Translating broad objectives into measurable ones
14. Identifying classes of variables for measurement
15. Selecting and developing measurement techniques

16. Assessing validity of measurement techniques
17. Using appropriate data-collection methods
18. Monitoring program to detect deviations from specified procedures
19. Choosing and using appropriate statistical analyses
20. Using electronic computers and computer-related equipment
21. Interpreting and drawing appropriate conclusions from data analyses
22. Reporting findings and implications
23. Making recommendations based on results
24. Providing immediate feedback for decisions on program modification
25. Obtaining and managing resources necessary to conduct the study

A comprehensive review of the AERA and related efforts is provided by Millman (1975). Ricks (1976) offers one of the most succinct and distinctive lists of "training needs for effective evaluators": demystified research techniques (to avoid "isolating research evaluators from clinicians and administrators"), effective communication (to avoid the "Yes, but what does this mean?" reaction from program directors), flexibility and creativity (becoming "unbound by our research or evaluation prejudices"), involvement in decision making ("the researcher should be willing to put his or her money on one or two alternatives"), consideration of ethics (including "the why of particular projects"), and systems theory and practice (to enable "a dynamic conceptualization of evaluation").

Acquiring Evaluation Competencies

Returning to our questionnaire, the items about the best way for future evaluators to obtain initial levels of competence in the various content areas and skills evoked as wide a range of comments and "qualified" responses as the importance ratings. These comments reflected two major points of view: getting beyond the initial levels of competency, and combining training methods, perhaps by adding

177

Table 8. Best Methods of Obtaining Initial Competence in Content Areas and Skills (Given by Number of Persons Recommending Each Method; N = 44)

Content Areas	Formal Instruction	Independent Study or Application	Supervised Field Experience	Some Combination	No Response and Other Unscorable Responses
Experimental design	39	0	1	1	3
Quasi-experimental design	37	0	3	1	3
Correlation and regression methods	37	0	1	3	3
Sampling	36	0	4	0	4
Survey methods	35	1	4	2	3
Descriptive statistics	35	1	1	4	3
Inferential statistics	35	1	1	4	3
Psychometrics (reliability, validity, scaling, equating, and so on)	33	1	2	2	6
Statistical analysis	31	3	3	4	3
Alternative models for program evaluation	27	8	1	2	6
Cost-benefit analysis	23	9	3	2	7
Major literature and reference sources useful for evaluators	22	14	2	2	4
Major constructs in education and the social sciences	22	9	3	1	9
Reactive concerns in measurement and evaluation	20	9	5	1	9

Data preparation and reduction	20	3	15	3	3
Legal and professional standards for empirical studies	19	10	7	0	8
Applications of tests (paper-and-pencil, situational, performance, and so on)	19	1	15	2	7
Content analysis	14	12	10	1	7
Case-study methodology	14	10	13	1	6
Applications of interviews, questionnaires, ratings	14	2	21	1	6
Techniques of seting goals and performance standards	13	11	12	2	6
Methods of controlling quality of data collection and analysis	13	4	20	3	4
Applications of observation techniques, unobtrusive measures	10	5	20	4	5
Job analysis	9	11	11	1	12
Contracts and proposals	8	9	17	2	8
Field operations	5	0	31	0	8

Skills

Expository skills (speaking and writing)	7	11	17	3	6
Professional and ethical sensitivity	7	7	20	4	6
Sensitivity to concerns of all interested parties	6	4	23	0	11
Interpersonal skills	4	6	24	1	9
Management skills	4	5	26	3	6
Public-relations skills	3	7	24	2	8

case studies. One expert summarized: "What sets off the top-flight evaluator is whether he gets past the *initial* level of competency. I suggest a combination of formal instruction and supervised field experience for attaining that." However, even one of the respondents who was willing to express preferences for the best ways to obtain most of the knowledge and skills listed was frustrated: "Most institutions offer courses in measurement and statistics and call this evaluation training. IT ISN'T! Those are tools used by evaluators, researchers, developers, administrators. But there are a lot more tools needed by the evaluator. I guess this argues that our best training source is field experience. BUT we have so few really competent with whom to apprentice!"

We tabulated the straightforward responses to the training items with the results shown in Table 8. Formal instruction wins out as the preferred source of initial competency in the content areas, and supervised field experience in the skills areas. Initial competency in the art of contracts and proposals and in field operations is evidently viewed as closer to initial competency in the skills areas. It is interesting to note that experts place confidence in independent study as a source of initial competence in many of the areas. However, several comments were of the "born-not-made" variety. For example, "personality," "unteachable," or "What I find most frequently lacking in evaluations is common sense, which I'm afraid is not obtained—you either have it or you don't!"

The liberal reporting of comments here betrays our attitude toward the summaries in Tables 6 and 8. The tabulations certainly do not tell the whole story. They may not even tell a true story. For example, the patterns of importance ratings and preferred training methods marked by professionals reputed to be of somewhat different persuasions appear to be somewhat different. However, our number of respondents is so small and the classification basis so subjective that formal analyses along these lines do not seem to be warranted.

Before moving on to a report on the data obtained about local training, we cannot resist one more quotation, this one summarizing reactions to the competency and training items by one of our favorite respondents: "Pretty funny this. It adds up to a well-trained, mature, discreet, experienced, diplomatic, literate, ethically concerned behavioral scientist. And, of course, formal instruction is *initially* most important and efficient—but then field experience and application also become indispensable."

The thirty-nine persons completing at least part of the last section of the questionnaire came from thirty-three well-known universities in eighteen states. Three of them noted explicitly that their institutions did not offer a degree program specifically oriented toward a "profession" of evaluation, observing that "such a graduate program would be too narrow and too lacking in substantive content" or "methodology divorced from content is a dangerous thing" or "evaluators will come into their roles fortuitously." Indeed, as the summaries in Parts B and C of Table 9 suggest, this state of affairs seems more typical than not. The numbers of students being trained in evaluation (Part D) do not suggest that competition for jobs in program evaluation will increase greatly in the future. Furthermore, it is estimated that only a little more than half of the graduate students who might reasonably conduct evaluations ever will. (We might note here that the numbers of students enrolled in the kinds of ecological-psychology programs described earlier are generally quite small; for example, the Michigan State program graduated only ten people during its first six years.) However, one respondent to our questionnaire noted that the number of students pursuing relevant study in his institution was "increasing rapidly," and another called program evaluation "one of the most promising fields for our graduates at this time."

Other Training Issues

In our report of the survey, we have just barely touched on three issues in the training of evaluators. First, the knowledge and skills that evaluators will need depend to a great extent on the kinds of programs they will be called upon to evaluate and the purposes of their evaluation efforts. The requirements would be very different, say, for a counselor given the added responsibility of providing feedback for program improvement to instructors using new remedial-

Table 9. Responses to "Current Practices" Questions

A. Do graduate students in your institution receive specific training designed to equip them . . . to evaluate?

Yes: 35[a]   No: 4

B. If so, in what school(s) or department(s)?

Education: 24   Administration: 1
Psychology: 13   Business: 1
Sociology: 5   Communication: 1
Statistics: 3   Community Medicine: 1
Human Development and   Social Services Administration: 1
Family Studies: 2

C. What graduate degree(s) do students who receive such training typically obtain?

Ph.D.   29   M.A.   4
Ed.D.   4   M.S.   22
                                    M.Ed.   2

D. (1) At the present time, about how many graduate students . . . in your institution . . . are pursuing study . . . which will equip them to become program evaluators?
   (2) What percentage of these . . . will ever become practicing evaluators?

Size of Graduate Student Population Receiving Evaluation Training	Number of Institutions in Size Category	(1) Total Number of Students Being Trained	(2) Estmated Total Number of Students Who Will Become Evaluators
0–5	8	25	15
6–10	4	36	16
11–15	2	28	13
16–20	8	165	102
21–30	2	55	21
31–40	3	115	87
41–50	1	50	1
Total	28[b]	474	255

[a]The 35 persons responding "yes" represent 29 institutions. Four institutions were doubly represented; one was triply represented.

[b]For each of the multiply represented institutions (see note a), a single representative set of figures was estimated, based on the other information provided. Student estimates were not provided for one institution.

reading materials, for an industrial manager charged with designing a program to train a large number of operators at the lowest possible cost, or for a clinician asked to make recommendations to a federal agency about continuing or discontinuing an ambitious parent-child health program; for an experimental psychologist drawn into the business of evaluating the effectiveness of television programs; for an officer of a state licensing board attempting to determine the influence of licensing requirements on the quality of service provided in the occupation of interest; or for a sociologist studying the impact of voter registration drives on election results.

If potential evaluators knew that their primary work would be in the area of needs assessment (estimating the frequency or intensity of student, societal, or other needs in order to plan appropriate action programs), they might "major" in survey methods, sampling, and descriptive statistics. Those planning to evaluate personnel-training efforts might take large doses of job analysis, quasi-experimental design, techniques of setting goals and performance standards, statistical analysis, and cost-benefit analysis. Unfortunately—or fortunately—this is not the way the world works. Evaluators, whatever their primary interest or basic discipline, are usually expected to behave like applied researchers and contribute their talents to a variety of information needs. If they are successful in conducting needs analyses, formative and summative evaluation requirements will probably not be far behind. If they limit themselves to conducting needs analyses, boredom will almost certainly ensue—and possibly unemployment. More fundamental, one of the evaluator's major challenges is to define problems, as well as approaches to their solutions, and definition frequently requires a broad range of experience and a kit with many tools.

A second issue revolves around the degree to which an evaluator needs to be expert in the field in which he or she performs evaluation services. Does the designer of a national evaluation of Head Start have to be a specialist in child development and early education? Does the evaluator of a Suzuki-method program need to know how to play the violin? Can anyone other than a cosmetologist evaluate the effectiveness of a licensing program in that area? Does the evaluator of a bilingual program have to be bilingual? Three responders in the questionnaire study added "substantive knowledge of the content of the program" as essential for the competent evaluator, but they did not specify how much knowledge. Certainly, the evaluator should have some understanding of the content of the program under study. But it is probably asking too much for evaluators to be expert in every substantive area where their evaluation skills might be applied— just as it is probably asking too much for chemists, psychiatrists, or Russian scholars to acquire a full range of evaluation skills just because they are involved in a program with an evaluation component. A team approach such as that advocated by one of the responders to the questionnaire on training and competencies is probably best in many instances, with the members of the team drawn from both evaluation and subject-matter specialties. However, a team approach does not relieve the evaluator from the responsibility of acquiring as much familiarity as possible with the content of the program or "a lively recognition . . . of the formal and informal context within which the program occurs" (Guttentag and Struening, 1975, p. 3). Further, the acceptability of evaluators on such teams may depend on their honest show of interest in the substance and workings of the program. The situation is not unlike that of the foreign visitor whose attempts at the language, however bad his pronunciation, meet with obvious pleasure from the natives.

Our attitude, then, is that the more the evaluator can grasp the content of the program, the better—within reasonable limits of time and effort. However, evaluators can be helpful even when their understanding of the subject matter is limited. We know of evaluators who have participated in evaluation efforts in fields that were initially completely strange to them, yet they were able to make substantial contributions. They also developed strong appreciation for the work of the practitioners in those fields before they had finished.

This discussion of the breadth of expertise of evaluators is closely related to a third issue. Perhaps a distinction needs to be drawn between the skills and knowledge a program evaluator needs to have personally and those he or she might obtain for particular projects by calling in technical consultants. Of course, this means that evaluators would have to have sufficient self-awareness to recognize where they were deficient and needed help. We might add "realistic appraisal of own abilities and limitations" to the skills lists in Tables 6 and 7. The corresponding content area, already listed in Table 6, is "major literature and reference sources useful for evaluators."

Evaluating Evaluators

Three approaches to evaluating the competencies of evaluators are analogous to those practiced or discussed in teacher evaluation and certification (Rosner, 1972): program approval, estimations of competency, and product evaluation. We might assume that if an evaluator was trained in a "good" program, he or she is competent. Definitions of "good" programs vary, of course, and are usually more global-subjective than analytical-objective. But personnel in agencies that let or work on many evaluation contracts seem to be able to agree at least among themselves about the strengths of various graduate departments in turning out people able to perform the evaluation functions they need. As Millman (1975) notes: "One should keep in mind that completion of course work is no guarantee that the individual will have the enablers needed to carry out R and E [research and evaluation] tasks. Nevertheless, training and experience do have some merit, since they are certain to have had some influence on the apprentice" (p. 8). There is little denying that, at present, hiring people for their first jobs in evaluation is predicated far more on where and with whom they studied than on direct assessment of their competencies.

Direct assessment is a possibility, of course. From time to time, there have been calls for certification mechanisms for program evaluators or those working in educational research and development (Gagné, 1975; Worthen, 1972), mechanisms which would provide that individuals have appropriate requirements to enter the "profession." However, none of the proposals has yet been implemented, nor have they received significant national backing, although the emergence of standards for program evaluation (see Chapter Eleven) may provide an impetus for individual certification. Furthermore, it is doubtful that the number of program-evaluation jobs in any single organization will be sufficient to justify that organization's setting up the kinds of elaborate assessment centers that have been used by

Table 10. Checklist for Rating Evaluator Competence

Knowledge and Content Areas

Experimental design
Quasi-experimental design
Survey methods
Sampling
Case-study methodology
Field operations
Legal and professional standards for empirical studies
Techniques of setting goals and performance standards
Job analysis
Alternative models for program evaluation
Major literature and reference sources useful for evaluators
Methods of controlling quality of data collection and analysis
Data preparation and reduction
Applications of observation techniques, unobtrusive measures
Applications of interviews, questionnaires, ratings
Applications of tests (paper-and-pencil, performance, and so on)
Content analysis
Psychometrics (reliability, validity, scaling, equating, and so on)
Reactive concerns in measurement and evaluation
Descriptive statistics
Inferential statistics
Statistical analysis
Correlation and regression methods
Cost-benefit analysis
Contracts and proposals
Major constructs in education and the social sciences

Skills Areas

Management skills
Public-relations skills
Interpersonal skills
Expository speaking skills
Expository writing skills
Professional and ethical sensitivity
Sensitivity to concerns of all interested parties

industry and government agencies to identify potential managers
(see, for example, Bray and others, 1974). Therefore, in the immediate
future, any direct assessment will probably be limited to self-report
measures (Bunda, 1973; Worthen and Brzezinski, 1971), locally developed tests (Worthen and Associates, 1971), or rating procedures—
the latter being the most common. As the medical profession seems to be
increasingly aware (see, for example, Barro, 1973), systematic rating

procedures, relying chiefly on observation and background information, can be useful—in the present case to those concerned with hiring evaluators and commissioning evaluation efforts or to those who train evaluators and want to check up on their training programs through a common look at all of their candidates. At a minimum, a rating procedure requires its authors to specify some of their own values. Such rating systems might also be used for self-evaluation by those of us concerned with whether our ranges and degrees of competency are up to date.

A sample checklist of evaluation competencies derived from the questionnaire and survey results reported in this chapter is provided in Table 10. We suggest that the would-be evaluator of evaluators who wants to try the list go through it first and eliminate the items judged "not very important" with respect to the job requirements or program goals of interest (very much as the questionnaire respondents did). Then additional items specific to the situation can be added (reference to Table 7 might be helpful here). Finally, a rating of 4 to 1 might be assigned to evaluators for each item on the checklist, according to the following scheme:

Knowledge or Skill Sufficient to Select
Appropriate Approaches and Techniques and
to Design and Implement Evaluation

	With technical consultation	*With minimal technical consulation*
No or minimal field experience	1—Lowest competence	2 or 3
Relevant successful field experience	2 or 3	4—Highest competence

The horizontal dimension of the chart relates to an issue discussed earlier: An evaluator may have the necessary skills and knowledge personally, or he may have sufficient sense to obtain technical consultation in areas where he is deficient. Either way is acceptable, although we would feel more comfortable if a person with major evaluation responsibilities had to obtain technical consultations only occasionally. (Consider, as an analogy, the level of skill you would prefer in your medical doctor.) Of course, it is possible to have necessary skills for evaluation without much practical experience (the vertical dimension). Again, however, we would feel more comfortable entrusting major responsibility for an evaluation to someone who has had some practice. (Return again to the medical analogy and consider your selection of the surgeon who is to operate on you.)

Clearly the highest rating (see the cell marked 4) would be earned by an experienced evaluator who needs only minimal technical consultation. The least competent level is represented by the cell marked 1 and defines an inexperienced evaluator with considerable need for technical consultation. Somewhere between these extremes lie the other two cells. Their ordering must depend on the judgment of the rater and must be based on situational factors. In practice, of course, it would be rare for an evaluator to obtain a rating of 4 on every item in the checklist.

What kinds of evidence would raters use in evaluating the competencies of evaluation candidates or students?* For senior candidates, they would probably employ many of the kinds of indicators used in determining faculty promotions and derived from vitae: relevant research and evaluation productivity, publications, fellowships and grants, invitations to participate in important seminars and conferences, estimates of reputation in professional circles, degrees and special study (Dressel, 1976, p. 333). In the case of students, consideration would be given to courses taken, grades, instructors' recommendations, assistantships, and special projects. In all instances, of course, the more specific the evidence with respect to a given item, the more confident the judge can be about assigning a rating. The reliability and validity of background data are not generally held in high

---

*Merrill (1976) would distinguish here between *competencies* and *attainments,* perhaps permitting us to rate the competencies of career evaluators, but allowing assessment of little more than the attainments of graduate students. "The concept of competency," he declares, "although much in vogue in education, is a concept inappropriate to the educational process. Competency is essentially a lifelong issue" (p. 3).

esteem. If feedback to a program designed to train evaluators is the object of running several students through such a rating procedure, the training institution will be particularly interested in the items considered essential but on which students tend to receive low ratings. Maybe a new course or an improved component of an existing course or practicum is needed.

Table 10 represents only one of many possible approaches to rating the competencies of evaluators. We suggest it as a starting point because it is short, relatively simple, and includes items endorsed by a large number of informed people. However, developers of rating forms might prefer to begin with the "universe" of evaluation competencies containing about 250 items (see Bunda, 1973; Stufflebeam, 1973), Coller's (1970) classification of evaluation tasks into sixteen general groups, or some of the AERA-related efforts referred to earlier.

A third approach to evaluating evaluators is through detailed examination of their products. Returning to the teacher-evaluation analogy, we find that one school maintains that "teaching effectiveness must be defined by the effect on students (that is, by changes in student behavior)" (Ragosta in Anderson and others, 1975, p. 269; see also McDonald, 1972). Unfortunately, up to the present time, many evaluators have received rather poor marks on their evaluation studies and reports (Gamel and others, 1975; Horst and others, 1975; Wargo and others, 1972). Some of these marks are no doubt deserved. For example, Tallmadge and Horst (1976) report "outrageous incoherencies" as "just a few of the 'horror stories' uncovered in the course of routinely examining real-world evaluation studies [in the area of compensatory education]. The sad part was that . . . irrationalities were so pervasive that not a single evaluation report was found which could be accepted at face value! Even more disheartening, many of these evaluations followed procedures officially sanctioned by one or more presumably authoritative groups of experts" (p. 2).

Tallmadge and Horst performed one kind of secondary evaluation: a critical review of primary evaluations. Another kind of secondary evaluation involves reanalysis of the data from the primary evaluation (Anderson and others, 1975, p. 363; Stufflebeam, 1974). Some of these secondary evaluations have produced new insights (for example, those by Mayeske and others, 1972; Elashoff and Snow, 1971). Others have produced equivocal results for the simple reason that the main purpose of the reanalysis was not checking the original results for accuracy or testing the reasonableness of the conclusions by using different methods. Rather, answers were sought to questions not asked in the primary evaluation, questions that were not directly answerable in terms of the original measures and design. If the evaluators' products are to be used as the basis for evaluating their competencies, direct critical review is probably in order. Specific instruments for appraising program evaluations (Cummings, 1975) and guidelines commissioned by such agencies as the U.S. Office of Education (Horst and others, 1975; Tallmadge and Horst, 1976) and the National Institute of Mental Health (Little, 1976) may be useful.

Of course, in some cases evaluators cannot be held strictly accountable for their products. They may not have complete freedom in selecting a compatible area of work; they may be pushed into compromises; they may have to work under frustrating organizational constraints (Weiss, 1973); they may have to collaborate with so many others that it is hard to disentangle their contributions (Millman, 1975, p. 9). Certainly, given that the real world offers different opportunities, it is very difficult to compare the competencies of two evaluators in terms of products alone. As Humphrey Bogart said of the Academy Awards, the only way they could be fairly awarded was to have everyone in a given category play the same part in front of the same judges.

Ten

Evaluations of Adult Technical Training Programs

Although program evaluation is still a relatively new field of endeavor, its advocates already suspect that the state of the science or art may be well ahead of practice. To verify or refute such suspicions in one "evaluatable" domain—adult technical training—we surveyed 142 programs sponsored by the Department of Defense, federal government departments and agencies other than the Department of Defense, state and local government agencies (usually through junior or community colleges), and industrial or commercial organizations (Ball and Anderson, 1975a). We were interested not only in the quality of evaluation efforts but also in whether studies addressed the broad range of purposes listed in Table 1 or were primarily of the summative or impact variety (Purpose II).

Fifty programs were selected in each category from complete listings available for the armed services and from less comprehensive listings developed by the project staff through diverse inquiries of agencies in the other three categories. An attempt was made to obtain a wide range of types of programs distributed over the entire United States. The samples were restricted to programs reputed to have evaluations, initiated within the five-year period preceding the survey, and, in keeping with the purpose of the investigation, devoted to technical training of persons over seventeen years of age. The processes of program selection, follow-up, and replacement (detailed in Ball and Anderson, 1975a) eventuated in complete returns from 70 percent, or 142, of the 200 target programs, with the highest response rates from Department of Defense and private business and industry programs—84 and 80 percent, respectively. Interestingly, the response rate correlated with the proportions of programs having some form of evaluation.

The questionnaire from which we derived our major conclusions about the state of program evaluation in adult training contained eighteen questions on program goals, trainees, length, level, instructional methodology, and trainee evaluation practices and thirty questions on program evaluation activities including purposes, funding source, design and measurement, analyses, and dissemination. Further information was obtained from site visits to fourteen of the programs judged on the basis of the questionnaire reports to be "exemplary" or, in a couple of cases, "typical." A picture of the great diversity of the total sample of programs can be obtained from brief descriptions of a few of the programs examined in depth:

• Drug Abuse Education Specialist Program (Navy) "to provide selected personnel with the knowledge and skill to assist command personnel with the development, implementation, and evaluation of drug and alcohol action programs." (Such programs were seen as a needed improvement over earlier "scare" programs that, it was felt, had only created the greater problem of turning experimenters into hard and proficient users.) Four components of the DAES program: pharmacology, political strategy and human motivation, communication, and program development and evaluation. At the time of the site visit, there were a total of 350 "graduates" (from five-week classes of twenty to thirty-five officers and enlisted men each). Internal and external evaluations, mostly of the "expert observer" type, had been carried out, focusing on whether "the DAES course was doing what it should do and how well" and on factors contributing to attrition in the school. The primary purpose of evaluation was program modification and improvement (Ball and Anderson, 1975a, pp. D1–D9).

• Digital Subscriber Terminal Equipment Repair Course (Army), fifteen to twenty weeks of "hands on" training for noncommissioned officers and other personnel in occupation specialties dealing with military communications and electronics. Evaluation was included in the seventh step of a formal model ("Systems Engineering of Training") continuously applied to courses at the Signal Center where this course was offered. Major steps in the model: job analysis, selecting tasks for training, training analysis, developing training materials, developing evaluation materials, conduct of training, and quality control. The evaluation employed both formal performance-based measures and less formal indicators (for example, trainee comments, faculty recommendations). Formal evaluation data were used for certifying the ability of trainees to perform specific tasks at the termination of the course and later on the job. Both formal and informal data were used in providing feedback for purposes of course improvement (pp. D10–D15).

• Program for training air-traffic controllers (Air Force) to meet Federal Aviation Administration requirements and to be ready for on-the-job training. A high level of electronic aptitude was required for the six hundred to one thousand trainees selected per year in some forty courses. All evaluation reports were organized as follows: statement of goals for the evaluation, sample selection, mail questionnaire (to program graduates or supervisors), field visit (on-site visits and interviews with graduates), staff evaluation of curriculum, analysis and report, follow-up. Primary goal of the evaluation: curriculum revision (not direct evaluation of either trainees or instructors). (See pp. D16–D19.)

• Management-by-Objectives Course (Social Security Administration), offered to groups of about twenty-five second-level supervisors at a time. The course involved three days of workshop activity within a thirty-day period, followed by consultation on request. Participants were familiarized with the "language" of MBO and encouraged to develop skills in defining target outputs and results. Evaluation, at the time of the site visit, was described as "informal" and "observational," using questionnaires for participant ratings (for example, of the degree to which the course met their expectations and of the effectiveness of course leaders) and a critique session three months after the last workshop. The observer speculated that the stimulus for the evaluation activity seemed to derive from the desire of the trainers to assure themselves that something worthwhile was going on, rather than from any charge from above to document the impact of the effort (pp. D22–D24).

• Supervisory Training Phase I, required of new supervisors and available to anyone within the U.S. Department of Agriculture who supervised other employees. The program was intended to develop management skills with emphasis on skills in a particular strategy, a problem-analysis approach. It involved two forty-hour blocks of time and much small-group interaction. "Graduates" numbered about 3,000 at the time of the site visit. Evaluation, entirely in-house, was limited to occasional attempts to gain feedback from trainees (for example, individuals were asked to cite examples of on-the-job use of the concepts acquired in the training). The program director felt this feedback was useful in program modification. The site visitor noted a discrepancy between "the details of training materials and scant attention to evaluation" (pp. D25–27).

• Program on clear writing (Forestry Services), one of the course options for employees required to take a minimum of forty hours of training each year. Ninety days after course completion, a general open-ended questionnaire was administered to a 10 percent sample of participants. The principal audience for the completed questionnaires: regional management. Secondary audience: the instructional agency, for review with respect to course content. Outstanding case studies were sought to document cost savings and other

194

on-the-job improvements that might be attributable to the training (pp. D28–29).

• Food and Beverage Management Program for employees of a large motel chain, generally a four-week program including interrelated units on employee-employer relations, cost and controls, advertising and promotion, restaurant operations, banquet and meeting rooms, bar operations and standards, goals and awards. The program was designed to develop and extend the expertise of trainees to ensure greater efficiency of operations at their own sites. (The thirty-five participants at the time of the visit to the program came from almost as many states.) Measurement included pre- and posttests of trainees' knowledge of course content, assessment of trainees' ability to operate relevant business machines, and instructor ratings of personal characteristics of trainees. The goals of the evaluation effort included review of course content for applicability to the field and profiles of individual and group growth. Summary evaluation results were shared with corporate executives and innkeepers; results for individual trainees, with franchise owners who sent participants to the program (pp. D33–D36).

• Sales Fundamentals Program or "Effectiveness of Ideas" (employee-development department of a large corporation), conducted by request and involving sixteen hours of in-class time. The objectives: provide participants with a "perfect standard for selling," develop a vocabulary for selling, acquire knowledge of fundamentals of selling, give new insight to "true" product knowledge, be able to teach others. Students completed "Program Evaluation Forms," which the director felt were useful in "getting an overall feel for departmental effectiveness" and modifying courses. Objective criteria (for example, increase in sales volume) were judged "possible," but if the evaluation showed no impact on sales, the director might be "cutting his own throat" (pp. D37–D39).

• Medical laboratory technician program (community college), a two-year program for fifteen to twenty students entering a year, leading to an associate in science degree, and designed to bring students to "a realistic level of training" to meet the needs of local employers. Students were evaluated by tests, performance examinations (for example, lab techniques), and simulations in worklike settings. Program evaluation involved study by an eleven-person committee including insiders and outsiders (future study committees will include consumers of health services) and feedback from supervisors after graduates went to work in the field. The course has been declared generally effective, but some changes have been made (for example, a change in math requirements, inclusion of more clinical training). (See pp. D43–D44.)

• Environmental-aide program (county vocational-education center), to prepare trainees for employment as assistants in soil conservation, public health, and air-pollution control. The program included two thousand hours of classroom lectures, laboratory and field experience, and supervised internships. A front-end analysis (Purpose I, Table 1) referred to environmental conditions in the region, increasing employment opportunities, and available resources for technical assistance in course development and cooperative training efforts. Three annual program evaluations conducted before the site visit had made use of follow-up surveys with former students and their employers and of supervisors' and instructors' factual and subjective reports (including information on job placement, suggestions for program improvement). (See pp. D45–D55.)

Conclusions

From the general survey of adult training programs, we drew the following conclusions. Our findings may not encourage the ardent evaluation theorist or the purist in experimental design, but they certainly indicate that evaluation activity abounds.

1. Over two thirds of the programs had been "formally" evaluated—with emphasis on Purpose III (formative) evaluation. Efforts in the name of Purposes I (to contribute to decisions about program installation) and VI (to contribute to an understanding of basic processes) were rarely mentioned. No one admitted and few suggested that evidence was being sought primarily to rally support or opposition for a program (Purposes IV and V, Table 1).
2. Almost all of the programs had a written statement of goals. Most of these had goals stated in behavioral terms.

196

3. Typically, evidence on program impact or information to be used for program modification was obtained through questionnaires or interviews with trainees and instructors or through observations.

4. The reliability and validity of the measures used did not particularly seem to concern most of those conducting the evaluations.

5. The general method of investigation employed in most of the evaluations was characterized as "observational study," corresponding to "survey" in Tables 1 and 2. Few claims were made that experimental or quasi-experimental designs were used, and the data in a large majority of the studies were not analyzed statistically.

6. In over 40 percent of the evaluations, evaluation was a continuing process, especially in the "systems-oriented" Defense Department and other federal programs.

7. Evaluations were usually called for, funded, and carried out by staff rather than by persons or agencies external to the program. There were, however, some external evaluations mandated for Defense Department training programs.

8. Respondents indicated that written reports were prepared for less than half of the evaluations; an even smaller percentage indicated that they would make these reports available to us.

9. In spite of the widely held belief that evaluation results are not often used, the respondents in this particular sample at least claimed that program changes had been made on the basis of the findings—81 percent in the case of evaluations conducted in the interests of program improvement, 61 percent even for impact studies.

Tabulations supporting or amplifying the nine conclusions are given in Table 11. The complete questionnaire and responses are included in the Ball and Anderson (1975a) report.

Finally, it may be enlightening to review some of the special lessons learned from the "case studies" of fourteen of the programs. It is important to remind ourselves that the evaluations were conducted and used by real people with real programs in the field; the intent was not to produce scholarly publications or methodological contribu-

197

Table 11. Selected Results from Survey of Evaluation Practices in Adult Training Programs

	Total		D.O.D.		Other Federal		State, Local		Industry	
	N^a	$\%^b$	N^a	$\%^b$	N^a	$\%^b$	N^a	$\%^b$	N^a	$\%^b$
About how many students/trainees have been trained in this program so far?										
0–49	29	20	6	14	7	21	8	30	8	20
50–99	12	8	3	7	1	3	4	15	4	10
100–149	15	11	3	7	4	12	2	7	6	15
150–199	11	8	2	5	2	6	5	19	2	5
200–249	8	6	3	7	3	9	1	3	1	3
250–999	30	21	9	21	8	24	4	15	9	23
1000 or more	23	16	7	17	8	24	1	3	7	18
Don't know or omit	14	10	9	21	0	0	2	7	3	8
Is this program offered in more than one center or location?										
Yes	49	35	6	14	24	73	4	15	15	38
No	93	66	36	86	9	27	23	85	25	63
If so, in how many other centers or locations?										
1	9	24	3	50	2	10	3	75	1	8
2–5	11	27	3	50	6	29	1	25	1	8
6–9	6	11	0	0	3	14	0	0	3	25
more than 9	17	38	0	0	10	48	0	0	7	58
Does the program have a written statement of goals?										
Yes	134	94	42	100	32	97	27	100	33	83
No	8	6	0	0	1	3	0	0	7	18

Are these goals written in behavioral terms; that is, indicating desired change in student/trainee behavior?										
Yes	108	77	36	86	29	91	22	82	21	53
No	32	23	6	14	3	9	5	19	18	45
Don't know	1	1	0	0	0	0	0	0	1	3
How long does it normally take a student/trainee to complete this program?										
Less than 1 month	56	40	4	10	28	85	0	0	24	62
1–3 months	36	26	24	57	1	3	2	8	9	23
4–6 months	15	11	11	26	2	6	0	0	2	5
7–12 months	13	9	3	7	1	3	8	31	1	3
More than 12 months	19	14	0	0	1	3	16	62	2	5
Has there been or is there currently any formal[c] evaluative effort to improve the program? Has there been or is there currently any formal evaluative effort to assess the impact (effects) of the program?										
Improvement but not impact	26	18	6	14	12	36	0	0	8	20
Impact but not improvement	3	2	0	0	2	6	0	0	1	3
Both improvement and impact	69	49	24	57	11	33	19	70	15	38
Neither improvement nor impact	44	31	12	29	8	24	8	30	16	40

Table 11 (continued)

	Total N[a]	Total %[b]	D.O.D. N[a]	D.O.D. %[b]	Other Federal N[a]	Other Federal %[b]	State, Local N[a]	State, Local %[b]	Industry N[a]	Industry %[b]
Who called for this program evaluation to be done?										
Improvement[d]										
Program administrator	55	56	16	53	14	56	6	32	19	79
Program's educational staff	45	46	7	23	17	68	11	58	10	42
Outside agency	11	11	6	20	2	8	3	16	0	0
Other	20	20	11	37	3	12	5	26	1	4
Impact[d]										
Program administrator	41	42	9	30	13	52	6	32	13	54
Program's educational staff	24	25	7	23	5	20	7	37	5	21
Outside agency	8	8	3	10	1	4	4	21	0	0
Other	19	19	11	37	0	0	6	32	2	8
Who carried out the evaluation?										
Improvement[d]										
Program administrator	33	34	8	27	10	40	5	26	10	42
Program developers	35	36	12	40	6	24	3	16	14	58
Program's educational staff	56	57	20	67	17	68	9	47	10	42
Outside agency	13	13	8	27	2	8	3	16	0	11
Other	16	16	6	20	0	0	6	33	4	32
Impact[d]										
Program administrator	38	39	9	30	12	48	6	32	11	46

Program developers	14	14	5	17	2	8	3	16	4	17
Program's educational staff	27	28	10	33	4	16	8	42	5	21
Outside agency	12	12	9	30	1	4	2	11	0	0
Other	18	18	8	27	0	0	6	32	4	17
Who funded the evaluation?										
Improvement[d]										
Internal funding (part of program)	81	87	24	83	21	96	18	95	18	78
External funding (outside grant, contract, and so on)	12	13	5	17	1	5	1	5	5	22
Impact[d]										
Internal funding	60	90	20	87	12	92	16	89	12	92
External funding	7	10	3	13	1	8	2	11	1	8
Was the evaluation monitored by some person or group independent of the evaluation?										
Improvement[d]										
Yes	39	42	19	63	10	46	7	37	3	14
No	50	54	10	33	11	50	10	53	19	86
Don't know	4	4	1	3	1	5	2	11	0	0
Impact[d]										
Yes	29	40	13	52	3	23	9	47	4	25
No	41	56	11	44	9	69	9	47	12	75
Don't know	3	4	1	4	1	8	1	5	0	0

Table 11 (continued)

	Total N^a	Total $\%^b$	D.O.D. N^a	D.O.D. $\%^b$	Other Federal N^a	Other Federal $\%^b$	State, Local N^a	State, Local $\%^b$	Industry N^a	Industry $\%^b$
How long did the evaluation take?										
Less than 1 week	7	9	0	0	1	6	3	19	3	21
Less than 1 month (more than a week)	4	5	1	4	1	6	1	6	1	7
1–4 months	9	12	2	7	2	13	3	19	2	14
5 months	11	15	3	11	3	19	1	6	4	29
6–12 months	7	10	4	14	0	0	2	13	1	7
More than 1 year	5	7	3	11	0	0	2	13	0	0
A continuing or ongoing process	31	42	15	54	9	56	4	25	3	21
Who or what was the focus of measurement?										
Improvement[d]										
Students	62	63	19	63	16	64	7	37	20	83
Classroom and teaching processes	45	46	12	40	11	44	13	68	9	38
Teachers	33	34	10	33	11	44	8	42	4	17
Curriculum	57	58	22	73	13	52	15	79	7	29
Other	13	13	6	20	0	0	6	32	1	4
Impact[d]										
Yes	32	46	13	54	5	42	6	33	8	50
No	23	33	7	29	5	42	8	44	3	19
Don't know	15	21	4	17	2	17	4	22	5	31

Was the validity of the measure assessed?

Improvement[d]										
Yes	41	44	20	69	6	26	9	47	6	27
No	39	42	5	17	16	70	8	42	10	46
Don't know	13	14	4	14	1	4	2	11	6	27
Impact[d]										
Yes	33	47	15	63	5	42	7	39	6	38
No	21	30	5	21	4	33	8	44	4	25
Don't know	16	23	4	17	3	25	3	17	6	38

What research design was used in this evaluation?

Improvement[d]										
True experiment	14	16	9	27	1	6	3	14	1	6
Quasi-experiment	11	13	6	18	0	0	2	9	3	18
Observational study	68	72	23	55	15	94	17	77	13	76
Impact[d]										
True experiment	10	15	5	23	0	0	3	17	2	13
Quasi-experiment	9	14	4	18	1	10	1	6	3	20
Observational study	46	71	13	59	9	90	14	78	10	67

Was there a statistical analysis of the results?

Improvement[d]										
Yes	24	26	10	36	3	13	2	11	9	43
No	56	62	14	48	19	83	14	78	9	43
Don't know	11	12	5	17	1	4	2	11	3	14
Impact[d]										
Yes	22	33	9	38	5	39	3	19	5	33
No	35	53	9	42	7	54	12	75	7	47
Don't know	10	15	5	21	1	8	1	6	3	20

Table 11 (continued)

	Total		D.O.D.		Other Federal		State, Local		Industry	
	N^a	$\%^b$	N^a	$\%^b$	N^a	$\%^b$	N^a	$\%^b$	N^a	$\%^b$
Was there a written report of the evaluation?										
Improvement[d]										
Yes	44	48	16	57	9	39	10	56	9	39
No	45	49	10	36	13	57	8	44	14	61
Don't know	3	3	2	7	1	4	0	0	0	0
Impact[d]										
Yes	33	49	10	46	8	62	9	56	6	35
No	31	46	10	46	4	31	6	38	11	65
Don't know	4	6	2	9	1	8	1	6	0	0
Could we have a copy?										
Improvement[d]										
Yes	10	20	4	24	2	20	2	17	2	20
No	30	61	7	41	7	20	9	75	7	70
Don't know	9	18	6	35	1	10	1	8	1	10
Impact[d]										
Yes	9	24	3	25	3	33	2	18	1	17
No	22	58	5	42	5	56	8	73	4	67
Don't know	7	18	4	33	1	11	1	9	1	17
Did any changes take place as a result of the evaluation?										
Improvement[d]										
Yes	66 /	79	23	82	20	87	15	88	8	50
No	9	11	4	14	2	9	2	12	2	13
Don't know	8	10	1	4	1	4	0	0	6	38

Impact[d]									
Yes	40	61	15	68	5	42	12	75	8	50
No	14	21	4	18	6	50	2	13	2	13
Don't know	12	18	3	15	1	8	2	13	6	38

[a]N may differ from question to question because of omissions by the respondents.

[b]Percentage totals may differ slightly from 100 because of rounding error.

[c]"By formal we mean some conscious, planned effort though it need not be a sophisticated effort. In contrast, an informal evaluation would mainly involve an after-the-fact looking over the program and data related to the program where this activity was not part of the overall plan" (from questionnaire instructions).

[d]Ns are inflated and percentages sum to more than 100 because some respondents checked more than one response. Based on a total of 98 cases.

tions. On the other hand, the observers by and large came from rather strict measurement and research backgrounds. The observers seemed to learn quite a few things from the practitioners, and we suspect that the reverse was also true.

Different evaluation strategies are needed for programs at different stages of development. For example, "innovative and developmental programs probably need less restricted or constrictive evaluation designs than are typically applied to static programs that are to be evaluated in relationship to cost-effectiveness, validity, or productivity." Further, newly conceived or initiated programs require new evaluation approaches and special expertise, while evaluations of continuing programs can become routine. In one case of a continuing program, an observer noted: "The procedures for instructional delivery *and* for evaluation are carefully developed, presented in written specifications, and implemented as specified—there is an almost total absence of ambiguity, irrelevance, or redundancy."

The most important factor in program implementation and evaluation may be the people factor. Special note was taken by observers of such matters as these:

> The strong points of the evaluation are that (1) the evaluation effort has the excellent support of the commander and (2) the personnel involved in the evaluations are subject-matter experts so that their credibility is quite eye-winning when results are reported back to instructional personnel.

> Where empathy and high fidelity communication exist between consultants/evaluators and personnel being assessed, there appears to be high likelihood that even somewhat critical and derogatory statements may be taken for self-improvement rather than rejected as self-destructive.

> The effectiveness of this evaluation was highly related to the personality characteristics of the principal staff members engaged in the program. . . . One may question whether summarizations about the relative effectiveness or usefulness of program evaluation may be as much a function of the attitudes and characteristics of the recipients as of the technical competence, comprehensiveness, or effectiveness of the evaluation conducted.

Evaluations of Adult Technical Training Programs

The confidence in the use of evaluation results is justified not only from previous experience but from the mutual respect between line officers and dedicated civil servants who lend professional stability to the enterprise.

It would appear judicious for organizations developing evaluation programs to seek outside professional assistance if the talent required does not reside in or is not available from the organization. This action will serve not only to provide professional quality to the evaluation program but also to allow interchange of ideas and values between internal and external professionals.

The most noteworthy aspect of the evaluation was its input of different points of view: employers, former students, instructors, and supervisors.

The involvement of industry staff members in the evaluation of a technical training program appears to be of major importance in accomplishing the program's goals.

At the same time, the "visitors" called specific attention to instances in which "the instructional personnel did not take kindly to the evaluation reports" or "the evaluator was acutely aware of the implications that any comprehensive evaluation might have" (in the latter case, the evaluator, who was also the program director, deliberately avoided comprehensiveness). In another instance, the site visitor commented on the "climate" for evaluation as follows: "The call for Executive Development Programs was issued as an edict. They are 'good' per se. Why would anyone go any further and gather data that might be analyzed to conclude that the whole thing is a waste and managers come into being by a political process rather than a merit procedure?" One observer summed up the situation nicely. "Yes, though I speak before many groups, I rarely find the clamor, 'Please come and evaluate me!' The enthusiasm for evaluation seems to swell largely in the evaluator rather than the evaluatee. The antidote for this generalization may be found in the involvement and maturity of the various persons who are intimately related to or affected by the evaluation."

Adequate planning and front-end analysis save a lot of diffi-

culties later on. In many of the programs visited, needs analysis prior to program development or evaluation was virtually ignored. As one observer put it, "The 'is-should' model appears to be a useful one that is easily understood by a staff relatively unsophisticated in evaluation. . . . After the fact, the staff discovered the importance of the needs assessment and lamented that it was now 'too late.' " Other comments in the same vein included: "Input from the field must be more representative, so that program content can be reflective of participants' perceived needs"; and, "More lead time was required for the planning of a program than was available, and the director believes the overall effectiveness of the program/evaluation would have been much more positive with greater lead time." Such charges were not made in the case of evaluation systems applied to continuing programs: "The systems engineering of courses is a carefully and logically developed background reconstruction of important analyses beginning and ending with analysis on the job which contributes tangible results and documents all along the way, and which can be refined further in successive efforts."

Sophisticated research designs and statistics are not necessary for effective evaluation studies oriented toward program improvement; prompt, interpretable feedback is. One of the particularly interesting evaluative efforts observed was characterized as stressing "the practical criteria of the evaluation data, such as relevance, importance, scope, credibility, and timeliness, . . . over criteria of reliability, predictive validity, and so on." And in another case: "This observer would speculate that some quantitative specialist bent on finding some methodological flaw in the thirty pages of tables and narrative would be rewarded; he might point out, for example, that apparent differences in proportions were not tested for significance or some effort to apply quasi-experimental design would strengthen the report, or that additional correlations between course grades, performance tests, supervisor ratings, etc., should be undertaken. In the opinion of the writer, however, this would be missing the point." The importance of quick feedback and turnaround was also emphasized; for example, "The ongoing professional judgment by the individual consultant allowing for prompt adjustment in the program seems worthwhile." And: "There appears to be an excellent rapport between the evaluation unit and the instruction unit. This might be attributed to the fact that oral reports are quite common, with the evaluation unit often reviewing their findings immediately with the instructional personnel long before they are put in writing."

Eleven

Trends in
Program Evaluation

In the preceding chapter we covered some of the trends in training evaluation as practiced in the field. Many of our conclusions are similar to those reported by Campbell and others (1970) and Campbell (1971), but the passage of only a few years seems to have brought both greater appreciation of the role of evaluation and increased concern for the quality of evaluation. Thus, our appraisal of practice in this domain may be more optimistic than that of the earlier authors. We must face the fact, however, that training programs may be easier to evaluate than many other kinds of human-service efforts. As stated in the Ball-Anderson (1975a) report: "Training programs frequently lend themselves to evaluation that can be characterized as systematic and where words such as 'feedback' and 'performance criteria' apply" (p. 27). General education programs and programs directed toward improving physical and mental health, long-term economic development, or the quality of the environment seem to be more difficult to conceptualize in concrete terms. In some cases, the "evaluability" of such programs is open to question (Zusman and Bissonette, 1970). Reviews of programs and evaluation efforts in some of these fields tend to bear out these contentions. See, for example, the reviews by Buchanan and Wholey (1972) of federal evaluation efforts; Goldmann (1975), of evaluation approaches taken by the Ford Foundation; Hall and Hall (1974), of programs designed to treat obesity; Kunce and others (1974), of rehabilitation programs; Crawford and Chapulsky (1973), of evaluation strategies used in programs for alcoholics; Sells and Watson (1971), of methadone treatment approaches and the implications for program evaluation; Gilbert and others (1975), cited extensively in Chapter Four, and Boruch (1974), of randomized field experiments for impact evaluation; and Glaser and Taylor (1973), of ten studies sponsored by the National Institute of Mental Health.

Some generalizations from the Glaser-Taylor study supplement and support the "lessons" we learned from the review of adult training program evaluations (Chapter Ten). Successful investigators sought involvement and understanding by others (including genuine criticisms), did not hesitate to raise controversial issues during planning stages, sought technical consultation when it was indicated, disseminated their findings widely—and saw many instances of their findings being used by practitioners.

Trends in Climate and Methodologies

We have seen that there are a great many social intervention programs "out there" and a large number of both program people and outsiders engaged in processes described as evaluation. It is probably not necessary to remind any readers of this book that these efforts do not spring entirely from the wisdom of program officers and a desire to come to an honest understanding of program needs, workings, and effects. Rather, many evaluations are mandated by the agency footing the bill for the program, usually some branch of the

211

federal government. That agency, in turn, is responsible to the Congress for its funds, and Congress ultimately is responsible to the public whose money and votes are at stake. Parallel lines of responsibility can be drawn if the funding source is a local government agency, a foundation, or a business-industrial organization. The popular term for all of this is *accountability,* which usually implies some obligation by the spenders to those whose money they are spending (or interests they are supposedly representing) to provide information about what they did, why they did it, and what the consequences were or are. In addition, some interpretations of accountability stress the right of those providing the money, or otherwise vitally concerned with the effort, to participate in decisions about program goals and implementation strategies (Anderson and others, 1975, pp. 1-4).

Increasingly since the mid 1960s, funds for large programs in the public interest have been allocated with the stipulation that the programs be evaluated. Increasingly since the early 1970s, the nature of those mandated evaluations has been prescribed and regulated. Title I of the Elementary and Secondary Education Act (ESEA) is a case in point. Title I authorizes financial assistance to Local Education Agencies with concentrations of economically disadvantaged children but makes State Education Agencies responsible for allocating funds and monitoring the special programs. When it was enacted in 1965, Title I was declared notable not only in its intent (to alleviate poor educational achievement by poor children) but also because "for the first time in educational legislative history [Congress] wrote the requirement of evaluation into the . . . act" (Spickler, 1966, p. 9). The original, rather general evaluation guidelines, published the year after the legislation went into effect, were also notable in their intent, but assumed a level of sophistication about program evaluation and a level of motivation to evaluate (and be evaluated) that were not realistic for educators in state and local agencies. It is thus not surprising that the quality of Title I evaluations has been unremarkable (Wargo and others, 1972; Gamel and others, 1975). As Title I appropriations have come up for reexamination, legislators have called for more evidence that the funds were being spent reasonably and productively. The next legislation dealing with Title I was far more specific (Educational Amendments of 1974, Section 151) on the issue of evaluation:

> (a) The Commissioner shall provide for independent evaluations which describe and measure the impact of programs and projects assisted under this title. Such evaluations may be provided by contract or other arrangements, and all such evaluations shall be made by competent and independent persons, and from program or project participants about the strengths and weaknesses of such programs or projects.
>
> (d) The Commissioner shall provide to State educational agencies models for evaluations of all programs conducted under this title.
>
> (j) The models developed by the Commissioner shall specify objective criteria which shall be utilized in the evaluation of all programs and shall outline techniques . . . and methodology . . . for producing data which are comparable on a statewide or nationwide basis.

The regulations pertaining to the "models" referred to in the law, including technical assistance in applying those models, are expected to achieve a level of specificity, if not restrictiveness, heretofore unknown in a country that prides itself on local educational autonomy. We readily admit that some national report card on the effectiveness of Title I is in order. To say the least, Title I is a major item in the budget of the Department of Health, Education and Welfare. However, we hope that the voluminous testing and reporting requirements oriented primarily toward reading and arithmetic will not discourage innovative local instructional and evaluation efforts that go beyond the requirements.

Program developers and evaluators in other areas are seeing the same kinds of trends. To name just a few, there are Head Start Program Performance Standards (U.S. Department of Health, Education and Welfare, 1975), Guidelines for Evaluating Continuing Education Programs in Mental Health (NIH, 1971), and Principles and Standards for Employing Water and Other Resources (Water Resources Council, 1973). We have already mentioned that evaluations are mandated for some Department of Defense programs.

Accountability is associated with built-in requirements for

213

program evaluation. It is also associated with such management-oriented concepts and techniques as zero-based budgeting (Minmier, 1975), Program Evaluation and Review Technique (PERT—see Cook, 1966; Case, 1969), management-by-objectives (Brady, 1973), cost-benefit or -effectiveness analysis (Dorfman, 1965), and "the systems approach" (Churchman, 1968). These in turn have found their place in the literature and practice of program evaluation in the last decade, where earlier program-evaluation concepts were likely to be limited to those of such social-behavioral sciences as psychology and sociology. For example, we have mentioned some instances of the application of the systems approach in developing and evaluating military training programs. Systems-analysis techniques have also been used in, or advocated for, such diverse kinds of programs and services as university counseling (O'Neil and others, 1973), mental health care service delivery (Levin and Bishop, 1972), special education (Lerner, 1973), and alcoholism programming (Holder and Stratas, 1972).

The relatively new "decision-theoretic" approach counts as another methodological trend that questions the relevance of classical research paradigms for program evaluation. The approach is associated with Edwards and others (1975) and involves aggregation of value decisions across program instances and decision makers through Bayesian statistics and utility theory. More detail on the approach is given in Chapter Three, and the reader is also referred to the summarization provided by Perloff and others (1976). They question whether the decision-theoretic approach in fact dispenses with the need for "some kind of design . . . in order to link program effects with program treatments" and suggest "that the contribution of the decision-theoretic approach to evaluation research is its capability for helping in the development of criterion variables" (p. 575). The decision-theoretic approach is just one approach to the general problem of aggregating data across different studies. Light (1977) thinks that, in spite of problems, it is "possible" to carry out such aggregations and "arrive at powerful conclusions" (p. 3), although Cronbach (1977) concludes that up to now "none of us knows what he is doing when he analyzes aggregate data" (p. 3).

Trends in Program Evaluation

In summarizing the findings from evaluations of technical training programs for adults, we noted, without disapproval, that sophisticated research designs and statistics were not necessary for feedback *useful in program improvement*. This trend has been noted and encouraged in other program areas. Some evaluation specialists most dedicated in their earlier writings to objectivity and relatively formal approaches have come increasingly to appreciate the advantages of close working relationships with program staff and informal approaches—when joint and timely decisions about program installation and processes are indicated. Stake (1975), for example, extols the relevance of such "responsive evaluation" to programs in the arts. He argues that such programs require "different readiness by the evaluators, different data, different sensitivities, and different interpretations" from, say, many conventional instructional programs (p. iv). Problems will arise, however, when attempts to determine the *impact* of social innovations are limited to nonexperimental approaches. As Gilbert and his colleagues (1975) point out so clearly, "uncontrolled and poorly controlled studies led to greater enthusiasm than was warranted on the basis of well-controlled studies" (p. 131), and poorly controlled studies "may not only generate conclusions with doubtful validity—they may actually delay the implementation of better evaluation." The result is that "an ineffective treatment or program may be administered for years. The opportunity cost of such a mistake can be high" (p. 134).

At least one more methodological trend in program evaluation deserves mention. Unfortunately, it is probably more of a niggling concern than a real trend, for, although the case for studying person-treatment interactions (as well as main effects of social interventions) has been strongly advanced in professional discussions, relatively little practical work in the area has been done. Yet there are important decision implications of finding out that treatment A works better for clients who have characteristics x while treatment B is more effective with clients who have characteristics y. If policy makers had such information, they could then match persons to treatments with the promise of maximum payoff. There are probably several overlapping reasons why the "press" has been better than the practice in this area:

The Profession and Practice of Program Evaluation

The conceptualization and analysis of such studies are complex; such interactions may represent relatively subtle effects; many persons may be flexible enough to benefit from "either" treatment (or treatments may be so eclectic that they include "something for everyone"); or it may not be considered "good" or feasible to allow such differentiation in operating programs (see Anderson and others, 1975, pp. 444–449). The recent review of the literature on person-treatment interaction by Cronbach and Snow (1975), Lo's (1973) guide to statistical methodologies in the area, and Cooley and Lohnes's (1976) exposition of how evaluators might approach the investigation of person-treatment interaction should all be influential in fostering any trend toward including searches for interactions in evaluation studies.

Professional Trends

During the past decade, the professionals have, if anything, been more active than the practitioners—if we may be permitted to use the word *professionals* to apply to those who prepare books, articles, and speeches about evaluation and invent journals, societies, and training programs with program evaluation as the theme.

As we indicated in the first chapter, program evaluation by different names has been going on for a long time. But the present burst of literature in the field began in the 1960s with such seminal books and articles as Campbell and Stanley (1966), Cronbach (1963), Glaser (1962), Guba and Stufflebeam (1970), Stake (1967), Suchman (1967), and Tyler, Gagné, and Scriven (1967). It was inevitable that handbooks and encyclopedias would come along (notably Bloom, Hastings, and Madaus, 1971; Anderson and others, 1975;* and Guttentag and Struening, 1975) and textbooks as well (for example, Cooley and Lohnes, 1976). Perloff and others (1976) uncovered the interesting fact that "program evaluation" did not appear as an index term in *Psychological Abstracts* until January 1973, and their

---

*There is even a "poverty alternative" to the *Encyclopedia of Educational Evaluation* according to the authors of *An Evaluation Thesaurus* (Scriven and Roth, 1977), a sure sign that a field is to be reckoned with.

216

article was the first one on the topic in the *Annual Review of Psychology*. The *Annual Review of Sociology* also included its first chapter on evaluation research in 1976. In spite of this lag in recognition by two societies who have many members actively engaged in program evaluation, the last few years have not been marked by any shortage of printed, xeroxed, and spoken words recounting evaluation efforts and advising others how to conduct them. For example, in the category of spoken words, 1977 saw about eighty symposia and paper sessions pertaining to program evaluation at the annual meeting of the American Educational Research Association in New York and another thirty or so at the American Psychological Association convention in San Francisco. By and large at such conventions, words are exchanged between people in the evaluation business, most of whom are already sold on program evaluation as a good idea. We do not see a strong parallel trend in explaining and promoting program evaluation to people outside the profession: educational administrators, training directors, government agency officials, legislators, and others. However, some new journals and societies appear to be interested in opening such communication channels.

One journal that is devoted exclusively to program evaluation and recognizes the multidisciplinary nature of the enterprise as well as the variety of social programs to which it may apply is called *Evaluation: A Forum for Human Service Decision-Makers*. It was established on an experimental basis in 1974 by the Program Evaluation Resource Center, Minneapolis Medical Research Foundation, Inc. Included on the editorial board are reviewers from the fields of alcoholism, biostatistics, community mental health, criminal justice, education, epidemiology, geriatrics, governmental planning, mental health, public health, rehabilitation, and research dissemination. A second, *New Directions for Program Evaluation*, launched in 1978, is characterized by its publishers (Jossey-Bass) as a series of "quarterly sourcebooks." Each issue focuses on a single theme or problem of increasing concern to evaluators and includes articles by authors from a variety of disciplines who are judged to be especially qualified to address the problem.

Another journal that has started arriving regularly adds an

217

international concern for evaluation of educational programs: *Studies in Educational Evaluation*, published by the School of Education, Tel Aviv University; Center for Study of Evaluation, University of California at Los Angeles; and Institute for Science Education, University of Kiel, West Germany. Other journals or newsletters in the evaluation area, most of them established recently and some of them issued on erratic schedules, include *Evaluation Quarterly, A Journal of Applied Social Science; Evaluation Comment*, published by the Center for the Study of Evaluation, UCLA; *Newsletter SIG:IE*, distributed by the Instructional Evaluation (IE) Special Interest Group (SIG) of the American Educational Research Association; *Division H Newsletter* of the School Evaluation and Program Development Division of AERA; *Evaluation Exchange*, an interdisciplinary newsletter produced by the University of Michigan, Institute of Labor and Industrial Relations, and Wayne State University; *Newsletter* from the California Educational Program Auditors and Evaluators; and *RIPPLE*, in the mental health field and focusing mainly on New York State, from the Bureau of Program Evaluation, Department of Mental Health, Albany.

A major solution to the problems "evaluation specialists . . . have . . . communicating with each other" is promised by the *Evaluation Studies Review Annual*. The first *Annual* (1976) was edited by Glass and, according to the publishers, "comprises an excellent survey of the latest and best in evaluation methods and theories—a realistic picture of the frontiers in an exciting interdisciplinary field." The volume is in fact of high quality and includes contributions to theory and methods of evaluation by such distinguished authors as Cronbach, House, and Scriven. Further, the series offers an opportunity for widespread dissemination of reports of exemplary evaluations of particular projects, reports that might otherwise be seen only by those immediately concerned with the projects.

At least three new associations with evaluation as a primary or major focus have been formed: the Council for Applied Social Research, "an interdisciplinary group of academic and entrepreneurial research types out to bridge the gap between policy researchers and policy makers, and a brainchild of Clark Abt, head of the

218

Cambridge-based Abt Associates, Inc."; the Evaluation Research Society, "also an interdisciplinary group which tilts a bit more toward the specialty of evaluation research, organized by Harvard psychologist Marcia Guttentag" (these descriptions from the *APA Monitor*, April 1977); and the Evaluation Network, proposed and initiated under a grant from Phi Delta Kappa, focusing on "evaluation in all areas of society," with an initial emphasis on "communication and educating evaluators and their clients at the pre-service and in-service levels" (from the announcement of the Second Annual Conference, November 8–10, 1976). *Evaluation News* is the Network's delightfully unorthodox publication.

One of the most telling indications that a field is coming of age occurs when the idea of standards and sanctions for its activities is broached. That happened in 1975 for the evaluation of educational programs. Under a grant from the Lilly Foundation, a Committee to Develop Guidelines and Standards for Educational Evaluation was appointed with Daniel L. Stufflebeam, Western Michigan University, as chairman. The committee includes representatives or monitors from the National Education Association, National Association of Elementary School Principals, American Society for Curriculum Development, National School Boards Association, American Educational Research Association, National Council on Measurement in Education, American Association of School Administrators, American Federation of Teachers, American Personnel and Guidance Association, Education Commission of the States, and the American Psychological Association. The initial set of standards was scheduled to appear in 1977. The President of the Evaluation Research Society has also recently announced the appointment of a Standards Committee. Presumably the purview of that committee will extend beyond educational evaluation.

It has been debated whether program evaluation qualifies as a profession or a discipline or is simply an activity or job (sometimes part-time). Our answer is "probably all of the above." It is certainly for many "an occupation . . . requiring extensive education in a branch of science or the liberal arts" and there is certainly a "body of persons engaged in such an occupation." If we are to believe the data in Chapter Nine, program evaluation is also "a branch of instruction or learning" (these definitions are taken from *The Random House Dictionary of the English Language,* college edition, 1969). As we have observed in the examples given throughout this book (and especially in Chapter Ten), evaluation is also an activity or job engaged in by many people who have not had the benefit of extensive education in the area—and many of whom are doing worthwhile work. The argument about evaluation as a profession, discipline, or job may be as useless as the one about whether evaluation is research; sometimes it is and sometimes it isn't. Clearly, program evaluation has room for people with several levels of skills and a variety of specializations, depending on the purposes, setting, and requirements of a particular program. It is also clear that the contributions of individuals to the theory and methodology of evaluation can be expected to vary with the skills and specializations they possess, as well as with their interests and motivation. As Perloff and others (1976) urge psychologists: "Arise! Reach for more of program evaluation's shiny brass rings. In so doing you may not only help to create more jobs for your younger cohorts now receiving their doctoral degrees and facing bleak job prospects, but also, as Wortman [1975] points out, awaiting you are opportunities in program evaluation for useful and exciting research . . . in clinical, educational, experimental, measurement, and social psychology" (p. 590). Similar advice seems in order for accountants, anthropologists, communications specialists, economists, educators, environmental experts, industrial engineers, medical and health professionals, military and business managers, operations researchers, political scientists, sociologists, statisticians, and urban planners. Program evaluation has evolved as a profession, discipline, or occupation that is not the exclusive province of any one group.

References

American Psychological Association. *Ethical Standards of Psychologists.* (Rev. ed.) Washington, D.C.: American Psychological Association, 1977.

American Psychological Association, American Educational Research Association, and National Council on Measurement in Education. *Standards for Educational and Psychological Tests and Manuals.* Washington, D.C.: American Psychological Association, 1974.

Anderson, S. B. "Educational Compensation and Evaluation: A Critique." In J. C. Stanley (Ed.), *Compensatory Education for Children Ages Two to Eight.* Baltimore, Md.: Johns Hopkins University Press, 1973.

Anderson, S. B., Ball, S., Murphy, R. T., and Associates. *Encyclopedia of Educational Evaluation: Concepts and Techniques for Evaluating Education and Training Programs.* San Francisco: Jossey-Bass, 1975.

Argyris, C. "Creating Effective Research Relationships in Organizations." *Human Organization,* 1958, *27,* 34-40.

Baker, E. L. "Lean Data Strategies for Formative Evaluation." Paper presented in the symposium "An End of Affluence: Educational Evaluation in Tight Money Times," at the annual meeting of the American Educational Research Association, San Francisco, April 1976.

Ball, S. "Achievement Grouping in Reading." *Australian Journal of Education,* 1957, *1,* 87-89.

Ball, S. "Methodological Problems in Assessing the Impact of Television Programs." *Journal of Social Issues,* 1976, *32,* 8-17.

Ball, S., and Anderson, S. B. *Practices in Program Evaluation: A Survey and Some Case Studies.* Princeton, N.J.: Educational Testing Service, 1975a.

Ball, S., and Anderson, S. B. *Professional Issues in the Evaluation of Education/Training Programs.* Princeton, N.J.: Educational Testing Service, 1975b.

Ball, S., and Bogatz, G. A. *The First Year of Sesame Street: An Evaluation.* Princeton, N.J.: Educational Testing Service, 1970.

Barber, B., Lally, J. J., Makaruska, S. L., and Sullivan, D. *Research on Human Subjects.* New York: Russell Sage Foundation, 1973.

Barcikowski, R. S. "A Monte Carlo Study of Item Sampling (Versus Traditional Sampling) for Norm Construction." *Journal of Educational Measurement,* 1972, *9,* 209-214.

Barro, A. R. "Survey and Evaluation of Approaches to Physician Performance Measurement." *Journal of Medical Education,* 1973, *48,* 1051-1093.

Becher, T. "The Times Educational Supplement No. 3232." *The London Times,* May 13, 1977, p. 2.

Berke, J. S. "Policy-Relevant Research." Internal memorandum, October 27, 1976. Educational Testing Service, Princeton, N.J.

References

Bernstein, E. N., and Freeman, H. E. *Academic and Entrepreneuring Research.* New York: Russell Sage Foundation, 1975.

Bersoff, D. N. "Internship Models in School Psychology." *Journal of School Psychology,* 1973, *11,* 155-156.

Bice, T. W., Eichhorn, R. L., and Klein, D. A. "Evaluation of Public Health Programs." In M. Guttentag (Ed.), *Handbook of Evaluation Research.* Vol. 2. Beverly Hills, Calif.: Sage, 1975.

Bissell, J. S. *Implementation of Planned Variation in Head Start: Review and Summary of First Year Report.* Washington, D.C.: Office of Child Development, U.S. Department of Health, Education and Welfare, 1971.

Blabolil, G. J. "Emergence of Needs Assessment as a Basis for Title I Planning." Paper presented in the symposium "Evaluating Title I in an Urban School System—A Decade of Happenings" at the annual meeting of the American Educational Research Association, San Francisco, April 1976.

Bloom, B. S., Hastings, J. T., and Madaus, G. F. *Handbook on Formative and Summative Evaluation of Student Learning.* New York: McGraw-Hill, 1971.

Boring, E. G. *A History of Experimental Psychology.* (2nd ed.) New York: Appleton-Century-Crofts, 1957.

Boruch, R. F. "Bibliography: Illustrative Randomized Field Experiments for Program Planning and Evaluation." *Evaluation,* 1974, *2* (1), 83-87.

Botein, B. "The Manhattan Bail Project: Its Impact on Criminology and the Criminal Law Processes." *Texas Law Review,* 1964-1965, *43,* 319-331.

Bowles, S., and Gintis, H. *Schooling in Capitalist America: Educational Reform and the Contradictions of Economic Life.* New York: Basic Books, 1976.

Brady, R. H. "MBO Goes to Work in the Public Sector." *Harvard Business Review,* March-April 1973, 65-74.

Bray, D. W., Campbell, R. J., and Grant, D. L. *Formative Years in Business: A Long-Term AT&T Study of Managerial Lives.* New York: Wiley, 1974.

Brayfield, A. H. "How to Create a New Profession: Issues and Answers." *American Psychologist*, 1976, *31*, 200-205.

Briggs, R. G. "What Philosophic Questions for Educational Evaluators?" Paper presented in the symposium "Philosophical Perspectives on Educational Evaluation" at the annual meeting of the American Educational Research Association, San Francisco, 1976.

Bronfenbrenner, U. "Is Early Intervention Effective?" In M. Guttentag (Ed.), *Handbook of Evaluation Research.* Vol. 2. Beverly Hills, Calif.: Sage, 1975.

Bruner, J. *Man: A Course of Study.* Occasional Paper, No. 3. Cambridge, Mass.: Educational Development Center, 1965.

Buchanan, G. N., and Wholey, J. S. "Federal Level Evaluation." *Evaluation*, 1972, *1*, 17-22.

Bunda, M. A. "A Partial Validation of the New Conceptualization of Evaluation Competencies." Paper presented at the annual meeting of the American Educational Research Association, New Orleans, La., 1973.

Burke, H. R. "A Study in Public School Accountability Through the Application of Multiple Regression to Selected Variables." Doctoral dissertation, Indiana University, 1972. Abstracted in *Dissertation Abstracts International*, 1973, *34*, 4661A-4662A. (University Microfilms No. 73-6965.)

Bussis, A. M., Chittenden, E. A., and Amarel, M. "Alternative Ways in Educational Evaluation." In V. Perrone, M. D. Cohen, and L. P. Martin (Eds.), *Testing and Evaluation: New Views.* Washington, D.C.: Association for Childhood Education International, 1975.

California State Department of Education. *The Evaluation Improvement Program: Program Evaluator's Guide.* Princeton, N.J.: Educational Testing Service, 1977.

Campbell, D. T. "Reforms as Experiments." In C. H. Weiss (Ed.), *Evaluating Action Programs: Readings in Social Action and Education.* Boston: Allyn & Bacon, 1972.

Campbell, D. T., and Erlebacher, A. "How Regression Artifacts in Quasi-Experimental Evaluations Can Mistakenly Make Compensatory Education Look Harmful." In J. Hellmuth (Ed.), *Disadvantaged Child.* Vol. 3: *Compensatory Education: A National*

References

Debate. New York: Brunner/Mazel, 1970. (Reprinted in E. L. Struening (Ed.), *Handbook of Evaluation Research*. Vol. 1. Beverly Hills, Calif.: Sage, 1975.)

Campbell, D. T., and Stanley, J. C. *Experimental and Quasi-Experimental Design for Research*. Chicago: Rand McNally, 1966.

Campbell, J. P. "Personnel Training and Development." In P. H. Mussen and M. R. Rosenzweig (Eds.), *Annual Review of Psychology*. Vol. 22. Palo Alto, Calif.: Annual Reviews, 1971.

Campbell, J. P., Dunnette, M. D., Lawler, E. E., III, and Weick, K. E., Jr. *Managerial Behavior, Performance and Effectiveness*. New York: McGraw-Hill, 1970.

Caplan, N., and Nelson, S. D. "On Being Useful: The Nature and Consequences of Psychological Research on Social Problems." *American Psychologist*, 1973, *28*, 199-211.

Cardon, B. W. "Law, Professional Practice and University Preparation: Where Do We Go from Here?" *Journal of School Psychology*, 1975, *13*, 377-386.

Caro, F. G. (Ed.). *Readings in Evaluation Research*. New York: Russell Sage Foundation, 1971.

Case, C. M. "The Application of PERT to Large-Scale Educational and Evaluation Studies." *Educational Technology*, 1969, *9*, 79-83.

Chazan, M. "Compensatory Education: Defining the Problem." In *Compensatory Education: An Introduction*. Occasional Publication, No. 1. Schools Council Research Project in Compensatory Education, Department of Education, University College of Swansea. Swansea, Wales: Schools Council Publishing, 1968.

Churchman, C. W. *Prediction and Optimal Decision*. Englewood Cliffs, N.J.: Prentice-Hall, 1961.

Churchman, C. W. *The Systems Approach*. New York: Delacorte Press, 1968.

Churchman, C. W. *The Design of Inquiring Systems*. New York: Basic Books, 1971.

Coller, A. R. *A Taxonomy of Programmatic Tasks in an Educational Evaluation, Facilitation, and Coordination System*. Northfield, Ill.: Cooperative Educational Research Laboratory, 1970. (ERIC Document Reproduction Service, No. ED 051 283.)

225

Convey, J. J. "A Validation of Three Models for Producing School Effectiveness Indices." Paper presented at the annual meeting of the American Educational Research Association, Washington, D.C., April 1975. (ERIC Document Reproduction Service, No. ED 051 283.)

Convey, J. J. "Determining School Effectiveness Following a Regression Analysis." Paper presented at the annual meeting of the American Educational Research Association, San Francisco, April 1976.

Cook, D. L. *Program Evaluation and Review Technique Applications in Education.* Washington, D.C.: U.S. Government Printing Office, 1966.

Cook, T. D., Appleton, H., Conner, R., Shaffer, A., Tomkin, G., and Weber, S. J. *Sesame Street Revisited: A Case Study in Evaluative Research.* New York: Russell Sage Foundation, 1972.

Cook, T. D., Appleton, H., Conner, R. F., Shaffer, A., Tomkin, G., and Weber, S. J. *Sesame Street Revisited.* New York: Russell Sage Foundation, 1975.

— Cook, T. D., and Campbell, D. T. "The Design and Conduct of Quasi-Experiments and True Experiments in Field Settings." In M. D. Dunnette (Ed.), *Handbook of Industrial and Organizational Research.* Chicago: Rand McNally, 1975.

Cooley, W. H., and Lohnes, P. R. *Evaluation Research in Education: Theory, Principles, and Practice.* New York: Irvington, 1976.

Corder, R. *The Information Base for Reading: A Critical Review of the Information Base for Current Assumptions Regarding the Status of Instruction and Achievement in Reading in the United States.* Washington, D.C.: U.S. Department of Health, Education and Welfare, 1971.

Cort, H. R., Jr., Henderson, N. H., and Jones, C. *Approaches to Further Evaluation of Man: A Course of Study.* Washington, D.C.: Educational Studies Development, Washington School of Psychiatry, 1971.

Coulson, J. E. "Problems and Approaches in Education Program Evaluation." Paper presented at the annual meeting of the American Educational Research Association, San Francisco, April 1976.

References

Crawford, J. J., and Chapulsky, A. B. "Evaluation Strategies Used in Current Alcoholism Rehabilitation Programs: Problems and Specifications for Improvement." *Proceedings 81st Annual Convention of the American Psychological Association*, 1973, *8*, 791-792.

Cremin, L. A. *The Transformation of the School*. New York: Knopf, 1961.

Cronbach, L. J. "Course Improvement Through Evaluation." *Teachers College Record*, 1963, *64*, 672-683.

Cronbach, L. J. "Remarks to the New Society." *Evaluation Research Society Newsletter*, 1977, *1*, 1-3.

Cronbach, L. J., and Snow, R. E. *Aptitudes and Instructional Methods*. New York: Irvington, 1975.

Cronbach, L. J., and Suppes, P. (Eds.). *Research for Tomorrow's Schools: Disciplined Inquiry for Education*. New York: Macmillan, 1962.

Cummings, F. W., Jr. "Identifying and Appraising Exemplary Program Evaluation of Projects in the Affective Domain." Unpublished doctoral dissertation, Saint Louis University, 1975.

Deming, W. E. "The Logic of Evaluation." In E. L. Struening (Ed.), *Handbook of Evaluation Research*. Vol. 1. Beverly Hills, Calif.: Sage, 1975.

Dennis, N. *Cards of Identity*. New York: Vanguard Press, 1955.

Ditman, K. S., Crawford, G. G., Forgy, E. W., Moskowitz, H., and MacAndrew, C. "A Controlled Experiment on the Use of Court Probation for Drunk Arrests." *American Journal of Psychiatry*, August 1967, *124*, 160-163.

Dorfman, R. (Ed.). *Measuring Benefits of Government Investments*. Washington, D.C.: Brookings Institution, 1965.

Dressel, P. L. *Handbook of Academic Evaluation: Assessing Institutional Effectiveness, Student Progress, and Professional Performance for Decision Making in Higher Education*. San Francisco: Jossey-Bass, 1976.

Dyer, H. "The Pennsylvania Plan." *Science Education*, 1966, *50*, 242-248.

Dyer, H., Linn, R., and Patton, M. *Feasibility Study of Educational Performance Indicators: Final Report to New York State Education Department*. Princeton, N.J.: Educational Testing Service, 1967.

Earle, H. H. *Police Recruit-Training: Stress Versus Nonstress.* Springfield, Ill.: Thomas, 1973.

Education Commission of the States. *National Assessment of Educational Progress Report 02-9-00: Reading Summary.* Denver: Education Commission of the States, May 1972.

Edwards, W., Guttentag, M., and Snapper, K. "A Decision-Theoretic Approach to Evaluation Research." Vol. 1. Beverly Hills, Calif.: Sage, 1975.

Eisner, E. W. "The Perceptive Eye: Toward the Reformation of Educational Evaluation." Occasional Paper. Stanford Evaluation Consortium, Stanford University, December 1975.

Elashoff, J. D., and Snow, R. E. *Pygmalion Reconsidered.* Worthington, Ohio: Charles A. Jones, 1971.

Everhart, R. B. "Between Stranger and Friend: Some Consequences of 'Long Term' Fieldwork in Schools." *American Educational Research Journal,* 1977, *14,* 1-15.

Federal Bureau of Prisons. *Rational Innovation: An Account of Changes in the Program of the National Training School for Boys from 1961 to 1964.* Washington, D.C.: Federal Bureau of Prisons, 1964.

Freedman, M. B. "The Promise and Problems of an Independent Graduate School." *American Psychologist,* 1976, *31,* 182-188.

French, J. W., and Michael, W. B. *Standards for Educational and Psychological Tests and Manuals.* Washington, D.C.: American Psychological Association, 1966.

Gagné, R. M. "Qualifications of Professionals in Educational R & D." *Educational Researcher,* 1975, *4* (2), 7-11.

Gamel, N. N., Tallmadge, G. K., Wood, C. T., and Binkley, J. L. *State ESEA Title I Reports: Review and Analysis of Past Reports and Development of a Model Reporting System and Format.* RMC Report UR-294. Mountain View, Calif.: RMC Research Corporation, 1975.

Gephart, W. J., Ingle, R. B., and Saretsky, G. "Similarities and Differences in the Research and Evaluation Processes." Unpublished report. National Symposium for Professors of Educational Research, 1972.

References

Gephart, W. J., and Potter, J. "The Generalizability Problem in Evaluation and a Borrowed Solution." *Cedar Quarterly,* Summer 1976, pp. 9-11.

Gibbon, S. Y., Jr., Palmer, E. L., and Fowles, B. R. "Sesame Street, The Electric Company, and Reading." In J. Carroll and J. Chall (Eds.), *Toward a Literate Society.* New York: Holt, Rinehart and Winston, 1976.

Gilbert, J. P., Light, R. J., and Mosteller, R. "Assessing Social Innovations: An Empirical Base for Policy." In C. A. Bennett and A. A. Lunsdaine (Eds.), *Evaluation and Experiment.* New York: Academic Press, 1975.

Glaser, E. M., and Backer, T. E. "A Clinical Approach to Program Evaluation." *Evaluation,* 1972a, *1,* 54-59.

Glaser, E. M., and Backer, T. E. "Outline of Questions for Program Evaluators Utilizing the Clinical Approach." *Evaluation,* 1972b, *1,* 56-60.

Glaser, E. M., and Taylor, S. H. "Factors Influencing the Success of Applied Research." *American Psychologist,* 1973, *28,* 140-146.

Glaser, R. (Ed.). *Training Research and Education.* Pittsburgh, Pa.: University of Pittsburgh Press, 1962.

Glass, G. V. *Evaluation Studies Review Annual.* Vol. 1. Beverly Hills, Calif.: Sage, 1976.

Glass, G. V., and Worthen, B. R. *Essential Knowledge and Skills for Educational Research and Evaluation.* Technical Paper, No. 5. Washington, D.C.: American Educational Research Association, 1970.

Goldmann, R. *Foundations and Evaluation: One Approach to Measuring Performance.* New York: Ford Foundation, 1975.

Gramlich, E., and Koshel, P. *Social Experiments in Education: The Case of Performance Contracting.* Washington, D.C.: Brookings Institution, 1975.

Grant, D. L., and Anderson, S. B. "Issues in the Evaluation of Training." *Professional Psychology,* 1977, *8,* 659-673.

Gray, S. W., and Klaus, R. A. "The Early Training Project: The Seventh-Year Report." *Child Development,* 1970, *41,* 909-924.

Grotberg, E. (Ed.). *Critical Issues in Research Related to Disad-*

vantaged Children. Princeton, N.J.: Educational Testing Service, 1969.

Guba, E. G. "Problems in Utilizing the Results of Evaluation." *Journal of Research and Development in Education,* 1975, *8,* 42-54.

Guba, E. G., and Stufflebeam, D. L. *Evaluation: The Process of Stimulating, Aiding, and Abetting Insightful Action.* Monograph Series in Reading Education, No. 1. Bloomington: Indiana University, 1970.

Gurel, L. "The Human Side of Evaluating Human Services Programs: Problems and Prospects." In M. Guttentag (Ed.), *Handbook of Evaluation Research.* Vol. 2. Beverly Hills, Calif.: Sage, 1975.

Guttentag, M. (Ed.). *Handbook of Evaluation Research.* Vol. 2. Beverly Hills, Calif.: Sage, 1975.

Guttentag, M. "Evaluation and Society." Presidential address to the Division of Personality and Social Psychology at the annual meeting of the American Psychological Association, Washington, D.C., September 1976.

Guttentag, M., and Struening, E. L. "The Handbook: Its Purpose and Organization." In M. Guttentag (Ed.), *Handbook of Evaluation Research.* Vol. 2. Beverly Hills, Calif.: Sage, 1975.

Hall, S. M., and Hall, R. G. "Outcome and Methodological Considerations in Behavioral Treatment of Obesity." *Behavior Theory,* 1974, *5,* 352-364.

Hanley, J. P., Whitla, D. K., Moo, E. W., and Walter, A. S. *Curiosity, Competence, Community. Man: A Course of Study—An Evaluation.* Cambridge, Mass.: Education Development Center, 1970.

Harless, J. H. "An Analysis of Front-End Analysis." *Improving Human Performance: A Research Quarterly,* 1973, *2,* 229-244.

Hastings, J. T. *Final Report to National Science Foundation Course Content Improvement Section.* Washington, D.C.: U.S. Government Printing Office, 1963.

Hess, R. D., and Shipman, V. "Early Blocks to Children's Learning." *Children,* 1965, *12,* 189-194.

Hill, D. B., and Veney, J. E. "Kansas Blue Cross/Blue Shield Outpatient Benefits Experiment." *Medical Care,* 1970, *8,* 143-158.

References

Holder, H. D., and Stratas, N. E. "A Systems Approach to Alcoholism Programming." *American Journal of Psychiatry,* 1972, *129,* 32-37.

Horst, D. P., Tallmadge, G. K., and Wood, C. T. *A Practical Guide to Measuring Project Impact on Student Achievement.* Washington, D.C.: U.S. Government Printing Office, 1975.

House, E. R. "The Conscience of Educational Evaluation." *Teachers College Record,* 1972, *73,* 405-414.

House, E. R. "Justice in Evaluation." In G. V. Glass (Ed.), *Evaluation Studies Review Annual.* Vol. 1. Beverly Hills, Calif.: Sage, 1976.

Hudson, L. *The Cult of the Fact.* New York: Harper & Row, 1972.

Inkeles, A., Coleman J., and Smelser, N. *Annual Review of Sociology 1976.* Vol. 1. Palo Alto, Calif.: Annual Reviews, 1976.

Jamison, D. "Definitions of Productivity and Efficiency in Education." Appendix A in A. Melmed (Ed.), *Productivity and Efficiency in Education.* Washington, D.C.: Educational Panel of Federal Council on Science and Technology, Commission on Automation Opportunities in the Service Areas, 1972 (draft).

Jurs, S. G. *Experimental Mortality.* Boulder: Laboratory of Educational Research, University of Colorado, 1970.

Kelly, G. *The Psychology of Personal Constructs.* Vol. 1. New York: Norton, 1955.

Kelman, H. C. "An Experiment in the Rehabilitation of Nursing Home Patients." *Public Health Reports,* 1962, *77,* 356-366.

Kelman, H. C. *A Time to Speak: On Human Values and Research.* San Francisco: Jossey-Bass, 1968.

Kourilsky, M. "An Adversary Model for Educational Evaluation." *UCLA Evaluation Comment,* 1973, *4* (2), 3-6.

Kunce, J. T., Miller, D. E., and Cope, C. S. "Macro Data Analysis and Rehabilitation Program Evaluation." *Rehabilitation Counseling Bulletin,* 1974, *17,* 132-140.

Langley Porter Institute. *Resource Materials for Community Mental Health Program Evaluation.* Washington, D.C.: National Technical Information Service, U.S. Department of Commerce, 1974.

Lerner, J. W. "Systems Analysis and Special Education." *Journal of Special Education,* 1973, *7,* 15-26.

231

Lesser, G. S. *Children and Television: Lessons from Sesame Street.* New York: Random House, 1974.

Levin, H. M. "Cost-Effectiveness Analysis in Evaluation Research." In M. Guttentag (Ed.), *Handbook of Evaluation Research.* Vol. 2. Beverly Hills, Calif.: Sage, 1975.

Levin, S., and Bishop, D. "An Evaluation Tool for Feedback and Leverage of Mental Health Delivery Systems." *Canadian Psychiatry Association Journal,* 1972, *17,* 437-442.

Levine, M. "Scientific Method and the Adversary Model: Some Preliminary Suggestions." *UCLA Evaluation Comment,* 1973, *4* (2), 1-3.

Lewin, K. "Group Decision and Social Change." In E. E. Maccoby, T. M. Newcomb, and E. L. Harley (Eds.), *Readings in Social Psychology.* New York: Holt, Rinehart and Winston, 1958.

Light, R. "Remarks at a Symposium on 'Evaluation and Social Policy.'" *Evaluation Research Society Newsletter,* 1977, *1,* 3.

Little, A. D. *A Working Manual of Simple Techniques for Community Mental Health Program Evaluation.* Washington, D.C.: U.S. Government Printing Office, 1976.

Lo, M. Y. "Statistical Analysis of Interaction and Its Application to Data from the Cooperative Research Program in Primary Reading Instruction." Unpublished doctoral dissertation, State University of New York at Buffalo, 1973.

Longood, R., and Simmel, A. "Organizational Resistance to Innovation Suggested by Research." In C. H. Weiss (Ed.), *Evaluating Action Programs: Readings in Social Action and Education.* Boston: Allyn & Bacon, 1972.

Lord, F. M. "Estimating Norms by Item Sampling." *Educational and Psychological Measurement,* 1962, *22,* 259-267.

Lynd, R. S. *Knowledge for What? The Place of Social Science in American Culture.* New York: Grove Press, 1939.

MacDonald, B. *Evaluation and the Control of Education.* Norwich, England: Center for Applied Research in Education, University of East Anglia, 1974.

McDonald, F. J. "Evaluation of Teaching Behavior." In W. R.

References

Houston and R. B. Howsam (Eds.), *Competency-Based Teacher Education*. Chicago: Science Research Associates, 1972.

MacMurray, V., Cunningham, P., Cater, P., Swensen, N., and Bellin, S. *Citizen Evaluation of Mental Health Services: An Action Approach to Accountability*. New York: Human Sciences Press, 1976.

Maehr, M. L. "Continuing Motivation: An Analysis of a Seldom Considered Educational Outcome." *Review of Educational Research*, Fall 1976, 433-462.

Maehr, M. L., and Stallings, W. M. "Freedom from External Evaluation." *Child Development*, 1972, *43*, 177-185.

Marco, G. L. "A Comparison of Selected School Effectiveness Measures Based on Longitudinal Data." *Journal of Educational Measurement*, 1974, *11*, 225-234.

Mayeske, G. W., Wisler, C. E., Beaton, A. E., Jr., Weinfield, F. D., Cohen, W. M., Okada, T., Prosher, J. M., and Tabler, K. A. *A Study of Our Nation's Schools*. Washington, D.C.: U.S. Department of Health, Education and Welfare, 1972.

Merrill, J. R. "Competence in the Natural Sciences." Paper presented at the annual meeting of the American Educational Research Association, San Francisco, April 1976.

Messick, S. "The Criterion Problem in the Evaluation of Instruction: Assessing Possible, Not Just Intended Outcomes." In M. C. Wittrock and D. E. Wiley (Eds.), *The Evaluation of Instruction: Issues and Problems*. New York: Holt, Rinehart and Winston, 1970.

Messick, S. "Research Methodology for Educational Change." *Educational Change: Implications for Measurement, Proceedings of the 1971 Invitational Conference on Testing Problems*. Princeton, N.J.: Educational Testing Service, 1972.

Messick, S. "The Standard Problem: Meaning and Values in Measurement and Evaluation." *American Psychologist*, 1975, *30*, 955-966.

Millman, J. *Selecting Educational Researchers and Evaluators*. TM Report 48. Princeton, N.J.: ERIC Clearinghouse on Tests, Measurement, and Evaluation; Educational Testing Service, 1975.

Minmier, G. S. *An Evaluation of Zero-Based Budgeting System in Governmental Institutions.* Research Monograph, No. 68. Atlanta: School of Business Administration, Georgia State University, 1975.

Moore, P. "Social Research Group Explores Policy Role." *APA Monitor,* April 1977, pp. 1-21.

Myers, A. E. "The Impact of Evaluative Research on Educational Program for the Poor." *Teachers College Record,* 1970, *71,* 371-379.

Myrdal, G. *An American Dilemma.* New York: Harper & Row, 1944.

National Academy of Sciences. *Final Report of the Panel on Manpower Training Evaluation. The Use of Social Security Earnings Data for Assessing the Impact of Manpower Training Programs.* Washington, D.C.: National Academy of Sciences, 1974.

National Institute of Health. *Guidelines for Evaluating Continuing Education Programs in Mental Health.* Washington, D.C.: U.S. Public Health Service, 1971.

Nozick, R. *Anarchy, State, and Utopia.* New York: Basic Books, 1974.

Nunnally, J. C. "The Study of Change in Evaluation Research." In E. L. Struening (Ed.), *Handbook of Evaluation Research.* Vol. 1. Beverly Hills, Calif.: Sage, 1975.

O'Neil, H. F., Jr., Richardson, F. C., Carver, D., and Iscoe, I. "A Systems Analysis of a Campus Community Mental Health Facility: A Preliminary Investigation." *American Journal of Community Psychology,* 1973, *1,* 362-376.

Pace, C. R. *Thoughts on Evaluation in Higher Education.* Iowa City, Iowa: American College Testing Program, 1972.

Palmer, E. L. "Sesame Street: Shaping Broadcast Television to the Needs of the Preschooler." *Educational Technology,* February 1971, pp. 18-21.

Palmer, E. L. "Applications of Psychology to Television Programming: Program Execution." *American Psychologist,* 1976, *31,* 137-138.

Perloff, R., Perloff, E., and Sussna, E. "Program Evaluation." In M. R. Rosenzweig and L. W. Porter (Eds.), *Annual Review of Psy-*

References

chology. Vol. 27. Palo Alto, Calif.: Annual Reviews, 1976.

Pfeiffer, J. *New Look at Education: Systems Analysis in Our Schools and Colleges.* New York: Odyssey Press, 1968.

Proper, E. C., and St. Pierre, R. G. "The Effects of Attrition on the National Evaluation of Follow Through." Paper presented at the annual meeting of the American Educational Research Association, San Francisco, April 1976.

Proshansky, H. M. "Environmental Psychology and the Real World." *American Psychologist,* 1976, *31,* 303-310.

Provus, M. *Discrepancy Evaluation.* Berkeley, Calif.: McCutchan, 1971.

Rawls, J. *A Theory of Justice.* Cambridge, Mass.: Belknap Press, 1971.

Renzulli, J. S. "The Confessions of a Frustrated Evaluator." *Measurement and Evaluation in Guidance,* 1972, *5,* 298-305.

Resnick, D. P., and Resnick, L. B. "The Nature of Literacy: An Historical Exploration." *Harvard Educational Review,* 1977, *47,* 370-385.

Ricks, F. A. "Training Program Evaluators." *Professional Psychology,* 1976, *7,* 339-343.

Riecken, H. W., and Boruch, R. F. (Eds.). *Social Experimentation: A Method for Planning and Evaluating Social Intervention.* New York: Academic Press, 1974.

Rippey, R. M. (Ed.). *Studies in Transactional Evaluation.* Berkeley, Calif.: McCutchan, 1973.

Roberts, A. O. H. "Foibles and Fallacies in Educational Evaluation." Paper presented at the annual meeting of the American Educational Research Association, San Francisco, April 1976.

Rodman, H., and Kolodny, R. "Organizational Strain in the Researcher-Practitioner Relationship." *Human Organization,* 1964, *23,* 171-182.

Rosenzweig, M. R., and Porter, L. W. *Annual Review of Psychology.* Vol. 27. Palo Alto, Calif.: Annual Reviews, 1976.

Rosner, B. *The Power of Competency-Based Teacher Education: A Report.* Boston: Allyn & Bacon, 1972.

Ross, L., and Cronbach, L. J. "Review of *Handbook of Evaluation*

The Profession and Practice of Program Evaluation

Research by M. Guttentag and E. L. Struening." *Proceedings of the National Academy of Education*, 1976, *3*, 87-107.

Rothenberg, J. "Cost-Benefit Analysis: A Methodological Exposition." In M. Guttentag (Ed.), *Handbook of Evaluation Research.* Vol. 2. Beverly Hills, Calif.: Sage, 1975.

Rubin, D. B. "Estimating Causal Effects of Treatments in Randomized and Nonrandomized Studies." *Journal of Educational Psychology*, 1964, *66*, 688-702.

Salasin, S. "Experimentation Revisited: A Conversation with Donald T. Campbell." *Evaluation*, 1973, *1*, 7-13.

Salcedo, J., Jr., "Views and Comments on the Report on Rice Enrichment in the Philippines." In Report No. 12 of the Food and Agriculture Organization of the United Nations. Rome: 1954.

Sassone, P. G., and Schaffer, W. A. "Cost-Benefit Analysis and Economic Evaluation of Business Activity." Seminar presented at Georgia Institute of Technology, March 10, 1977.

Scriven, M. "The Methodology of Evaluation." *Perspectives of Curriculum Evaluation.* American Educational Research Association Monograph Series on Curriculum Evaluation, No. 1. Chicago: Rand McNally, 1967.

Scriven, M. *Evaluation Skills.* Tape 6B. Instructional cassette recording produced by W. J. Popham. Washington, D.C.: American Educational Research Association, 1971.

Scriven, M. "An Introduction to Meta-Evaluation." In P. D. Taylor and D. M. Cowley (Eds.), *Readings in Curriculum Evaluation.* Dubuque, Iowa: William C. Brown, 1972.

Scriven, M. "Evaluation Perspectives and Procedures." In W. J. Popham (Ed.), *Evaluation in Education: Current Applications.* Berkeley, Calif.: McCutchan, 1974.

Scriven, M. "Evaluation Bias and Its Control." In G. V. Glass (Ed.), *Evaluation Studies Review Annual.* Vol. 1. Beverly Hills, Calif.: Sage, 1976a.

Scriven, M. *A Procedure for Assessing the Performance of a Particular School.* Report to the San Francisco Public Schools Commission. Regis, Calif.: Edge Press, 1976b.

Scriven, M., and Roth, J. *An Evaluation Thesaurus.* 1977. Available

References

from the senior author at 1384 Queens Rd., Berkeley, Calif. 94708.

Scriven, M., and Ward, J. (Eds.). *Evaluation News: The Newsletter of the Evaluation Network,* 1977, *2* (entire issue).

Sechrest, L., and Campbell, D. T. "Overview of a Summer Training Program in Health Care Research Methodology." Paper presented at the annual meeting of the American Psychological Association, Chicago, September 1975.

Sells, S. B., and Watson, D. D. "A Spectrum of Approaches in Methadone Treatment: Relation to Program Evaluation." *Journal of Psychedelic Drugs,* 1971, *4,* 198-204.

Shaw, L. W., and Chalmers, T. C. "Ethics in Cooperative Clinical Trials." *Annals of the New York Academy of Sciences,* 1970, *169,* 487-495.

Sherwood, C. C., Morris, J. N., and Sherwood, S. "A Multivariate, Nonrandomized Matching Technique for Studying the Impact of Social Interventions." In E. L. Struening (Ed.), *Handbook of Evaluation Research.* Vol. 1. Beverly Hills, Calif.: Sage, 1975.

Shoemaker, D. M. *Principles and Procedures of Multiple Matrix Sampling.* Cambridge, Mass.: Ballinger, 1973.

Skipper, J. A., Jr., and Leonard, R. C. "Children, Stress and Hospitalization: A Field Experiment." *Journal of Health and Social Behavior,* 1968, *9,* 275-287.

Smith, E. R., and Tyler, R. W. *Appraising and Recording Student Progress.* New York: Harper & Row, 1942.

Smith, M. B. "Is Psychology Relevant to New Priorities?" *American Psychologist,* 1973, *28,* 463-471.

Smith, M. S., and Bissell, J. S. "Report Analysis: The Impact of Head Start." *Howard Educational Review,* 1970, *40,* 51-104.

Snygg, D., and Combs, A. W. *Individual Behavior.* (Rev. ed.) New York: Harper & Row, 1959.

Sommer, R. "No, Not Research. I Said Evaluation!" *APA Monitor,* April 1977, *8,* pp. 1-11.

Southern Regional Education Board. *Program Evaluation in the State Mental Health Agency.* Atlanta, Ga.: Southern Regional Education Board, 1975.

Spickler, M. W. "The Role of Evaluation in Title I Programs." *On*

Evaluating Title I Programs, the proceedings of a conference held at Educational Testing Service. Princeton, N.J.: Educational Testing Service, 1966.

Stake, R. E. "The Countenance of Educational Evaluation." *Teachers College Record,* 1967, *68,* 523-540.

Stake, R. E. "To Evaluate an Arts Program." In R. Stake (Ed.), *Evaluating the Arts in Education—A Responsive Approach.* Columbus, Ohio: Merrill, 1975.

Stake, R. E. "Overview and Critique of Existing Evaluation Practices and Some New Leads for the Future." Paper presented at the annual meeting of the American Educational Research Association, San Francisco, April 1976.

Stake, R., and Gjerde, C. *An Evaluation of T City: The Twin City Institute for Talented Youth.* Urbana: Center for Instructional Research and Curriculum Evaluation, University of Illinois, 1971.

Struening, E. L. (Ed.). *Handbook of Evaluation Research.* Vol. 1. Beverly Hills, Calif.: Sage, 1975.

Stufflebeam, D. L. "A New Conceptualization of Evaluation Competencies." Paper presented at the annual meeting of the American Educational Research Association, New Orleans, La., 1973.

Stufflebeam, D. L. *Meta-Evaluation.* Occasional Paper, No. 3. Kalamazoo: Evaluation Center, Western Michigan University, 1974.

Stufflebeam, D. L., Foley, W. J., Gephart, W. J., Guba, E. G., Hammond, R. L., Merriman, H. O., and Provus, M. M. *Educational Evaluation and Decision-Making.* Itasca, Ill.: Peacock, 1971.

Suchman, E. A. *Evaluative Research: Principles and Practice in Public Service and Social Action Programs.* New York: Russell Sage Foundation, 1967.

Szaniawski, K. "Formal Analysis of Evaluative Concepts." *International Social Science Journal,* 1975, *27,* 446-457.

Tallmadge, G. K., and Horst, D. P. *A Procedural Guide to Validating Achievement Gains in Educational Projects.* Washington, D.C.: U.S. Government Printing Office, 1976.

Tallmadge, G. K., and Wood, C. T. *User's Guide ESEA Title I Evalu-*

References

ation and Reporting System. Mountain View, Calif.: RMC Research Corporation, 1976.

Taylor, J. C., and Bowers, D. J. *Survey of Organizations: A Machine-Scored Standardized Questionnaire Instrument.* Ann Arbor: Center for Research on Utilization of Scientific Knowledge, Institute for Social Research, University of Michigan, 1972.

Temp, G., and Anderson, S. B. *Final Report Project Head Start—Summer 1966, Section 3, Pupils and Programs.* Princeton, N.J.: Educational Testing Service, 1966.

Thorndike, E. L. "Mental Discipline in High-School Studies." *Journal of Educational Psychology,* 1924, *15,* 1-22 and 83-98.

Tornatzky, L. G. "How a Ph.D. Program Aimed at Survival Issues Survived." *American Psychologist,* 1976, *31,* 189-192.

Trachtman, G. M. "Pupils, Parents, Privacy, and the School Psychologist." *American Psychologist,* 1972, *27* (1), 37-45.

Trismen, D., Waller, M. I., and Wilder, G. *A Description and Analytic Study of Compensatory Reading Programs.* (2 vols.) Princeton, N.J.: Educational Testing Service, 1973.

Tumin, M. M. "Evaluation of the Effectiveness of Education: Some Problems and Prospects." *Interchange,* 1970, *1* (3), 96-109.

Tyler, R. W., Gagné, R. M., and Scriven, M. *Perspectives of Curriculum Evaluation.* American Educational Research Association Monograph Series on Curriculum Evaluation, No. 1. Chicago: Rand McNally, 1967.

U.S. Department of Health, Education and Welfare. *Head Start Performance Standards.* Washington, D.C.: Office of Human Development, U.S. Department of Health, Education and Welfare, 1975.

U.S. Department of Health, Education and Welfare. *Evaluation Procedures for Handicapped Children.* Washington, D.C.: Bureau of Education for the Handicapped, Office of Education, U.S. Department of Health, Education and Welfare, 1976.

Vallance, T. R. "The Professional Neuropsychology Graduate Program for Psychologists." *American Psychologist,* 1976, *31,* 193-199.

Wallace, D. *The Chemung County Research Demonstration with*

Dependent Multi-Problem Families. New York: State Charities Aid Association, 1965.

Walsh, J. "Antipoverty R and D: Chicago Debacle Suggests Pitfalls Facing OEO." *Science,* 1969, *165,* 1243-1246.

Ward, D. A., and Kassebaum, G. G. "On Biting the Hand That Feeds: Some Implications of Sociological Evaluations of Correctional Effectiveness." In C. H. Weiss (Ed.), *Evaluating Action Programs: Readings in Social Action and Education.* Boston: Allyn & Bacon, 1972.

Wargo, M. J., Tallmadge, G. K., Michaels, D. D., Lipe, D., and Morris, S. J. *ESEA Title I: A Reanalysis and Synthesis of Evaluation Data from Fiscal Year 1965 Through 1970.* Palo Alto, Calif.: American Institutes for Research, March 1972.

Warren, R. *Social Research Consultation.* New York: Russell Sage Foundation, 1963.

Water Resources Council. "Water Resources Council: Water and Related Land Resources. Establishment of Principles and Standards for Planning." *Federal Register,* September 10, 1973, *38,* Part III.

Watts, H. W. (Ed.). *Final Report of the New Jersey Graduate Work Incentive Experiment: A Social Experiment in Negative Taxation.* Madison: Wisconsin University Institute for Research on Poverty and Mathematics, 1973.

Webb, E. J. "Unconventionality, Triangulation, and Inference." In *Proceedings of the 1966 Invitational Conference on Testing Problems.* Princeton, N.J.: Educational Testing Service, 1967.

Weinstein, A. S. "Evaluation Through Medical Records and Related Information Systems." In E. L. Struening (Ed.), *Handbook of Evaluation Research.* Vol. 1. Beverly Hills, Calif.: Sage, 1975.

Weiss, C. H. "The Politicization of Evaluation Research." *Journal of Social Issues,* 1970, *26,* 57-68.

Weiss, C. H. "Utilization of Evaluation: Toward Comparative Study." In F. G. Caro (Ed.), *Readings in Evaluation Research.* New York: Russell Sage Foundation, 1971.

Weiss, C. H. (Ed.). *Evaluation Action Programs: Readings in Social Action and Education.* Boston: Allyn & Bacon, 1972.

References

Weiss, C. H. "Between the Cup and the Lip." *Evaluation*, 1973, *1* (2), 49-55.

Weiss, C. H. "Evaluation Research in the Political Context." In E. L. Struening (Ed.), *Handbook of Evaluation Research.* Vol. 1. Beverly Hills, Calif.: Sage, 1975.

Weiss, R. S., and Rein, M. "The Evaluation of Broad-Aim Programs: A Cautionary Case and a Moral." *Annals of the Academy of Political and Social Science*, 1969, *385*, 118-132.

Welch, W. W., and Walberg, H. J. "A Natural Experiment in Curriculum Innovation." *American Educational Research Journal*, 1972, *9* (3), 373-383.

Westinghouse Learning Corporation and Ohio University. *The Impact of Head Start Experience on Children's Cognitive and Affective Development.* Contract OEO B89-4536. Washington, D.C.: Office of Economic Opportunity, 1969.

Wholey, J. S., Duffy, H. G., Fukumoto, J. S., Scanlon, J. W., Berlin, M. A., Copeland, W. C., and Zelinsky, J. G. "Proper Organizational Relationships." In C. H. Weiss (Ed.), *Evaluating Action Programs: Readings in Social Action and Education.* Boston: Allyn & Bacon, 1972.

Wilner, D. M., Walkley, R. P., Pinkerton, T. C., Tayback, M., with the assistance of Glasser, M. N., Schram, J. M., Hopkins, C. E., Curtis, C. C., Meyer, A. S., and Dallas, J. R. *The Housing Environment and Family Life.* Baltimore: Johns Hopkins University Press, 1962.

Witkin, B. R. "Needs Assessment Models: A Critical Analysis." Paper presented at the annual meeting of the American Educational Research Association, San Francisco, April 1976.

Wixon, R., Kell, W. G., and Edford, N. M. (Eds.). *The Accountant's Handbook.* (5th ed.) New York: Ronald Press, 1970.

Worthen, B. R. "Certification for Educational Evaluators: Problems and Potential." Paper presented at the annual meeting of the American Educational Research Association, Chicago, 1972.

Worthen, B. R., "Competencies for Educational Research and Evaluation." *Educational Researcher*, 1975, *4*, 13-16.

Worthen, B. R., and Associates. *Development of a Pilot Test of*

Selected Competencies in Educational Research, Evaluation, Development, and Diffusion. Technical Paper, No. 29. Washington, D.C.: Task Force on Training Research and Research-Related Personnel, 1971.

Worthen, B. R., and Brzezinski, E. J. *Development of a Self-Report Instrument for Selected Skills and Knowledge in Educational Research, Development, Diffusion, and Evaluation.* Technical Paper, No. 30. Washington, D.C.: American Educational Research Association, 1971.

Worthen, B. R., and Gagné, R. M. *The Development of a Classification System for Functions and Skills Required of Research and Research-Related Personnel in Education.* Technical Paper, No. 1. Washington, D.C.: American Educational Research Association, 1969.

Wortman, P. M. "Evaluation Research: A Psychological Perspective." *American Psychologist,* 1975, *30,* 562-575.

Wright, S. R. "The First Two Years of the Summer Institute in Evaluation Research." *Evaluation Quarterly,* 1977, *1,* 183-187.

Young, M., and Willmott, P. *Family and Kinship in East London.* London: Routledge & Kegan Paul, 1957.

Zeisel, H. "Reducing the Hazards of Human Experiments through Modification in Research Design." *Annals of the New York Academy of Sciences,* 1970, *169,* 475-486.

Zusman, J., and Bissonette, R. "The Case Against Evaluation: With Some Suggestions for Improvement." *International Journal of Mental Health,* 1970, *2,* 111-125.

Name Index

Index

Index

Index

Index

Subject Index

Index

Communication *(continued)*
ation staff, 98-99; leadership
style and, 93-94; role of funding
agent, 95-96
Comparability problems, 46-50
Content of programs, 31-32
Context of program, 32-33, 53-54.
See also Political context
Correlation methods, 50-52, 85-86
Cost analysis, 22, 23-27
Cost-benefit analysis (CBA), 24-26
Cost-effectiveness analysis, 25-27

D

Decision-theoretic approach, 214
Dissemination, 99-104

E

Ethical responsibilities, 141-164;
APA statement of, 142, 221; and
confidentiality, 145-146; draft
statement of, 149-164; and privacy, 145-146
Evaluating evaluators, 185-190
Evaluation competencies, 169-181;
acquisition of, 176-181; and
AERA task force, 176-177
Evaluation methods, 3-6, 43-66; and
Purposes IV and V, 63-64
Evaluation purposes, 3-6, 14-42;
and program changes, 22-30; and
program installation, 15-22; and
program modification, 30-33; to
obtain evidence, 34-35; and un-
derstanding basic processes, 35.
See also Front-end analysis
Evaluation strategies, 5
Evidence, 67-90; and other evalu-
ation questions, 85-90; of pro-
gram impact, 69-85
Experimental studies, 44-50
Expert judgment, 68, 88-89
Expert panels, 58

External relationships, 126-140; and
ethical considerations, 136-137;
and practical considerations,
137-140
Extracontractual relationships, 159-
162

F

Feasibility study. *See* Front-end
analysis
Federal Bureau of Prisons, 74, 238
Formative evaluation, 3, 10, 11, 30-
35, 54
Front-end analysis, 3, 11, 15, 207-
208. *See also* Evaluation purposes

H

"Hard" and "soft" evaluations, 65-
66
Horse-race approach, 28

I

Impact: of programs, 69, 74-85
Impact evaluation. *See* Summative
evaluation
Independence of evaluators, 131-136
Informal observation, 62-63
Informed consent, 145-146
Internal relationships, 126-140; and
ethical considerations, 136-137;
and practical considerations,
137-140
Interviews, 52-54

J

Journals on evaluation, 217-218
Judgments, 57-60, 112-113

L

"Lawnmower" effect, 48

250

Index

Licensing, 22-30
List of evaluators, 169-170
Literacy, example of changing definition, 20
Long-term effects, 28-29

M

Man, A Course of Study (MACOS), 53-54
Matching, 47
Method-bound evaluator, 43-44
Methodology of programs, 32

N

National assessment, 21
National Science Foundation (NSF), evaluation methods and, 53-54
Needs assessment, 17-22, 23; and adult programs, 207-208; "models" of, 19. *See also* Front-end analysis
Net Present Value (NPV), 25-26
Nonrandom comparisons. *See* Quasi-experimental studies

O

Objectives of programs, 31
Obligations of evaluators, 127
Organizational effectiveness, 60-61
Outliers, 50-51

P

Personality factors, 138-140
Personnel assessment, 54-57
Personnel policies, 33
Policy relevance, 106, 107-108
Political context, 126-140
Predispositions of evaluators. *See* Values
Problem-oriented evaluator, 43-44

Product checklist, 15
Program, definition of, 2-3
Program continuation, 22-30
Program evaluation: beginnings of, 1-2, 10-11; definition of, 14; mandated by law, 212-214; "models" of, 4-5; targets for, 2-3; when to avoid, 12-13
Program expansion, 22-30
Program modification, 4, 30-35
Program monitoring, 5-6

Q

Quasi-experimental studies, 46-50
Questionnaires, 52-54

R

Regression analysis, 50-52
Representativeness, 46
Research versus evaluation, 9-11, 35-36
Responsive evaluation, 215
Roles of evaluators, 6-7, 128-140, 148

S

Sampling, 56-57. *See also* Experimental studies; Quasi-experimental studies
Secondary evaluation, 162-164
Self-selection, 47
"Sesame Street," 10, 32, 100, 118-119, 132, 135-136
Short-term effects, 28
Side effects, 29-30
Standards: in needs assessment, 20; for program evaluation, 219
Standardized tests, 87
Summative evaluation, 3, 10, 22-23; and ethics, 144-146
Surveys, 52-54, 68

251

Index